STAYING TOGETHER

The G8 and Global Governance Series

Series Editor: John J. Kirton

The G8 and Global Governance Series explores the issues, the institutions, and the strategies of the participants in the G8 network of global governance, and other actors, processes, and challenges that shape global order in the twenty-first century. Many aspects of globalisation, once considered domestic, are now moving into the international arena, generating a need for broader and deeper international co-operation and demanding new centres of leadership to revitalise, reform, reinforce, and even replace the galaxy of multilateral institutions created in 1945. In response, the G8, composed of the world's major market democracies, including Russia and the European Union, is emerging as an effective source of global governance. The G8 and Global Governance Series focusses on the new issues at the centre of global governance, covering topics such as finance, investment, and trade, as well as transnational threats to human security and traditional and emerging political and security challenges. The series examines the often invisible network of G8, G7, and other institutions as they operate inside and outside established international systems to generate desired outcomes and create a new order. It analyses how individual G8 members and other international actors, including multinational firms, civil society organisations, and other international institutions, devise and implement strategies to achieve their preferred global order.

Also in the series

Guiding Global Order
Edited by John J. Kirton, Joseph P. Daniels and Andreas Freytag
ISBN 0 7546 1502 2

New Directions in Global Economic Governance
Edited by John J. Kirton and George M. von Furstenberg
ISBN 0 7546 1698 3

The New Transatlantic Agenda
Edited by Hall Gardner and Radoslava Stefanova
ISBN 0 7546 1780 7

New Directions in Global Political Governance
Edited by John J. Kirton and Junichi Takase
ISBN 0 7546 1833 1

Governing Global Trade
Theodore H. Cohn
ISBN 0 7546 1593 6

The New Economic Diplomacy
Edited by Nicholas Bayne and Stephen Woolcock
ISBN 0 7546 1832 3 (Hbk) ISBN 0 7546 4318 2 (Pbk)

The G8, the United Nations, and Conflict Prevention
Edited by John J. Kirton and Radoslava N. Stefanova
ISBN 0 7546 0879 4

From Traditional to Group Hegemony
Alison Bailin
ISBN 0 7546 1979 6

Staying Together

The G8 Summit Confronts the 21st Century

NICHOLAS BAYNE
The London School of Economics and Political Science, UK

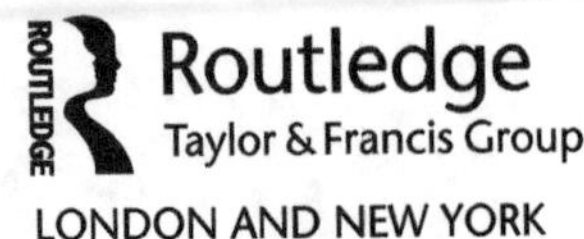

LONDON AND NEW YORK

First published 2005 by Ashgate Publishing

Reissued 2018 by Routledge
2 Park Square, Milton Park, Abingdon, Oxon OX14 4RN
711 Third Avenue, New York, NY 10017, USA

Routledge is an imprint of the Taylor & Francis Group, an informa business

First issued in paperback 2018

© Nicholas Bayne 2005

Nicholas Bayne has asserted his right under the Copyright, Designs and Patents Act, 1988, to be identified as the author of this work.

All rights reserved. No part of this book may be reprinted or reproduced or utilised in any form or by any electronic, mechanical, or other means, now known or hereafter invented, including photocopying and recording, or in any information storage or retrieval system, without permission in writing from the publishers.

A Library of Congress record exists under LC control number: 2004028610

Notice:
Product or corporate names may be trademarks or registered trademarks, and are used only for identification and explanation without intent to infringe.

Publisher's Note
The publisher has gone to great lengths to ensure the quality of this reprint but points out that some imperfections in the original copies may be apparent.

Disclaimer
The publisher has made every effort to trace copyright holders and welcomes correspondence from those they have been unable to contact.

ISBN 13: 978-0-815-39719-9 (hbk)
ISBN 13: 978-1-138-62066-7 (pbk)
ISBN 13: 978-1-351-14860-3 (ebk)

Contents

List of Tables

Preface and Acknowledgements

This volume completes a trilogy of books on summitry. Volume I, *Hanging Together*, which I wrote with Professor Bob Putnam, first appeared in 1984. We produced German, Japanese and Italian versions over the next three years and an updated English edition in 1987. Volume II, *Hanging In There*, my sequel to the first book, was published in 2000. The two books together covered the whole cycle of G7 summits in the last quarter of the 20th century and the first appearance of the G8.

This new book covers the first sequence of G8 summits, from 1998 to 2004, in which every member country held the Presidency (except Russia, whose first turn comes in 2006). During this period the G8 fully absorbed its eighth member and re-invented itself to confront the new demands of the 21st century. The book tells the story of these summits and offers some judgements on them.

In the first two volumes I drew heavily on the knowledge of the summits I had gained as a member of the British Diplomatic Service. But after 1996, when I retired, that was no longer available to me. Instead, thanks to the good offices of the G8 Research Group of the University of Toronto, I was able to attend all the summits from 1997 onwards, apart from Cologne in 1999, with media accreditation. In 1997-1998 and again in 2002-2004 I represented *LSE Magazine*. During 2000 and 2001 I was part of the team sent by the Canadian *Financial Post* (later *National Post*). Following the summits as a journalist gave me an entirely new perspective. Rather than getting the inside story from my complete knowledge of one country's position, I had to reconstruct it from the public statements and briefings of all the members, especially from the contradictions between them. All the narratives of the G8 summits in this book (except Cologne 1999) are derived from 'Impressions' written at the time and based on such briefings, supported by published G8 documents.

I owe a great debt to John Kirton, Director of the G8 Research Group, and to Madeline Koch, the Managing Director, for making me so welcome in the Group and especially for encouraging me to create this book. The writing of it brought back vividly the entertaining times and the lively discussions I had with them and other members of the Group at the summits over the years, especially Joe Daniels, Peter Hajnal, Paul Jacobelli, Ella Kokotsis, Marc Lalonde, Christine Lucyk, Victoria Panova, Gina Stephens, Shinichiro Uda, Heidi Ullrich, George von Furstenberg and Helen Walsh.

Before every summit, the G8 Research Group has organised, with a local partner institution, an academic conference in the country where the summit is being held. I have attended these conferences every year since 1997, in Denver, London, Bonn, Tokyo, Okinawa, Rome, Calgary, Fontainebleau (INSEAD) and Bloomington, Indiana. In 2005 the conference will be at Glasgow University. I have profited greatly from the guidance and encouragement of scholars I met there, as well as in other academic contexts. These include: Ted Cohn, Michele Fratianni, Olivier Giscard d'Estaing, Jeffrey Hart, the late Mike Hodges, Karl Kaiser, Seiichi Kondo, Richard Layard, Malcolm McLeod, Cesare Merlini, Sylvia Ostry, Bob Reinalda, Alan Rugman, Paolo Savona, Junichi Takase, Bertjan Verbeek and Bob Wolfe, together with three gifted Canadian diplomats - David Angell, Len Edwards and Bob Fowler.

In London between summits, I have gained great benefit from the openness and expertise of my former colleagues in the Foreign and Commonwealth Office, especially Michael Arthur, Colin Budd, Creon Butler, Martin Donnelly, Graham Fry, Charles Hay, James Kariuki, Richard Lawrence and Joe McClintock. I have been encouraged by the continuing support of my colleagues at the LSE, especially Steve Woolcock, my partner in 'Economic Diplomacy', Chris Alden, Robert Falkner, Daphne Josselin, Razeen Sally, William Wallace, Andrew Walter and Judith Higgin, the Editor of *LSE Magazine*.

Finally I express my abiding gratitude to three people whose contribution has been indispensable to the creation and publication of this book: to Kirstin Howgate (with her team) at Ashgate Publishing; to Christine Hunter, for her skill in getting my words to look better than they deserve; and to Diana, my beloved wife.

Nicholas Bayne
Hampton Court
October 2004

List of Abbreviations

ACP	African, Caribbean and Pacific associates of the EU
AGOA	Africa Growth and Opportunity Act
AIDS	Acquired Immune Deficiency Syndrome
APR	Africa Personal Representative
ASEAN	Association of South-East Asian Nations
AU	African Union
BIS	Bank for International Settlements
CAP	Common Agricultural Policy (of the EU)
CDU	Christian Democratic Union (of Germany)
CEP	Centre for Economic Performance (of the LSE)
CFMM	Commonwealth Finance Ministers' Meeting
CHOGM	Commonwealth Heads of Government Meeting
CTAG	Counter-Terrorism Action Group
DOT-Force	Digital Opportunity Task Force
EBRD	European Bank for Reconstruction and Development
EC	European Community
ECA	Economic Commission for Africa
EU	European Union
FAO	Food and Agriculture Organisation
FATF	Financial Action Task Force
FCO	Foreign and Commonwealth Office (of the UK)
FDI	Foreign Direct Investment
FDP	Free Democratic Party (of Germany)
GATT	General Agreement on Tariffs and Trade
GDP	Gross Domestic Product
GMOs	Genetically Modified Organisms
GNP	Gross National Product
G5	Group of Five (finance ministers)
G7	Group of Seven (summit, finance ministers and other groups)
G8	Group of Eight (summit and other groups)
G10	Group of Ten (finance ministers and officials in the IMF)
G20	Group of Twenty (part of new financial architecture) or Group of Twenty (larger developing countries in WTO)
G22	Group of Twenty-Two (predecessor of financial G20)
G24	Group of Twenty-Four (countries helping Central Europe)
G77	Group of Seventy-Seven (developing countries in UN)
G90	Group of Ninety (smaller developing countries in WTO)
HIPC	Heavily Indebted Poor Countries
HIV	Human Immunity Virus, often combined with AIDS
IAEA	International Atomic Energy Agency

IAIS	International Association of Insurance Supervisors
ICAO	International Civil Aviation Organisation
IDA	International Development Association (in World Bank group)
IFF	International Finance Facility
ILO	International Labour Organisation
IMF	International Monetary Fund, also known as the Fund
IMFC	International Monetary and Financial Committee (of the IMF)
IMO	International Maritime Organisation
IOSCO	International Organisation of Securities Commissions
IT	Information and Communications Technology (sometimes ICT)
LSE	London School of Economics and Political Science
MANPADS	Man-Portable Air Defence Systems
MAP	Millennium Africa Plan
MCA	Millennium Challenge Account
MDB	Multilateral Development Bank
MDG	Millennium Development Goal
NATO	North Atlantic Treaty Organisation
NEPAD	New Partnership for Africa's Development
NGO	Non-Governmental Organisation
NPT	Nuclear Non-Proliferation Treaty
OAU	Organisation for African Unity
OECD	Organisation for Economic Cooperation and Development
OPEC	Organisation of Petroleum Exporting Countries
OSCE	Organisation for Security and Cooperation in Europe
PRSP	Poverty Reduction Strategy Paper
PSI	Proliferation Security Initiative
SAFTI	Secure and Facilitated International Travel Initiative
SARS	Severe Acute Respiratory Syndrome
SDP	Social Democratic Party (of Germany)
TRIPS	Trade-Related Intellectual Property Rights (in WTO agreement)
UK	United Kingdom
UN	United Nations
UNCED	United Nations Conference on Environment and Development
UNCTAD	United Nations Conference on Trade and Development
UNDP	United Nations Development Programme
UNEP	United Nations Environment Programme
US	United States of America
USSR	Union of Soviet Socialist Republics (also Soviet Union)
USTR	United States Trade Representative
WHO	World Health Organisation
WMD	Weapons of Mass Destruction
WSSD	World Summit on Sustainable Development
WTO	World Trade Organization

INTRODUCTION

Chapter 1

The Summit at 30: Transition to a New Century

This book is about how governments cooperate in response to advancing globalisation as the 21st century begins. It concentrates on the G8 summit, which brings together the heads of state or government of a small group of major powers.[1] As G7 the summit had met regularly for a quarter of a century, but it needed a change of direction to confront the demands of globalisation. From 1998 onwards, the heads have simplified the format of their meetings and each G8 country has since hosted a new-style summit, except for Russia, the newest member.[2] The new format has made the G8 members better able to strike deals among themselves, launch new initiatives and provide collective management to an international economic system that is being transformed by globalisation. It has also encouraged outreach from the G8 to both non-G8 countries and the private sector, to make its leadership more transparent and acceptable.

Since 2001 the G8 summit has had to turn its attention to the political threat of international terrorism. But its capacity to integrate politics and economics has meant it can treat these issues too in the context of globalisation. Only intractable international problems, which cannot be settled at lower levels, come up to the summit. The solutions agreed by the G8 have not always worked: some have had to be revisited and strengthened; others have proved to be inadequate. The G8 has been weakest not in reaching out world-wide, but in building domestic support for the tough policies needed for strong international measures. Better reconciliation of domestic and international pressures is a task outstanding for the future.

The summits began on 16-17 November 1975, when six heads of government met at the chateau of Rambouillet outside Paris. They were: President Valéry Giscard d'Estaing of France, the host and convenor: President Gerald Ford of the United States; Chancellor Helmut Schmidt of Germany; and Prime Ministers Takeo Miki of Japan, Harold Wilson of the United Kingdom and - a late addition - Aldo Moro of Italy. Each was supported by their foreign and finance ministers and by their personal representatives chosen to prepare the summit, later called 'sherpas'.[3] The next year Canada, led by Prime Minister Pierre Trudeau, became the seventh member, while from 1977 the European Community (later European Union) was represented by the European Commission and Presidency.

The G7 was the first international summit consecrated to economic issues. The aim of the heads was to resolve serious economic differences among themselves that were damaging the international system. Their differences affected exchange rate policy, growth and inflation, energy policy and multilateral trade negotiations.

The heads of government believed their intervention was justified for three main reasons:

- Their *political leadership* would enable them to launch new ideas and resolve disputes that had persisted at lower levels;
- They could take effective and far-reaching decisions by virtue of their capacity to *reconcile domestic and international pressures* on policy-making;
- Together they could introduce a system of *collective management*, where Europe, North America and Japan would share responsibilities hitherto exercised by the United States alone.

These common objectives proved durable and generated enough impetus to sustain an annual cycle of summits for the rest of the 20th century.[4]

The approach of the new millennium brought fresh demands on the summits, which were now meeting in a very different environment. Some of the changes concerned the international context for the summit. Others affected the interaction of domestic and external factors in policy-making. The main changes were:

- A great increase in the range of economic issues treated internationally;
- Deeper penetration of international commitments into domestic policies 'within the border';
- Greater involvement of non-state actors in policy-making, especially private business and civil society;
- An international system that embraced the whole world, with many more countries active;
- The removal of the security threat from a hostile super-power, which had served as a spur to settle economic disputes;
- But continued political unrest, especially the growing threat of international terrorism.

These changes flowed from the advance of globalisation, which had accelerated since the end of the Cold War.[5]

The response of the summits to these new challenges forms the subject-matter for this book. It examines the record of each of the summits held since fundamental reforms were introduced at the Birmingham summit in 1998. It assesses the performance of these summits in the principal economic and political issues they selected for treatment. It explores the consequences of the reforms both for the summit format, agenda and participation and for the wider G8 apparatus. It looks at how far the reforms have met the aims of simplifying the summit and giving the heads greater freedom to intervene personally. It judges whether the summits since 1998 have improved their performance against their original objectives of political leadership, collective management and reconciling domestic and international pressures. Finally, it considers whether the summits of the 2000s have developed wholly new objectives, which would set them apart from the cycle that began at Rambouillet 30 years ago.

The rest of this chapter begins with an overview of the summits of the 20th century, developed more fully in Chapter 2. This overview explains the context for reform. The central part of the chapter gives an initial account of the reforms and their consequences. The chapter concludes by explaining the structure of the book, composed of interwoven chapters of narrative and assessment.

Overview of 20th Century Summits

In the summits of the 1970s the heads concentrated on their economic agenda, especially as many of them were former finance ministers. Under US President Jimmy Carter, who arrived in 1977, the preparatory process managed by the sherpas became more elaborate and systematic. This led the summit to adopt increasingly complex decisions, notably the three-way, cross-issue deal at the Bonn summit of 1978.

But political issues soon began to appear, like hijacking and hostage-taking. When President Ronald Reagan replaced Carter in the early 1980s, political issues, which interested him more than economics, encroached further on the agenda. The main achievements of the summits in Reagan's time were political: agreement on stationing US missiles in Europe in 1983; and joint action against terrorism in 1986. Much of the economic agenda returned to the finance ministers, especially after the Tokyo summit of 1986 expanded the G5, who had been meeting in secret for over a decade, into the G7 finance ministers.[6] The summit itself began to be called the G7 summit. By the end of the 1980s, as Reagan left office, the G7 summit had lost much of its early dynamism. This emerges from *Hanging Together*, the history of the summits up to 1987.[7]

The end of the Cold War gave the summit a new lease of life. As first the countries of Central Europe and then the Soviet Union itself abandoned communism, the summits from 1989 to 1993 mobilised action to help them build working democracies and market economies. The end of communism in Europe also made the international economic system truly universal, which brought new items onto the summit agenda, such as the global environment and debt relief for poor developing countries. By the mid-1990s the summits began to recognise the impact of globalisation. From Naples in 1994 to Denver in 1997, they conducted a review of international institutions, to see if these could stand the new strains that globalisation would place upon them.

The G7 heads invited President Mikhail Gorbachev as a guest to the 1991 London summit, in almost the last international appearance of the Soviet Union. A year later they invited President Boris Yeltsin to Munich, to discuss a programme of economic reform for Russia. Reform proved difficult and Yeltsin kept coming back every year. From Naples 1994 the G7 heads began admitting Yeltsin to the summit on equal terms, first to their political discussions and then even to economic ones, so that US President Bill Clinton could call Denver in 1997 'the Summit of the Eight'. *Hanging In There*, the second volume of summit history, brings the record up to the closing years of the 20th century.[8]

By this time the summits had accumulated a massive agenda of recurrent themes, both economic and political. New items kept being added, but few could ever be removed. Efforts to lighten the load in the 1990s had proved in vain and the summit seemed to be sinking under its own weight. At the Birmingham summit of 1998, British Prime Minister Tony Blair launched a series of reforms. Their aim was to rationalise and simplify the summit process, so as to give the heads greater freedom to concentrate on issues that really needed their intervention. These reforms were confirmed by Chancellor Gerhard Schroeder at Cologne in 1999 and have shaped all the summits of the 21st century so far - see Table 1.1. In 2005 Blair expects once again to hold the G8 presidency, the first British Prime Minister to host a summit twice.

The Birmingham Reforms and Their Consequences

The reforms agreed at Birmingham in 1998 focused on three aspects of the summit format:

- Full admission of Russia, converting G7 into G8;
- Decision that heads of government would meet on their own, without supporting ministers;
- Concentration on a few selected topics, thus reducing the volume of summit documentation.

These three reforms had further consequences as the G8 entered the 2000s.

Admitting Russia

The Russians had served a long apprenticeship, since they had been coming to the summit as guests since 1991. They came as full members on probation to Denver in 1997; but Birmingham was the first recognised G8 summit. The Russians were admitted to all the sherpa meetings and to economic as well as political discussions.

Economically, however, the Russians were not in the same class as the G7 powers. They were not yet members of the World Trade Organization (WTO). In August 1998 they failed to meet the conditions of their programme agreed with the International Monetary Fund (IMF), leading to default on their public debt and the collapse of their currency. In consequence, the G7 heads still needed to meet at the start of every summit, before Yeltsin or his successor Vladimir Putin had arrived. As long as separate G7 meetings were needed, it was difficult to contemplate holding a summit in Russia. With time, however, the Russian presence became fully accepted. At Kananaskis in 2002 the heads agreed that Russia should host the summit of 2006; and from Evian in 2003 the G7 heads no longer met separately.

Table 1.1 The Summits of the First G8 Sequence

Year	*Site*	*Host*	*Country*
Sixth Summit Series - Globalisation and Development			
1998	Birmingham	Tony Blair	United Kingdom
1999	Cologne	Gerhard Schroeder	Germany
2000	Okinawa	Yoshiro Mori	Japan
2001	Genoa	Silvio Berlusconi	Italy
Seventh Summit Series - Fighting Terrorism and its Causes			
2002	Kananaskis	Jean Chrétien	Canada
2003	Evian	Jacques Chirac	France
2004	Sea Island	George W. Bush	United States
Start of Second G8 Sequence			
2005	*Gleneagles*	*Tony Blair*	*United Kingdom*
2006	*Site not known*	*Vladimir Putin*	*Russia*

Note

A summit *sequence* denotes a run of seven summits, each chaired by a different country. Thus the sequence that began at Birmingham in 1998 concluded at Sea Island in 2004. A summit *series* is a group of summits focused on a particular set of issues. The first five series, from 1975 to 1997, are covered in Table 2.1 below. The sixth series began with reforms to the format and concentrated on the G8 response to globalisation. The seventh series took over in 2002, when the summit began paying more attention to terrorism and related political issues after 11 September 2001. The summit *cycle* means all the summits from Rambouillet in 1975 to the present day - 30 in all so far.

The formal admission of Russia, on political rather than economic grounds, opened up the question of the G8's relationship with other non-G8 countries. While China was identified as the next potential member of the group, on both economic and foreign policy grounds, it did not meet the democracy test of summit membership. The G8 was in no hurry to take a decision on further expansion and China itself was not pressing. But all the G8 members saw merit in more systematic links with the world outside their exclusive circle.

The first move towards greater outreach came in 2000, when Japan, as host, invited a group of leaders from developing countries and international institutions to meet G8 members over dinner before the summit proper. The guests included three African Presidents - Thabo Mbeki (South Africa), Olusegun Obasanjo (Nigeria) and Abdulaziz Bouteflika (Algeria) - who were developing a plan for the economic and political renaissance of their continent. They arranged to be invited back to the Genoa summit of 2001, with a fourth member of their group (Abdoulaye Wade of Senegal) and stimulated the launch of the G8's 'Genoa Plan for Africa', which led to the G8 Africa Action Plan a year later. As a result, these African leaders were invited to the next three summits as participants, rather than guests, and can expect to be there again at Gleneagles in 2005.

The French hosts in 2003 did not want the G8's outreach to be limited to Africa. So they invited to Evian a selection of other leading developing countries, including China, India, Brazil and Mexico, for an informal session before the summit began. France wanted such a meeting to be a regular feature of the summit. However, the Americans in 2004 decided not to follow this formula. To support the launch of the broader Middle East initiative, the main innovation at the Sea Island summit, they invited a group of leaders from the region, from Algeria to Afghanistan. So while the G8 members were committed to the principle of outreach to other countries, they retained flexibility over deciding who should be invited to join them each year.

Heads-Only Summits

Back in 1975 Giscard and Schmidt, the summit founders, had intended that only heads of government should attend. But the US Secretary of State, Henry Kissinger, and the Treasury Secretary, William Rogers, had not trusted Ford to go alone to such an important meeting. So the Americans had insisted that the heads be accompanied to Rambouillet by their foreign and finance ministers. This format had persisted at all subsequent summits. Not only the Americans, but also the Germans and Japanese found it useful, as it allowed junior coalition partners or other factions of the ruling party to be present at the summit.

By the time of Birmingham, however, all the G8 members were ready to follow Blair's proposal to lighten the overloaded summit structure. The new format provided for the foreign and finance ministers to hold separate meetings a few days before the heads themselves met on their own. This was welcomed by the heads as giving them greater informality and greater freedom of action. They could now choose their own agenda and develop a close personal rapport among themselves, in a way that had not been possible even in the earliest experimental days of the summit. There were now only nine or ten chairs round the summit table and no one else in the room except the sherpas sitting silently behind each of the heads.[9]

Despite this thinning at the top, some G8 members, especially the United States and Japan, still brought huge delegations of supporting officials to the summit. But external events caused these delegations to be cut back drastically. In July 2001 the G8 summit in Genoa had been besieged by crowds of rioting demonstrators, while the terrorist attacks of 11 September on the US made security an overriding concern. So Canada, as host in 2002, held the summit in the secluded mountain resort of Kananaskis, where there was only room to accommodate delegations limited to 30 people. The same pattern was repeated in 2003 and 2004 and would still apply at Gleneagles in 2005.

Because the G8 heads had detached themselves from their official apparatus, they had more opportunity to engage with non-official forces, such as private business firms and civil society organisations. At Birmingham 1998 and Cologne 1999 this was limited to contacts between the summit hosts and representatives of public demonstrations. But from 2000 onwards non-official links became much more systematic. Business firms and NGOs were involved in the preparation of certain topics and in the groups created to follow up summit decisions. The G8 host government would consult business and civil society as part of the run-up to the summit and provide facilities for NGOs near the summit site.[10]

The format of 'heads-only' summits had detached the official G8 apparatus from the heads themselves. But this did not cause the apparatus to fade away. On the contrary, it continued to proliferate with the easing of tight control from the top. G7 finance ministers and G8 foreign ministers not only met just before the summit, but at other times throughout the year. In addition, there were periodic meetings of G8 ministers of environment, employment, energy, education, development and justice and home affairs. Each ministerial meeting was supported at the official level, while there were separate official groups meeting regularly on issues such as crime, terrorism and nuclear non-proliferation.

While all these groups originated from a summit decision, they steadily detached themselves from the summit and pursued their own agendas, only rarely seeking endorsement or decisions from the heads. Furthermore, while these subsidiary groups retained the G8 as a nucleus, they were much freer than the summit itself to invite other countries to join them if the theme of their meeting justified it. Some groups established a set 'G8-plus' format, notably the G20 finance ministers. Thus while the move to the heads-only format simplified the proceedings at the summit, it did not serve to simplify the G8 process as a whole.

Limited Agenda, Shorter Documents

Blair's intention at Birmingham was to bring the summit back to a limited agenda and shorter documents. He wanted the summit to revive its economic vocation, treating politics only on the side. The summit's review of international institutions in the light of advancing globalisation had run its course. Blair wanted the summit to address directly those aspects of globalisation that caused most concern, both within G8 populations, such as the threat to jobs and high-tech crime, and in the world at large, such as financial panic and persistent poverty.

Some parts of the rigorous approach favoured by Blair endured better than others. Birmingham and Cologne gave some attention to domestic issues, like employment, crime, education and social protection. But they were more concerned with international problems, like debt relief for poor countries and reform of the world financial system. These had some direct impact on G8 members, but required much greater action or adjustment by developing countries, whether poor or middle-income. This trend was taken further at Okinawa and Genoa, which were almost wholly devoted to development issues of concern to poor countries, especially in Africa.

These first four summits of the sequence were largely devoted to economic issues. The main political subject that demanded summit treatment was Kosovo in 1999, because it could only be settled by Yeltsin in person. Kosovo generated a broader G8 interest in conflict prevention, which was pursued by foreign ministers before Okinawa and formed an element of the Genoa Plan for Africa.

The pattern changed abruptly after the terrorist attacks of 11 September 2001. Canada, as host to the 2002 summit, rigorously kept the agenda to Africa, terrorism and the world economy. But the decisions of the summit were as much political as economic and even combined the two, as in the G8 Africa Action Plan. Thereafter France, as host in 2003, and the United States, host in 2004, relaxed the tight control over the agenda. They chose broad, open-ended themes for the summit, while the documents issuing from both Evian and Sea Island were more copious than any previous summit.

In the shift away from economics in favour of politics, Kananaskis marked the start of a new summit series. The sixth series, focused on the G8 response to globalisation, covered Birmingham 1998 to Genoa 2001 inclusive. The seventh series, focused on the G8 response to terrorism, began with Kananaskis 2002 and is likely to run till the 2006 summit held in Russia.[11]

Plan of the Book: Narrative and Assessment

The first two chapters of this book serve as its introduction. In addition to the present chapter, Chapter 2 gives a summary account of the summits of the 20th century, from the inaugural meeting at Rambouillet in 1975 to the Denver summit of 1997, on the eve of the first G8 sequence that began at Birmingham. Those already familiar with summit history can safely skip this chapter.

The next ten chapters divide into seven of narrative and three assessing summit performance. The narrative chapters form the core of the book. Each one covers a single summit and is based on 'impressions' written at the time.[12] Though these contemporary impressions have been lightly amended to give consistency between them, they are intended to give a sense of how each summit seemed at the time that it was happening. In this way the book differs both from *Hanging Together*, which constructed narratives of the early summits some time after most of them had taken place, and from *Hanging In There*, which only gave schematic accounts of what happened at the later summits of the 20th century.

The assessment chapters examine groups of subjects that formed the principal themes from Birmingham onwards. These themes are judged against a consistent set of criteria, to be explained more fully below. Finally, two chapters of conclusions examine how far the summit format has changed over the first G8 sequence and how far today's summit is succeeding in meeting its objectives.

Summit Narratives

Chapter 3 looks at the 1998 Birmingham summit; Chapter 4 at the 1999 Cologne summit. These two summits introduced and confirmed the reforms to the summit format, making G7 into G8. They also re-directed the summits' response to globalisation away from international institutions to the policies that the G8 members should adopt themselves.

Tony Blair and Gerhard Schroeder, who presided over these summits, had much in common. Both had recently come to power at the head of parties that had been out of office for over 15 years. They were leaders of governments that leant towards the left but had finally gained office by the skilful occupation of the middle ground. This made them keen to rejuvenate old structures, open to new ideas and ready to intervene in economic policy, despite strong attachment to the market. They saw the summits as influencing domestic policy-making as well as acting on the international scene. All these factors shaped their impact on the summits they chaired.

Chapters 6 and 7 tell the story of the Okinawa summit of 2000 and the Genoa summit of 2001. These two summits were prepared by leaders who did not survive in power to preside over them. Keizo Obuchi, as Japanese Prime Minister in 1999-2000, was determined that the Okinawa summit should focus on issues of development. He decided that the summit should be held in Okinawa, the first time Japan had hosted a summit outside Tokyo. But he died in May 2000, well before the summit date in July. In Italy Giuliano Amato, Prime Minister in 2000-2001, took a far more systematic approach to summitry than any of his predecessors. He maintained the focus on development issues, to complete work that had been begun at Okinawa. But his government was voted out of office two months before the Genoa summit.

Yoshiro Mori in Japan and Silvio Berlusconi in Italy, who took over power, wisely did nothing to upset or divert the careful preparations of their predecessors. But their lack of personal involvement in the process weakened their chairmanship of the summits of 2000 and 2001, which showed a slight slackening of performance.

A new summit series began with Kananaskis 2002, described in Chapter 9, and continued with Evian 2003 and Sea Island 2004, covered in Chapters 10 and 11. In contrast to the preceding summits in the sequence, the first two of the presiding heads of government were G7 veterans and were chairing the summit for the second time. The first summits chaired by Jean Chrétien of Canada (Halifax 1995) and Jacques Chirac of France (Lyon 1996) had been successful events that had carried forward effectively the G7 review of international institutions. But despite their previous experience, they produced very different results in the 2000s.

For Kananaskis (Chapter 9) Chrétien staked everything on brevity and simplicity: a short agenda, small delegations and a 'chair's summary' instead of a formal communiqué. This led to good results, to which the heads made a personal contribution. At Evian (Chapter 10) Chirac was more ambitious: he chose broad, open-ended themes and provided for elaborate outreach meetings. The outreach worked well, but the G8 summit itself sacrificed quality for quantity, so that documents of record number and length produced few decisions worthy of heads of government.

As Chapter 11 shows, George W. Bush in 2004 ended by following the French example, without originally intending to. Once again, broad summit themes led to a mass of G8 documents without much original content, while the outreach to the Middle East and Africa seemed rather improvised. But improvements in the situation in Iraq just before the G8 met enabled the Sea Island summit to launch an innovative programme to encourage political and economic reform in the Middle East and North Africa.

Assessing Summit Performance

The three chapters of assessment use a consistent set of six criteria for judging the results of the summits since Birmingham in major areas of policy-making. These criteria are:

1. Leadership;
2. Effectiveness;
3. Solidarity;
4. Durability;
5. Acceptability;
6. Consistency.

Each is defined more fully below.[13]

Leadership The first criterion judges how far the G8 summit was able to exercise its political authority. This authority could enable the heads to resolve disputes that had been blocked at lower levels and overcome bureaucratic inertia or deadlock. It could also give them the capacity to impart decisive momentum to new ideas and initiatives.

Effectiveness The second criterion assesses the summits' ability to reconcile the tensions between different pressures on the member governments, so as to reach agreement. The summits could seek to reconcile international and domestic factors; this was the major concern of the G7 summits when they began in the 1970s. But they could equally reconcile and integrate political and economic components of international policy. The G7 had rarely done this, but the G8 increasingly turned to this new element in the 2000s.

Solidarity The third criterion considers whether all the G8 countries were committed to the decisions taken at the summit, so that they could be fully implemented. The aim of the summit was collective management, with responsibility shared among the G8 partners. Where an initiative launched by one or two G8 members was only weakly supported by the others, this was unlikely to lead to successful collective management.

Durability The fourth criterion tests whether the agreement reached at the summit produced a lasting solution to the problem. This criterion recognises that summits were no longer isolated events, but part of a regular institutional series. It was often necessary for the summit to return to a problem several times before it no longer needed their attention.

Acceptability The fifth criterion examines whether the solutions reached at the summit commanded the support not only of the G8 members but also of the world community as a whole. This criterion reflects the growing number of actors in the international system caused by the advance of globalisation. The G8 could no longer expect their pronouncements to be accepted by other countries without question; they had to convince and persuade others to endorse them. The G8's decisions had to be acceptable not only to other governments and international institutions, but also to an expanding circle of non-state actors, including business, civil society and public opinion generally.

Consistency The sixth and last criterion is concerned with whether G8 decisions in one policy area, such as finance, fitted in with the policies the G8 adopted on other subjects, like trade or development. This criterion had always applied to the summits to some degree. But it had become harder to meet as the G8 agenda had expanded, so that more subjects had to be made compatible with one another.

The first three criteria correspond to the original objectives of the summits: political leadership, reconciling external and domestic tensions and collective management. They have always been relevant and would be sufficient for judging the results of an individual summit in terms of the effect on G8 members. But summits now take place in a much broader context. They pursue issues over several years, seeking solutions that will stand the test of time. They make their impact on a wider international system that is being transformed by globalisation. They address a greater range of potential issues, both economic and political. This makes it necessary to add the latter three criteria, which have grown in importance as the summit cycle has extended over 30 years.

Subjects for Assessment

Chapter 5, the first assessment chapter, considers the summits' achievements in international finance during the first G8 sequence. The two major issues were the new international financial architecture and debt relief for low-income countries. These two issues received their most detailed treatment at Birmingham 1998 and

Cologne 1999. Later summits also gave them some attention, especially debt relief.

Chapter 8, the second assessment chapter, judges the progress made in international trade and in a range of development issues (excluding debt relief), such as IT and the 'digital divide', infectious diseases and primary education. These all came to the top of the agenda at Okinawa 2000 and Genoa 2001, in parallel with the adoption of the 'Millennium Development Goals' at the United Nations. Other development issues, such as clean water and food security, were added at later summits, while trade was a recurrent concern throughout the sequence.

The last assessment chapter, Chapter 12, examines the G8's record on Africa and on terrorism and non-proliferation of weapons of mass destruction. While interest in Africa first surfaced at Genoa, the main achievements emerged at Kananaskis 2002 and subsequent summits, combining economic and political elements. Terrorism and non-proliferation likewise became major G8 subjects from Kananaskis onwards, following the terrorist attacks of 11 September 2001. Though the main focus of these issues was political, economic aspects were also relevant.

Grading the Summits

In addition to Chapters 5, 8 and 11, the performance criteria will also be used in the narrative chapters, as a means of judging the overall achievement of each G8 summit. This will underpin the grades given to the G8 summits, as set out in Table 14.1 and explained in Chapter 14. The grades already allocated to the G7 summits are provided in Table 2.1, for purposes of comparison.

This method of grading the summits from A to E was developed by Professor Bob Putnam and first applied to the summits from 1975 to 1986 analysed in *Hanging Together.*[14] It measures the degree of cooperation achieved at each summit in terms of the agreements achieved that would not have been possible without the intervention of the heads of government. The basis of the grading was adjusted to cover innovation, including institutional innovation, and consistency over time, when it was applied to the later G7 summits in *Hanging In There.*[15] Taken together, the summits of the first G8 sequence show a higher average score than any sequence of G7 summits. However, for reasons given in Chapter 14, no recent summit has attained the highest grades of A and A-. These have only been awarded to two of the earliest summits of the 1970s and have not been equalled since then.

Conclusions

Chapter 13, the first chapter of conclusions, draws out the implications of the reforms since Birmingham for the summit process. It analyses the different contributions made by the heads of government themselves; by the sherpas and the rest of the summit apparatus; and by outside forces, both non-G8 governments and non-state actors. Its main findings are that, while the heads may intervene independently, they do so mainly in procedural issues and for political motives. They are most effective in substantive decision-making when they act to complete and supplement the summit preparations. Greater outreach has given the summit essential transparency, at the cost of some efficiency.

Chapter 14, the second chapter of conclusions, gives an overall judgement of the summit's achievements against its objectives during the first G8 sequence. It finds that in political leadership - striking deals and launching initiatives - summit performance has clearly improved. The impetus for collective management has been maintained, despite some serious threats. The summit has developed new capacities for integrating politics and economics. However, in reconciling domestic and international pressures summit performance has got worse. Finally, in the light of what is on balance a positive assessment, the chapter takes the view that the G8 summit will endure and offers some thoughts on where it may be going in the near future.

Notes

1 Three of the members of the G8 - the Presidents of the United States, France and Russia - are heads of state as well as heads of government. But the term 'heads of government', or simply 'heads', will be used to cover all of them.

2 Russia will first host a summit in 2006.

3 For a complete list of summit participants - heads, supporting ministers and sherpas - from 1975 to 2000, see Sherifis and Astraldi 2001, pp. 217-253.

4 For more on the origins of the summit, see Chapter 2 below. A full account is in Putnam and Bayne 1987, pp. 25-35.

5 The literature on globalisation is vast. A concise and accessible account is in Cable 1999. Recent authoritative analyses are in Bhagwati 2004 and Wolf 2004.

6 The G5 finance ministers (US, Japan, Germany, France and UK), who were originally formed as the 'Library Group', had in fact contributed to the genesis of the summit itself in the mid-1970s. See Putnam and Bayne 1987, pp. 29-30.

7 Putnam, R. D. and Bayne, N. (1987), *Hanging Together: Cooperation and Conflict in the Seven-Power Summits,* SAGE, London.

8 Bayne, N. (2000), *Hanging In There: the G7 and G8 Summit in Maturity and Renewal,* Ashgate, Aldershot.

9 The exact numbers depend on the make-up of the EU delegation, which consists of the President of the European Commission and the prime minister of the country holding the six-month Presidency. When the Presidency is held by a European G8 member, there are eight heads of government plus the Commission at the table - nine in all. When the EU Presidency comes from a non-G8 member state, that adds an extra head of government and a tenth seat. See Tables 13.1 and 13.2 for the EU Presidency holders of the G8 sequence.

10 The developing relationship between the G8 summit and civil society is analysed in Hajnal 2002. The Americans departed a bit from this tradition in 2004, by providing no NGO facilities, but the British are likely to restore it in 2005.

11 For the five earlier summit series, see Table 2.1 and Chapter 2 generally.

12 I have attended all the summits since Denver 1997 with media accreditation, except for Cologne 1999.

13 I have previously used these criteria to assess the summits' record in finance (Bayne 2000a and 2002) and trade (Bayne 2001). But for those analyses I only used five criteria - 'solidarity' is new for this book. This assessment technique is different from the compliance monitoring pioneered by George von Furstenberg and Joseph Daniels and continued by Ella Kokotsis - see Von Furstenberg and Daniels 1992 and Kokotsis 1999.

14 See Putnam and Bayne 1987, pp. 269-270.

15 See Bayne 2000, pp. 193-195.

Chapter 2

The Story So Far: The G7 Summits 1975-1997

This chapter explains the origins of the summit and then gives a brief account of all the summits held from 1975 to 1997, grouped in five series of unequal length. The summits are enumerated in Table 2.1 overleaf, together with their main achievements and their grades, which measure the extent of cooperation achieved at each summit. This is based on Table 11.1 of *Hanging Together*, updated by Table 12.1 of *Hanging In There*.[1]

Origins

The G7 summit was born out of a cumulative economic crisis. Throughout the 1950s and 1960s the world had enjoyed sustained growth with low inflation. In the 1970s everything began to go wrong. The monetary system based on fixed but adjustable parities collapsed, as the United States refused to defend the dollar against gold. The Organisation of Petroleum Exporting Countries (OPEC) forced a four-fold increase in the price of oil. As Western countries were heavily dependent on imported oil, this produced a simultaneous drop in growth and surge in inflation. The economic institutions created after World War II - the IMF, the General Agreement on Tariffs and Trade (GATT) and the Organisation for Economic Cooperation and Development (OECD), the heir to the Marshall Plan - grappled with these problems but seemed unable to resolve them. Successive meetings ended in deadlock.[2]

The political impulses that had driven economic cooperation since the 1940s were weakening. The revival of fascism now seemed remote. The fear of communist encroachment was declining. American hegemony was being challenged, especially by the growth of the European Community. In particular France, under Presidents Charles de Gaulle and Georges Pompidou, sought to define Europe in terms of opposition to the United States.

Table 2.1 G7 Summits and their Achievements, 1975-1997

Year	*Summit Site*	*Achievements*	*Grade*
First Series - Reviving Growth			
1975	Rambouillet	Monetary reform	A-
1976	San Juan, Puerto Rico	Nothing significant	D
1977	London I	Trade, growth, nuclear power	B-
1978	Bonn I	Growth, energy, trade	A
Second Series - Holding Down Inflation			
1979	Tokyo I	Energy	B+
1980	Venice I	Afghanistan, energy	C+
1981	Ottawa (Montebello)	Trade ministers' quadrilateral	C
1982	Versailles	East-West trade, surveillance	C
Third Series - The Rise of Politics			
1983	Williamsburg	Euromissiles	B
1984	London II	Debt	C-
1985	Bonn II	Nothing significant	E
1986	Tokyo II	Terrorism, surveillance, G7 finance ministers	B+
1987	Venice II	Nothing significant	D
1988	Toronto	Debt relief for poor countries	C-
Fourth Series - The End of the Cold War			
1989	Paris (Arch)	Helping Central Europe, environment, debt	B+
1990	Houston	Trade - no net advance	D
1991	London III	Helping USSR	B-
1992	Munich	Nothing significant	D
1993	Tokyo III	Trade	C+
Fifth Series - Institutions for Globalisation			
1994	Naples	Russia into political debate	C
1995	Halifax	Institutional review, IMF and UN reform	B+
1996	Lyon	Debt, development	B
1997	Denver	Russian participation, Africa	C-

In the mid-1970s, however, after the death of Pompidou and the disgrace of President Richard Nixon in the US and Chancellor Willy Brandt in Germany, new leaders arose who owed no debts to the past. In particular President Giscard of France, encouraged by his friend Chancellor Schmidt of Germany, was ready for a reconciliation with US President Ford. Giscard and Schmidt had been frustrated by the unproductive international meetings they had attended when they were finance ministers. They believed - especially Giscard - that a small and select group of heads of government could break the deadlock that persisted in bureaucratic institutions.

Giscard called the first summit at Rambouillet, in November 1975, originally with five participants (US, Japan, Germany, France and UK) but adding Italy at the last moment. A non-bureaucratic group of personal representatives was charged to conduct minimal preparations and support the heads at the summit. Under American pressure, Giscard reluctantly agreed that foreign and finance ministers could also attend.

The First Summit Series, 1975-1978: Reviving Growth[3]

Rambouillet, November 1975 The topics chosen for Rambouillet became the standard agenda for the early summits: macro-economic policy, the monetary system, international trade, energy policy and relations with developing countries. But for Giscard the key topic was exchange rates. Since 1971, the Bretton Woods monetary system based on fixed par values had broken down to the point that all major currencies were floating, though the EC currencies were still linked to each other in the 'snake'.[4] Strictly, the IMF Articles only permitted floating as an emergency measure. Most other countries, led by the US, wanted the Articles amended to make floating an acceptable permanent regime, but so far France had refused.

Giscard planned to make the summit the occasion for France to agree, in return for an understanding among the summit countries to cooperate informally to stabilise exchange rates. The key provisions of this deal were worked out bilaterally between France and the US at official level and unveiled at the summit. The others were taken by surprise, but were happy to acquiesce. The Rambouillet monetary agreement was carried forward to the IMF and the Articles were quickly amended, to embody the regime still in force today. The informal stabilisation arrangement, however, did not survive for long.

Rambouillet showed good results in two other areas. In trade, the Tokyo Round of multilateral negotiations in the GATT, launched in 1973, was marking time. The heads set a deadline of 1977 for completing the Tokyo Round. They also made a firm undertaking to resist all forms of protectionism, which was soon invoked to discipline the United Kingdom. In macro-economic policy, all the participating economies had shown loss of growth and rising unemployment, as a result of the quadrupling of oil prices. During 1975, the summit governments had taken action to stimulate growth and the revival was just beginning as the heads met in November. The leaders forecast a recovery and, as their timing was good, they were proved right without the summit itself having to take any action.

Puerto Rico, June 1976 Giscard had originally intended the summits to be isolated, free-standing events, to be called when needed. But Rambouillet had produced such good results and been so well received by public opinion that Ford, who was facing elections, soon decided to call another one, at San Juan, Puerto Rico in June 1976. The agenda and the participating countries were the same, except that Ford invited Canada to help offset the weight of the four Europeans. This brought the numbers to seven - the G7.

But the results were much less substantial than in 1975. On money, the heads had nothing to add. On trade they could only reaffirm the 1977 deadline for completing the Tokyo Round. The stance of macro-economic policy had shifted in 1976, as many countries feared a resurgence of inflation. The US, Japan, Germany and France had all brought in measures to hold down prices, while Britain and Italy were facing insolvency. Nonetheless, the summit confidently forecast that the economic recovery would continue. But this time the heads' timing was bad and growth fell away as the year ended.

London I, May 1977 The third meeting in London in 1977 marked the establishment of the G7 summit as a regular annual event, held over 2-3 days some time between May and July. Jimmy Carter, the new US President, was enthusiastic about making use of the summit. His personal representative, Henry Owen, launched moves to institutionalise the summit preparations, which became known as the sherpa process. On the European side, Giscard, after long resistance, agreed that from now on the European Community (EC) should be represented at the summit by the President of the European Commission and the head of government of the country holding the EC Presidency.[5] Of the eight leaders thus present at London in 1977 and Bonn in 1978 six were former finance ministers - Giscard, Schmidt, Takeo Fukuda (Japan), James Callaghan (UK), Giulio Andreotti (Italy) and Roy Jenkins (European Commission).

Macro-economic policy and trade again dominated the summit. Carter had defeated Ford on a platform of stimulating the US economy and had already acted in this direction. But he feared that America's inflation rate, its balance of payments and the value of the dollar would suffer if its economy grew much faster than others. At London he advocated the 'locomotive approach', whereby strong G7 economies - US, Japan and Germany - would stimulate their growth and enable weaker ones, like Britain and Italy, to benefit also. But Schmidt and Fukuda were too much concerned about inflation to be willing locomotives. They accepted targets for economic growth but did not promise measures to meet them, so that in fact both countries fell short.

In trade the target of completing the Tokyo Round by the end of that year was clearly out of reach. But the heads agreed to make a sustained effort to resolve all the differences between them by the time they met in 1978. This gave Bob Strauss, Carter's energetic US Trade Representative, the impetus he wanted. Carter also raised the linked issues of nuclear energy and non-proliferation.

The G7 heads could not agree on the substance, but reached a procedural compromise on future discussions, which led to tighter disciplines on proliferation.

Bonn I, July 1978 The failure of the locomotive approach left Carter's economic strategy dangerously vulnerable. As he feared, the dollar was weakening and the US was sucking in huge volumes of imports, especially oil imports. Carter renewed his pressure on Schmidt and Fukuda to stimulate their economies. Schmidt in fact saw grounds for action to revive growth in Germany, but he faced domestic opposition. He and Fukuda were also insistent that the US should curb its demand for imported oil by raising domestic prices. This provided the basis for a three-way, cross-issue bargain, whereby Germany and Japan acted to revive growth in return for the US undertaking to raise domestic oil prices to international levels. Detailed preparations before the summit enabled this deal to be announced at Bonn, in terms of the measures each would take, and all three parties met their commitments fully.[6]

Meanwhile Strauss had been active in pushing forward the Tokyo Round agenda. Shortly before the summit, G7 representatives in Geneva had agreed the main points of a deal and they came on to Bonn to continue negotiating behind the scenes. This added a trade component to the growth and energy deal and brought in the other G7 members, including the EC. The deal struck at the summit gave enough impetus to the Tokyo Round to bring substantive agreement in the GATT by the end of the year. The Bonn summit also saw the first G7 agreement on a non-economic subject - a declaration on hijacking proposed without warning by Schmidt and concluded over a working lunch.

Judgement on the First Summit Series By the end of the first series, the summits had proved their worth and become an institution. They had mainly stuck to their economic agenda and successfully resolved disputes among the G7 members on the monetary system, international trade and macro-economic policy, though not always at the first attempt. Rambouillet 1975 and Bonn I 1978 are considered to have been the most productive summits in the entire cycle up to the present, with grades of A- and A on the Putnam Scale.

The summits were successful in overcoming the policy deadlock of the early 1970s and in restoring growth to the G7 and other OECD economies after the setbacks of the first oil crisis. But with hindsight it emerged that, in their pursuit of growth, the G7 heads had taken risks with inflation that left them vulnerable to a further rise in oil prices. OPEC saw their benefits from the first increase in oil prices being eroded by inflation, while the decline in the dollar reduced the value of their investments and monetary reserves, which were all held in US dollars. When the fall of the Shah shut off oil supplies from Iran at the end of 1978, OPEC was happy to see oil prices surge by another threefold increase and acted to keep prices up at that level. In these circumstances, the measures of economic stimulus agreed by the first Bonn summit looked like the wrong choice and they were rapidly discredited.

The Second Summit Series, 1989-1982: Holding Down Inflation[7]

Tokyo I, June 1979 The Tokyo summit was the first to be dominated by energy issues, as the heads struggled to respond to the unpredictable rise in oil prices, which was producing near-panic conditions in the United States. The chosen policy instrument was a set of national targets for energy imports in 1979 and 1980, which developed from an unexpected deal between the US and France and was agreed in tough negotiations at the summit itself.

The other main topic was again macro-economic policy, where the strategy adopted in the four previous summits was completely reversed. Instead of targets or fiscal measures to stimulate growth, the G7 heads gave absolute priority to holding down inflation through strict monetary policy. This produced a much simpler message than before, with a focus on corrective action by each country on its own, rather than collective or coordinated measures. British Prime Minister Margaret Thatcher, at her first summit, was surprised to find how closely her colleagues agreed with her.

Venice I, June 1980 The same austere macro-economic message persisted at Venice a year later. US monetary policy had been severely tightened, even though 1980 was an election year for Carter. Once again, energy policy was the main economic subject. The targets adopted at Tokyo were reinforced by a series of structural measures intended to make the G7 economies less energy-intensive and to diversify away from oil to other energy sources.

The Venice summit met in conditions of growing international tension, provoked by the persistent hostility of Iran (which was holding US hostages) and the Soviet invasion of Afghanistan. For the first time the heads set aside a day for political discussions and issued a series of foreign policy documents that had been prepared for them in advance.

Ottawa (Montebello), July 1981 This year's summit marked the arrival of US President Ronald Reagan and the replacement of Giscard, the founder, by François Mitterrand. Reagan had already launched the combination of loose fiscal policy and tight monetary policy that marked his first term. But he proved impervious to the complaints of the rest of the G7 about the problems this caused for them. Reagan was clearly more interested in politics than economics and the political content of summits continued to expand.

The only lasting outcome of the summit was a decision to form the Quadrilateral or 'Quad' composed of the US Trade Representative, the EC Trade Commissioner and the trade ministers of Japan and Canada. This was the first example of an enduring lower-level body linked to the summit.[8] Pressure from the media also began to make itself felt. The Canadian hosts had wanted the press held in Ottawa, while the heads met in seclusion in Montebello, 43 miles (70km) away. But the Americans contrived to circumvent this.

Versailles, June 1982 The 1982 summit marked the start of a new sequence of summits, following the same order of hosts as the first - France, US, UK, Germany, Japan, Italy and Canada. Mitterrand and his new sherpa, Jacques Attali, decided the summit should be held in great splendour at the palace of Versailles and should reach precise decisions on a limited set of economic topics, with no politics.

Mitterrand wanted a revival of monetary cooperation and stabilisation of exchange rates, reverting to Giscard's theme at Rambouillet. Reagan sought agreement on strict restraint on economic relations with the Soviet Union and its Central European allies. In particular the Americans wanted the Europeans to reduce their reliance on natural gas imported from the Soviet Union and backed up this pressure with the threat of sanctions. Though this was ostensibly an economic subject, Reagan's motives were political. He sought to sharpen the rivalry between East and West, in the conviction that Soviet power would crumble.

The preparations for Versailles were tense and agreement on both main subjects was elusive. Finally a cross-issue deal was struck at the summit, at which the Americans appeared to accept monetary intervention in return for promises by the others of greater restraint in economic dealings with Eastern Europe. But the agreement was so fragile that it broke down within a few hours of the end of the summit. The only abiding result was the decision that the finance ministers should conduct periodic surveillance of their economic policies, with the IMF Managing Director in attendance.

Judgement on the Second Summit Series In the summits of the second series, the heads still kept to a mainly economic agenda and sought to resolve differences among themselves. On macro-economic policy a broad consensus prevailed that, in responding to the second surge in oil prices, fighting inflation must have absolute priority, whatever the costs to growth. The consequence of this was a prolonged, worldwide recession during the years 1979-1982.

The energy measures agreed in 1979 and 1980 had a good short-term effect in calming the markets and restoring G7 solidarity. But with growth so weak, energy imports never approached the targets agreed so painfully at Tokyo, while many of the structural measures set out in Venice proved superfluous. The recession also made it much harder for developing countries to service their debts. But though Schmidt warned of the impending debt crisis at Versailles, his last summit, the G7 leaders took no action.

On the other economic topics, little was done on trade and the deal linking the monetary system with East/West economic relations soon collapsed. But political subjects made distinct advances during this series. They were never the main topic and preparations were less systematic. But the G7 began to debate and reach decisions both on broad foreign policy issues like hostage-taking and refugees and on regional crises like Afghanistan and Lebanon.

The Third Summit Series: the Rise of Politics[9]

Williamsburg, May 1983 By this time, none of the founders of the summit survived in office and none of the present heads were former finance ministers. A period of remarkable continuity among the heads was beginning. Reagan, Mitterrand, Thatcher and German Chancellor Helmut Kohl were there for all six years of this series. Yasuhiro Nakasone stayed for five years, more than twice the usual life for Japanese Prime Ministers and Brian Mulroney of Canada was also there from 1984 onwards. Adding Kohl and Mulroney to Reagan and Thatcher pushed the political balance among the G7 towards the right.

The main outcome from Williamsburg was agreement on the response to the threat from Soviet medium-range missiles, which endangered both Europe and Japan. This was the first time the summit had addressed an East/West strategic issue or made a political topic its dominant theme. The discussions were heated at times, but the outcome resolved the multiple tensions between the G7 members, which the Russians were trying to exploit.

The missiles agreement arguably provided the single most important achievement of this entire series. In contrast, the economic discussions at Williamsburg were insubstantial. Economic recovery was at last visible after the long downturn and this proved to be sustained. But the G7 heads were content to leave the markets to be the driving force behind the revival. The debt crisis, provoked by Mexico's default in August 1982, was ignored.

London II, June 1984 The London summit took place while Reagan was seeking re-election and this inhibited its ambitions. It did little on macro-economic policy and failed to agree on trade. The proposal for a new round of multilateral trade negotiations, advocated by Japan and the United States, was resisted by the Europeans. The summit did, however, give its authority to the technique of multi-year debt rescheduling, developed by the finance ministers as part of the response to the debt crisis. Political issues, such as Libyan terrorism and the outbreak of the Iran-Iraq war, occupied half the exchanges among the heads, but without yielding major decisions.

Bonn II, May 1985 In Reagan's second Administration, James Baker became US Treasury Secretary. He found the US economy under severe strain. Growth was strong, but the budget and external deficits were gaping, the dollar had risen steadily over five years and protectionist pressures were becoming intolerable. One way to defuse such pressures would be to launch a new round of trade negotiations. The US pressed strongly for this, as did Japan, but the EC was still divided, with France the most reluctant. Trade emerged as the main economic issue for the second Bonn summit, but this ended in open disagreement over whether the new round should start in the following year. Kohl, Thatcher and Bettino Craxi (for Italy) could agree to this, but Mitterrand refused. So Bonn II receives the lowest grade of all in the Putnam Scale, as it actually made matters worse than before.

Politically the summit was also tense, as all the Europeans, including Thatcher, and Nakasone as well, were worried that Reagan's new 'Strategic Defence Initiative' would weaken their protection from nuclear attack. Later in the year Reagan invited the other leaders to New York for a discussion of arms control before he met Gorbachev, but Mitterrand refused to attend. The second Bonn summit, however, enabled Kohl to pursue his concern for the global environment by getting this topic formally on to the G7 agenda for the first time.

Tokyo II, May 1986 Baker unveiled the rest of his economic strategy in September 1985, at the first published meeting of the G5 finance ministers, who had hitherto met in strict secrecy. The Plaza Accord brought about a lasting decline in the dollar, eased US protectionist pressures, and revived the process of macro-economic policy coordination.[10] This became the main economic issue for the 1986 Tokyo summit, though more for organisation than substance. Now that the G5 was out in the open, Italy and Canada insisted that they too must join. The heads endorsed the creation of two parallel groups of finance ministers - the existing secret G5 and a new public G7 - though the G5 soon atrophied. This decision at Tokyo marked the effective move of macro-economic policy and monetary issues away from the heads and back to the finance ministers. Henceforth these issues, though often discussed by the heads, would rarely lead to decisions at summit level.

The question of a new round of trade negotiations, so divisive at Bonn, was largely resolved by the time of Tokyo II. The new Uruguay Round would be launched at a GATT ministerial meeting in September 1986. One contentious issue, however, was agriculture, which deeply divided the US and Canada from Europe and Japan. The heads had a useful exchange on agriculture at Tokyo, which helped to ensure that it was fully treated in the new trade round. This was a rare example of the summit going beyond macro-economics to address a structural economic issue. The nuclear disaster at Chernobyl, which happened only a few days before the summit, also captured the heads' attention and led to sustained G7 interest in nuclear safety both in the Ukraine and elsewhere.

The main issue for the heads, however, was terrorism, another political theme. The American bombing raid on Libya, intended to punish President Muammar Gadaffi for his sponsorship of terrorism, had deeply divided the G7. Mitterrand had refused to let the American bombers overfly French airspace, while Thatcher only backed the US because she needed Reagan's support over Northern Ireland. But the Europeans reacted to Reagan's aggressive approach by agreeing an alternative, politically based strategy. Thanks to vigorous advocacy by Thatcher, this won Reagan's acceptance at the summit and G7 unity was successfully restored. Though this unity was later undermined again, when it emerged that the US was making clandestine deals with Iran to get American hostages released, Tokyo II was the most productive summit of the third series.

Venice II, June 1987 Baker kept up the pressure for economic policy coordination, especially on Germany and Japan. This led to a further agreement between the finance ministers on differentiated economic measures at the Louvre in February

1987.[11] This agreement served to stabilise the dollar after two years' decline. The Louvre measures were essentially confirmed at the Venice summit in June, so that it looked as if macro-economic policy coordination might return to the summit. But this proved an illusion. A severe fall on G7 stock exchanges in October 1987 was blamed on the markets' reaction to the consequences of the Louvre measures. Policy coordination was once again discredited. Politically, the Venice summit was the occasion for a major debate on the Soviet Union, but without foreseeing the historic changes only two years away.

Toronto, June 1988 The Toronto summit rounded off the Reagan era with an air of self-congratulation at the strength of the economic recovery, which had persisted since 1983 without reviving inflation. The main economic issue was debt relief for low-income countries. Hitherto the Americans had driven the response to the crisis that had been provoked in 1982 by the default of large Latin American countries - Mexico, Brazil, Argentina, Venezuela - whose debts were largely to banks. Now the UK, France and Canada had realised that the same strategy would not work for low-income countries, whose debts were mainly to governments. They promoted debt relief for poor countries that were following corrective policies agreed with the IMF, so as to reduce their debt burden by up to one-third. 'Toronto terms' were agreed among the G7 and later adopted by the Paris Club of creditor governments, the IMF and the World Bank. But the US, Germany and Japan were reluctant participants and limited the scope of the offer. Politically, Toronto was insubstantial and the heads still showed no awareness of the fundamental transformation at work in Central and Eastern Europe.

Judgement on the Third Summit Series This series was marked by sustained economic recovery, a welcome contrast to the recession years of the second series. But much of the initiative in economic issues passed back from the heads to their finance ministers, especially with Baker at the US Treasury, who engineered the emergence of the G7 finance ministers. Baker revived macro-economic policy coordination, which had been in abeyance since 1978. This did not really survive his departure from office, but the initiative hereafter always remained with the finance ministers.[12] As for other economic subjects, the record in trade was very mixed. Open discord over launching a new trade round was later offset by useful exchanges on how agriculture should be treated in the round. The global environment, nuclear safety and debt relief for poor countries emerged as summit issues.

The most substantial achievements of this series were in political subjects, especially missiles in 1983 and terrorism in 1986. But despite these two successes, the treatment of foreign policy issues was episodic rather than sustained. The summits never achieved effective continuity in dealing with major political issues like East/West relations or tensions in the Middle East. At the same time they were losing the capacity for sustained treatment of economic issues, as responsibility shifted back to the finance ministers.

In part these trends were due to the way the summit process was changing during the 1980s. Not only the G7 finance ministers but the foreign ministers too were beginning to meet on their own, away from the summit. The authority of the sherpas to bring issues together for resolution by the heads was being eroded. Altogether, by the end of the Reagan era, the G7 summit had lost much of its original impetus and capacity.

The Fourth Series: The End of the Cold War[13]

Paris (Arch), July 1989 The continuity among the heads began to break up from 1989, with George Bush (the elder) replacing Reagan and a run of short-lived prime ministers in Japan and Italy. But Mitterrand, like Kohl, remained in office and decided to combine the second summit he would host (and the start of a third summit sequence) with the celebrations of the 200th anniversary of the French Revolution. His sherpa Attali, innovative, energetic and abrasive, led the preparations for what proved to be the most productive summit for over a decade.

There were solid results in three economic subjects. France's original choice for the summit was the global environment. For the first time, the G7 heads agreed substantive provisions on how to integrate environmental protection into all government policies. The Americans, however, wanted to give priority to debt relief. Bush's Treasury Secretary, Nicholas Brady, had concluded that the long-running debt crisis affecting loans from banks to middle-income developing countries could only be solved by debt reduction, ie the banks would not get all their money back. When this proved too radical for the IMF to accept in spring 1989, Brady pursued it through the G7 finance ministers. Agreement on the 'Brady Plan' was reached in time for the new approach to be endorsed at the summit, which eased its adoption by the IMF in September. Finally the heads agreed, on joint French and American initiative, to set up a Financial Action Task Force (FATF) to penalise the laundering of the proceeds of the illicit drugs trade.

Late in the preparations, Attali and his fellow sherpas woke up to the transformation taking place in Central and Eastern Europe. Poland and Hungary had broken free from Soviet domination and Russia under Gorbachev was ready to let them go. The Paris summit agreed to set up a mechanism to coordinate technical and financial assistance to Central European countries escaping from communism and trying to create working democracies and market economies. This was known as the G24, as all OECD countries joined, and the summit gave the chair of the group to the European Commission, the first time it would preside over an international body.

This early response to the end of the Cold War gave the G7 a new lease of life and dominated the summits of the fourth series. Attali's ambitions in fact went further.[14] Before the summit he used his links with Moscow to stimulate a letter from Gorbachev seeking a place at the summit table. But the rest of the G7, led by the US, fended off this approach. They likewise rejected Attali's proposal that the G7 heads should meet a selection of leaders from other countries who had been invited by Mitterrand to Paris for the bi-centenary celebrations.

Houston, July 1990 One year after the Arch summit, all the countries of Central Europe had escaped from Soviet control and the Berlin Wall had fallen. The G24 mechanism was working well. Late in 1989 Attali had used the sherpa network to launch his initiative that led to the European Bank for Reconstruction and Development (EBRD). So by the Houston summit attention had shifted to relations with the Soviet Union. The Europeans, led by Germany, wanted to reward Gorbachev for his enlightened policies in Central Europe and his moves towards economic reform. They proposed that the G7 should make a joint offer of assistance to the USSR. But the Americans doubted the strength of the Soviet commitment to political and economic change. Japan shared these doubts, reinforced by an unresolved territorial dispute with the Russians. So the Houston summit could only agree to ask a group of economic institutions to prepare a study on how best the Soviet Union might be helped.

The second major issue was trade. The Uruguay Round of GATT negotiations was meant to finish in December 1990, but many issues were still unresolved. The summit made good progress on institutional questions, like dispute settlement and the idea of a new 'World Trade Organization'. But exchanges on agriculture were marked by sharp divisions between the US (with Canada) and the EC (with Japan), reflecting persistent disagreement at the GATT in Geneva and the OECD in Paris. After tense discussions, the G7 agreed a compromise, but this proved too fragile to survive in Geneva. The Uruguay Round failed to conclude in 1990 and trade remained firmly on the G7 agenda.

Houston continued work on the global environment, moving away from domestic policy-making to international issues such as global warming, biodiversity and protecting forests and oceans. But the G7 conclusions were usually couched in very general terms.

London III, July 1991 In August 1990 Thatcher, at a meeting with Bush, suggested 'bringing the Soviet Union gradually closer into association with the economic summit'.[15] When the next summit met in London, Thatcher had been replaced by John Major. But the decision had been taken to invite Gorbachev to a session with the G7 heads after the main summit, the first time the G7 had entertained a guest. In substance, however, this innovation had mixed success. By the time Gorbachev reached London, the G7 members were having serious doubts about whether his economic reforms were well-judged and whether he could implement them. So their promises of help and support were guarded and conditional. Shortly afterwards a coup against Gorbachev hastened both his own downfall and the break-up of the Soviet Union.

The summit tried to help in resolving the deadlock in the Uruguay Round, not by detailed negotiations but by getting the heads personally committed to concluding the Round that year. In practice this commitment proved too weak and the Round dragged on into 1992. The heads addressed the environment again, looking forward to the UN Conference on Environment and Development (UNCED), due in June 1992. Annual meetings of G7 environment ministers began from now on. But as discussion moved from statements of general principle to more formal commitments on climate change or biodiversity, transatlantic differences opened up between the ambitious Europeans and the sceptical Americans.

Debt relief for poor countries, always a British priority, marked a further advance. Since debt reduction had been accepted for middle-income countries under the Brady Plan, it became available to low-income countries too. Thus the relief of one-third of eligible debt under 'Toronto terms' could be raised to one-half under 'London terms'.

Munich, July 1992 By the time of the Munich summit the Soviet Union had broken up. Boris Yeltsin was firmly installed as President of Russia and his Prime Minister, Yegor Gaidar, had launched an ambitious strategy for transforming the Russian economy. So help for Russia became the principal item for the G7 heads and Yeltsin was invited to Munich, as Gorbachev had been the year before. The summit promised very substantial funds for Russia - $24 billion in total - but tied them to the observance of an IMF programme. When this programme ran into trouble and Yeltsin removed Gaidar, most of these funds could not be disbursed.

In other respects too, Munich proved a frustrating summit. The G7 heads again undertook to complete the Uruguay Round of trade negotiations within the year, but failed once more as the Bush Administration ran out of time.[16] At the summit, Bush was inhibited by his re-election campaign (which he lost) and Mitterrand was preoccupied by the French referendum on the Maastricht Treaty (which passed only by the smallest margin). All the heads were unhappy at the inexorable growth of the agenda and the overloading of the summit process. Shortly after Munich Major circulated proposals for reforms to simplify the summit format.

Tokyo III, July 1993 Russia was again a major topic at the third Tokyo summit. This time the preparations were more systematic. The new US President, Bill Clinton, had early established personal contact with Yeltsin. The measures agreed at the summit, with Yeltsin present, were more realistic, though they still proved not enough to put the Russian economy on a steady path to growth.

The main achievement of this Tokyo summit, however, was in trade. This looked like the last chance for the Uruguay Round, after successive failures to conclude. This time the G7 heads did not simply rely on their own authority, but obliged their trade ministers to meet as the Quad shortly before their own summit. The heads then endorsed the Quad's understanding on tariffs - the last major unresolved issue - and provided enough impetus to enable Peter Sutherland, the new Director-General of the GATT, to bring the Round to a final conclusion in December.

The short-term effect of the Major reform proposals was to cut back the summit declaration to six pages (from a maximum of 20 pages at Houston 1990), but this improvement proved to be short-lived.

Judgement on the Fourth Summit Series The summits of the fourth series gave a new sense of purpose to the G7 process, after the decline of the Reagan years. The end of the Cold War provided a double stimulus. First, it obliged the G7 to concentrate on bringing former communist countries fully into the international system - initially Central Europe, then Russia. Second, it transformed the international system itself, making it truly universal. This opened up a variety of economic issues and brought them to G7 attention. These included both traditional subjects, like trade and debt, and new ones like the environment and drugs and money-laundering.

While the summit thus had more work to do, agreement among the G7 often proved elusive, so that the results were disappointing. The European Union members worked together better, but at the cost of friction with the United States. Without an external security threat there was less incentive to resolve economic disputes quickly, for example over agricultural trade, climate change or attitudes to Russian reform. At the same time, the overloading of the summit process made it harder for the heads to exert any personal impact, so as to resolve problems that had defied settlement at lower levels.

The Fifth Summit Series: Institutions for Globalisation[17]

Naples, July 1994 The Naples summit was not rich in substantive decisions, except in debt relief for poor countries, where 'Naples terms' raised the relief available on eligible debt to two-thirds. But it launched two important procedural moves that mark it as the beginning of a new summit series.

The first was a change in the position of Russia. Yeltsin was asked to the summit again, but a new package of economic help was not on offer. Instead, Yeltsin was invited to take a full part in the political discussions, to ease his dislike of always being a supplicant. This made Russia a participant in part of the summit, not merely a guest, and marked a first step towards full membership.

The second was the G7 decision to launch a review of international institutions. This derived from an initiative from Clinton, who was proving a far more confident summit player than Bush had been. He had already proposed the first meeting of G7 employment ministers, held in Detroit early in 1994. Shortly before Naples, he suggested a new programme of trade liberalisation, to follow the Uruguay Round. But the Europeans thought this came too soon after the protracted GATT negotiations, whose results were not yet in force. They proposed that the G7 should look instead at the rest of the international economic system. The G7, for the first time, explicitly recognised the advance of globalisation that had been stimulated by the end of the Cold War. The summit agreed to conduct a review of international institutions, to see what adaptation they might need to meet the demands of globalisation.

Halifax, June 1995 The Canadian Prime Minister, Jean Chrétien, who had first appeared at Naples, decided to make the institutional review the centrepiece of the summit he would host in Halifax, Nova Scotia. From the list of potential issues and institutions, Canada gave priority to the international monetary regime and the United Nations system. Other topics - trade, development, crime and drugs and the environment - were reserved for later treatment.

The monetary regime deserved priority because of the severe financial crisis that had hit Mexico at the end of 1994. The massive rescue package put together by the United States and the IMF had gained only grudging support from the Europeans and Japan. At Halifax, however, the G7 heads were able to agree on a substantial set of measures to treat and deter future crises. These comprised: better standards of economic data; enlarged sources of IMF finance; improved financial regulation; and work towards an international bankruptcy regime. All these measures were well-judged and gained early support from the full IMF membership. But implementation of the measures was slow and they were overtaken by the outbreak of the Asian crisis in 1997.

The review of the United Nations machinery made less progress, because the subject was so diffuse. But at Halifax the heads decided they could not let the UN's 50th anniversary pass without a major effort, carried forward into the next year. They also commissioned serious work on international crime. Yeltsin's position was strengthened by G7 acceptance of his proposal for a special summit on nuclear safety, which took place in Moscow in April 1996. Overall, Halifax emerged as a highly productive summit, especially for its work on the institutional review.

Lyon, June 1996 President Jacques Chirac, who had succeeded Mitterrand in 1995, decided to host the summit away from Paris, in the provincial city of Lyon. He continued the institutional review by focusing on development, especially the World Bank and the economic arms of the United Nations. The heads of the World Bank, UN, IMF and WTO were invited, for the first time, to a joint session with the G7 leaders and Russia.

The Lyon summit agreed on a major advance in debt relief for poor countries, so as to provide relief on their debts to institutions, like the IMF and World Bank, as well as to governments. The summit decision built on a British initiative, first launched at the Commonwealth Finance Ministers Meeting in 1994, and was rapidly adopted by the IMF and World Bank as the Heavily Indebted Poor Countries (HIPC) programme. As before, France, Britain and Canada were strong backers of debt relief, while the United States under Clinton had also moved in favour. But Germany and Japan were still sceptical.

The remaining provisions of the Lyon summit documents on development and United Nations reform were extensive, but couched in very general terms. The treatment of international crime, though prepared by a dedicated group of officials (the Lyon group) and a meeting of G7 interior and justice ministers late in 1995, was sidetracked by the need to respond to a terrorist attack on US servicemen in Saudi Arabia just before the summit. So Lyon, though industrious, was not quite as successful as Halifax had been.

Denver, June 1997 The institutional review, which had yielded good results at Halifax and Lyon, made little progress at Denver. It was difficult for the United States to lead on further UN reform because of the persistent arrears in its subscription. The summit could only promise support for measures being prepared by Kofi Annan, the new UN Secretary-General. Decisions on international crime were prepared for the summit by the Lyon group, but the heads were not satisfied and called for more action in a year's time. Discussions on the environment exposed deep differences between the United States and Europe over climate change and forests, which could not be bridged at Denver.

Clinton's preferred economic topic for the summit was Africa. This followed logically from the Lyon summit's emphasis on development. Clinton hoped the summit would assist in getting his measures to improve US aid and trade access for Africa adopted by Congress. But the Europeans had been irritated by Clinton's claims that America was economically far more dynamic than Europe. The European Union's programme of help for Africa was well in advance of anything that the US proposed to do. The Europeans were thus disinclined to make new commitments at American urging and the results on Africa were disappointing.

Denver marked a further advance towards summit membership by Russia. In order to reconcile the Russians to several Central European countries joining NATO, Clinton invited Yeltsin to take part in much of the economic discussion, for example on Africa, crime and the environment, as well as the political exchanges. Denver was known as 'the Summit of the Eight'. But the G7 heads still met on trade and finance, before Yeltsin arrived, and Russia did not join the finance ministers' meetings.

Judgement on the Fifth Summit Series The fifth series marked a further advance of the summits from their low point of the late 1980s. The new arrivals among the heads, such as Clinton, Chrétien, Chirac and Blair (who arrived in 1997), were more active and innovative participants than their predecessors. Russia became more deeply integrated into the process, without preventing the G7 from making progress on economic issues. The institutional review provided a useful framework for concentrating the agenda of successive summits. All this produced some good results in specific subjects, such as monetary reform and debt relief. The G7 began to focus on the implications of advancing globalisation.

But by Denver in 1997 the institutional review had run its course and familiar frustrations were re-appearing. The summits were now less ceremonial, so that the heads spent more working time together. All the hosts were choosing to hold their summits in provincial centres, away from the distractions of capital cities. But the subject-matter handled by the summit was still heavily overloaded. One safety-valve was to develop lower-level meetings to take the strain off the heads. Not only foreign and finance ministers, but also environment ministers, employment ministers and justice and home affairs ministers were meeting annually or at wider intervals. But the agenda coming to the summit itself was still far too long for a two-day meeting and the documentation was inflated to match, having lost all the progress made at Tokyo III. The documentation from Denver was the longest yet - 29 pages endorsed by the heads, plus eight from the foreign ministers and seven from the finance ministers.

Conclusion

Over 30 years, the summits moved a long way from their origins at Rambouillet. They made a successful start in economic decision-making in the 1970s. The innovation of bringing together heads of government of major powers proved its worth and the summit became an institution. But the G7 process suffered a slow decline during the 1980s. The summit went deeper into politics, which interested Reagan, but only produced occasional results. Much of the summit's economic responsibilities moved back to the finance ministers.

The end of the Cold War and its transformation of the international system provided new challenges to the heads of government and generated a revival of the summit. There were some substantial achievements in the 1990s and the heads began to perceive the impact of globalisation. But while they were promoting change in other institutions, their own efficiency in responding to globalisation was still hampered by the inadequacies of the summit process. Fundamental reform was needed to liberate the personal capacities of the heads of government, so that they could meet their objectives of political leadership, collective management and reconciling domestic and international pressures.

Notes

1 As recorded in Chapter 1, the details are in Putnam and Bayne 1987, pp. 269-277 and Bayne 2000, pp. 192-200.

2 A good summary account of this period is in Kenen 1994, pp. 21-41.

3 Accounts of the summits of the first series are in Putnam and Bayne 1987, pp. 36-47, and pp. 62-94. See also De Menil and Solomon 1983, pp. 18-27.

4 In the Smithsonian Agreement of December 1971, all IMF members agreed to set par values again for their currencies and defend them within a band of 4.5%. The EC countries undertook to keep their currencies in a narrower band of 2.25%, which became known as 'the snake in the tunnel'. Very soon the 'tunnel' crumbled, but the 'snake' survived, to become the ancestor of the EU Exchange Rate Mechanism. See Kenen 1994.

5 In the early years the four Europeans at the summit - Germany, France, Britain and Italy - always contrived that the summit was held at a time when one of them held the Presidency. But this was impossible in 1982 and happened increasingly rarely as the EU expanded. See Putnam and Bayne 1987, pp. 150-154.

6 The cross-issue deal agreed at the first Bonn summit provided the inspiration for Professor Bob Putnam's model of 'two-level games'. See Putnam 1988, Putnam and Henning 1989 and Evans, Jacobson and Putnam 1993.

7 Accounts of the summits of the second series are in Putnam and Bayne 1987, pp. 110-144 and De Menil and Solomon 1983, pp. 28-41.

8 Earlier groups of officials set up by the summit had only a limited duration. The Quad later developed a life of its own, entirely detached from the summit - see Cohn 2002, especially pp. 123-166.

9 Accounts of the summits of the third series are in Putnam and Bayne 1987, pp. 170-226, with 252-254. See also Bayne 2000, pp. 31-44, especially for Venice II and Toronto.

10 For the Plaza Accord and its consequences, see Funabashi 1988.

11 In fact Italy did not attend the Louvre meeting, in protest because the G7 gathering was preceded by a G5. The result was that the G5 never met again.

12 The work of the G7 finance ministers on macro-economic policy continued to attract the attention of scholars in the 1980s and 1990s. As well as Funabashi 1988 (see note 10) these include Dobson 1991 and Bergsten and Henning 1996.

13 Accounts of the summits of the fourth series are in Bayne 2000, pp. 59-74.

14 His ideas and ambitions are well chronicled in Attali 1995, pp. 281-286.

15 The quotation is from a speech by Thatcher in Aspen, Colorado, on 5 August 1990. The main topic of the Bush/Thatcher meeting, however, was Saddam Hussein's invasion of Kuwait.

16 However, the Blair House agreement, which created the basis for an agreement on agriculture, was concluded just before Bush handed over to Clinton.

17 Accounts of the summits of the fifth series are in Bayne 2000, pp. 113-132.

THE FIRST G8 SEQUENCE, 1998-2004

Chapter 3

Breaking Free: Birmingham 1998

By the Denver summit of 1997, it was clear that the institutional review launched in 1994 was running out of steam. Although the British had been among the strongest advocates of the institutional review, Tony Blair, as host to the 1998 summit, could see that a new impetus was needed. He decided to focus the Birmingham summit - the first to meet in the UK outside London - on the reform of the summit process itself. Birmingham 1998 was a highly innovative summit in organisation and procedure. It was the first summit where heads of government met alone, without their ministers. This fulfilled the aspiration of the founders Giscard and Schmidt, which had never been achieved before. It was the first G8 summit with the Russians as permanent members. This completed a process of assimilation, which began in earnest at Naples 1994 and in fact went back to Paris 1989, when Gorbachev first wrote to the G7 seeking entry. Birmingham therefore marked the beginning of a new summit series, which would embrace the next four summits, up to Genoa 2001.[1]

The New Summit Format

Preparations for a Heads-Only Summit

Six years before, in 1992, Blair's predecessor John Major had tried to get his colleagues to agree to reshape the summit. His aims had been: more informal discussions, among leaders alone; lighter preparations and a shorter agenda; concise and simple summit documents. Only limited progress had been made in this direction during the fifth summit series. But Blair at Birmingham achieved almost all these objectives:

- Heads of government came to Birmingham without supporting ministers. They met for a full day 'in retreat' at a country house, far from the media and all but a few members of their delegations.[2]
- The summit had a limited agenda of three items, two of which - employment and crime - had been publicly identified in advance.
- The Birmingham economic communiqué was only ten pages long, together with a G7 document of four pages and a foreign policy statement of three pages. This was less than half the length of the Denver summit documentation.

This did not mean that total G7 and G8 activity was reduced or simplified; quite the opposite. Birmingham was preceded by more intense preparations than ever, in the sherpa network, in specialist groups and in other ministerial meetings. Employment was prepared by a meeting of employment and finance ministers in London in February; crime by interior ministers in Washington in December 1997. Environment ministers met in Leeds Castle, England, in April and energy ministers in Moscow in March. A major innovation was the series of meetings of foreign and finance ministers in London on 8-9 May, 1998, a week before the summit, to prepare some items for Birmingham and dispose of others which did not need the leaders' attention.

These ministers met in four combinations and issued documents totalling over 40 pages. The G7 finance ministers did the groundwork for the summit on the world economy, the new financial architecture and financial crime. A short meeting of G8 finance ministers issued national employment plans. G8 foreign and finance ministers, meeting jointly, disposed of development (leaving debt relief for the summit) and electronic commerce. The G8 foreign ministers dealt with the environment, issuing a separate paper on forests but reserving climate change for the leaders. They also disposed of UN issues, nuclear safety and non-proliferation, land-mines, human rights, terrorism and 17 regional issues, only two of which (Kosovo and Middle East) were picked up again by the leaders.

The British preparations were purposeful and well organised. By limiting the main summit agenda to three items and settling two of these well in advance, they prevented extra subjects from cluttering up the list. The financial crisis which broke out in Asia a few weeks after the Denver summit determined the choice of the third item, to which the British hosts successfully attached the problem of debt relief for low-income countries, which they had promoted at earlier summits. On the political side, two sudden crises that had blown up in the week before Birmingham - riots in Indonesia and Indian nuclear tests - were inevitably added to the agenda.

From G7 to G8

Denver 1997 had been called the 'Summit of the Eight'. Birmingham was billed as the first G8 summit. One immediate consequence was Yeltsin's conclusion that Russia was now eligible to host a future summit. At Birmingham, he bid to do this in 2000, taking over Japan's turn in that year. Japanese Prime Minister Ryutaro Hashimoto refused to yield; but Yeltsin pressed his point, saying that he wanted to host a summit no later than 2000, when his presidential term expired. Birmingham broke up with the matter unresolved and by Cologne a year later Yeltsin seemed to have forgotten about it.

Blair had chosen subjects for Birmingham that were intended to encourage Russian integration into the G8. The Russians made some real contributions to the discussions on crime and employability and even on debt, as they were now in the Paris Club. But this process did not get far. During the preparations on G8 topics there were occasions when the Russians tried to water down economic commitments that the other seven could accept, though this did not visibly weaken the summit documents. The work on financial architecture was all done by the G7, as were the preparations on debt relief for poor countries, though this topic formed part of the G8 communiqué at Birmingham and thus appeared to involve the Russians.

The Birmingham Summit, 15-17 May 1998

The political context for Birmingham 1998 tended to encourage harmony among the participants. The imbalance in economic performance between Europe and the United States, which had caused friction at Denver in 1997, was now correcting itself. The European economies began to recover and eleven EU countries were preparing to launch the new European currency - the euro - on 1 January 1999. Among European leaders, Blair and Chirac were electorally secure. But Kohl was facing elections later in the year (which he lost) and Romano Prodi would soon hand over to Massimo d'Alema as Italian Prime Minister.

Though the US economy remained very buoyant, Clinton had lost ground politically. Difficulties with Congress made him unable to obtain 'fast-track' authority for trade negotiations and delayed the release of new money for the IMF. Negotiations took place on the margins of Birmingham to resolve outstanding EU/US disputes over Cuba, Iran and Libya, where new American legislation threatened economic sanctions.[3] These led to agreement at the EU/US summit on 18 May, while Chrétien had a good EU/Canada summit just before Birmingham. Blair hosted both these summits, as the UK also held the EU Presidency.

Hashimoto was hampered by the persistent sluggishness of Japan's economy. But he benefited from Birmingham's focus on Asian political problems, like India and Indonesia. These gave an Asian slant to the summit, so that Japan had something to contribute and Clinton had an incentive to be helpful to Hashimoto. The leader in greatest difficulty was Yeltsin. He was fighting against Russia's economic collapse and his own failing health and shortly before Birmingham had dismissed his long-serving Prime Minister, Viktor Chernomyrdin.[4]

G7 Economic Issues

The G7 leaders met for two hours on the afternoon of 15 May, before Yeltsin arrived. They issued a four-page chairman's statement, which was supported by a detailed report by G7 finance ministers on the new financial architecture.

World Economy

Birmingham continued the practice, revived at Denver, of short recommendations on national economic policies, largely reflecting what countries were doing already. While the other recommendations were uncontroversial, there was a risk of friction over Japan, if Clinton pressed Hashimoto too hard to stimulate the economy. In the event, the other G7 members decided to give a message of confidence in Japan's economic strategy, helped by Hashimoto's promise of action on the bad debts of Japanese banks.

New International Financial Architecture

It was not part of the original British plan to have this on the agenda at Birmingham. But the Asian financial crisis, which had started in July 1997 and led to the collapse of the Thai, Korean and Indonesian economies, demanded the attention of the leaders. After the initial rescue operations orchestrated by the IMF and the World Bank, the G7 finance ministers had been active in devising measures to deter future crises and deal with them if they came.

At Birmingham the crisis seemed under control. The leaders endorsed the detailed report of their finance ministers on proposed reforms of the IMF, World Bank and other institutions. These reforms, described more fully in Chapter 5, focused on getting better economic data; on closer and more transparent policy surveillance; and on better standards and more cooperation in financial supervision. This was all solid, sensible work, which revealed close advance consultation with the Fund and Bank. The strong endorsement from the summit was intended to ensure that steady progress continued over the months ahead.

The lull in the crisis, however, was deceptive.[5] In August Russia, having used up an IMF drawing in a few weeks, was obliged to abandon the defence of the rouble and defaulted on government debt. In early October financial collapse threatened Brazil and a major American hedge fund, Long-Term Capital Management, needed a massive rescue. Blair prepared to call together the G7 leaders for an emergency summit - the first of its kind.

At this point the tide turned. During October the IMF began to put together a substantial package for Brazil. The G7 finance ministers agreed a strategy for reform, helped by a new informal G22 that had been earlier called together by the Americans and included many Asian and other developing countries affected by the crisis. The G7 leaders issued a written declaration on 30 October 1998 endorsing their ministers' work, without needing to meet.[6] But this subject had to come back to the summit at Cologne in 1999.

G8 Foreign Policy Issues

The summit had to deal with two unexpected crises in Asia - India and Indonesia - but still managed to dispose of all the foreign policy issues before it during the first G8 dinner on 15 May. A three-page statement covered the two main items as well as Northern Ireland, Kosovo, Bosnia, and the Middle East. The Indonesian crisis was soon resolved by the departure of President Suharto, but the tension in South Asia persisted.[7]

Indian Nuclear Tests

The Indian nuclear tests shortly before the summit had taken all G8 countries by surprise and their reactions diverged.[8] US legislation obliged Clinton to introduce economic sanctions. Japan did the same, because of its horror of nuclear war. This made Clinton and Hashimoto allies, while Canada was also in this camp. But the Europeans traditionally disliked sanctions; Blair wanted to try persuasion first; and Chirac was reluctant to punish India for doing what France itself had done in 1995.

The leaders did not allow these differences to turn into the sort of dispute they had had over economic sanctions in the past.[9] Clinton made no real effort to get the Europeans to impose sanctions. Instead the heads focused on what should happen next and - after condemning the Indian tests - put all their weight behind getting India to sign up to the Comprehensive Test Ban Treaty and the Non-Proliferation Treaty. The leaders also urged restraint on Pakistan, though without success - Pakistan also conducted nuclear tests a few weeks later.

The G8 foreign ministers followed up Birmingham promptly, meeting in June with other countries that had renounced nuclear weapons to put pressure on India and Pakistan to do likewise.[10] Sustained diplomatic activity over the next year, especially by the Americans, seemed to be having its effect, with both countries inching towards accepting the treaty commitments. Shortly before Cologne, however, all this was set back by an ill-advised incursion into Kashmir from Pakistan. But the G8 leaders gave this little attention, being by then wholly preoccupied with Kosovo.

G8 Economic and Global Issues

The G8 leaders spent 16 May 'in retreat', discussing their main agenda. On 17 May they issued a ten-page declaration, half the usual length. In their discussions they spent most time on debt relief and international crime. Other items, including the main item of employability, were taken more rapidly.

Employability

Detailed preparations before Birmingham on the theme of 'employability and inclusion' involved the preparation of employment plans by each country. These plans were endorsed by G8 finance ministers when they met a week before the summit.[11] When the leaders themselves turned to this topic, the discussion was harmonious, with none of the transatlantic clashes of earlier years, but it was brief and general. The communiqué endorsed the substantial work accomplished by employment and finance ministers during the year, but added nothing new. The main achievement of the summit in this field was to give impetus to work at lower levels, in an atmosphere of greater readiness to learn from the experience of others.

International Crime

The G8 leaders had their longest discussion at Birmingham on international crime, beginning with a briefing from the head of the UK National Crime Squad, supported by videos. They responded well to this original approach and agreed without difficulty on a series of points focusing on hi-tech crime, money-laundering and other financial crime, trafficking in persons and the illegal manufacture and smuggling of firearms. They undertook to support current UN work on drugs and on drawing up a convention on transnational organised crime. They agreed to hold a G8 ministerial meeting on crime in Moscow in 1999.[12]

This was the first time the leaders had a well-prepared discussion on this theme. Cooperation among the G8 was already quite far advanced. But even here it was clear that cooperation between law-enforcement agencies had gone further than judicial cooperation; it was easier to catch the criminals than to bring them to justice. In the wider UN context there was still a long way to go before the G8 leaders could think they were winning the war against international crime.

Debt Relief

The British had always wanted Birmingham to focus on debt relief for low-income countries, which is discussed in more detail in Chapter 5.[13] It was a topic which attracted much public interest. While the leaders met 'in retreat', Birmingham was the scene of a massive demonstration sponsored by the Jubilee 2000 Campaign, when 50,000 people walked round the conference site urging complete debt forgiveness for poor countries by 2000.[14]

The summit was intended to accelerate the Heavily Indebted Poor Countries (HIPC) initiative. This had been agreed by the G7 at Lyon in 1996, but was now flagging. Birmingham endorsed the aim of having all eligible countries engaged in the HIPC process by the year 2000. When countries had the necessary track record in IMF-approved policies, they should get the relief they needed for 'a lasting exit' from their debt problems. Interim debt relief should be available to them if needed; and accelerated measures were offered to African countries emerging from conflict.

The summit thus did make some advances in getting better debt relief for poor countries. But there was still plenty of scope for foot-dragging. The Germans remained unenthusiastic about the whole process, as emerged clearly from briefings by Kohl and his officials.[15] The issue of IMF gold sales (left open at Lyon back in 1996) was still unresolved, so that the financing of the HIPC process remained uncertain. The sums available for low-income countries, whether in debt relief or from other sources, looked meagre when compared with the huge rescue packages assembled for Thailand, Korea and Indonesia. The organisers of the big demonstration were very disappointed at the outcome.[16]

Other Economic Issues

A number of other issues were covered more cursorily:

- *Economic Policy* The G8 considered the wider implications of the Asian financial crisis and issued a warning against the revival of protectionism. At a late stage - too late for inclusion in the communiqué - the leaders decided to commend China for its responsible role in the crisis.
- *Trade* Even though a WTO ministerial in Geneva followed immediately after the summit, there was only a short exchange on trade.[17] The Europeans argued

that the next series of WTO negotiations, due to begin in 2000, should be a comprehensive 'Millennium Round', but they did not convince the US. The opportunity was wasted for a serious discussion on trade and investment and the protectionist pressures unleashed by globalisation. Clinton's failure to get fast-track authority put him in a weak position. The presence of the Russians, who were not even members of the WTO, also inhibited discussion.

- *Environment* The British had allowed plenty of time for this topic at Birmingham, expecting a difficult exchange on climate change as at Denver in 1997. But no one was in the mood for that. Agreement was easily reached on exhortations to all to sign the Kyoto Protocol within the next year, to bring in the necessary domestic measures to meet their commitments and to work together with developing countries.
- *Development* The leaders endorsed the OECD's 21st Century Strategy for economic and social development; they promised work on untying aid; they supported the World Health Organisation (WHO) campaign against malaria and other campaigns against AIDS; and they offered some trade and investment measures for least-developed countries. All these were welcome confirmations of support, at summit level, of international work in hand. But they fell short of the expectations raised at Denver, especially on help for Africa.

Assessment of the Birmingham Summit

Procedurally, the Birmingham summit was very successful. The new 'heads-only format' worked well and was highly welcomed by the participating heads. It enabled them to concentrate on a well-selected and well-prepared agenda and their discussions were focused and harmonious. The ceremonial aspects of the summit were kept to a minimum, but the heads were free to wander the streets as they had at Halifax in 1995. Clinton was observed drinking in a canal-side pub, to the amazement of the pensioner couple whose table he shared. In short, Birmingham came closer than any previous summit to the informal, personal encounter envisaged by the founders. The leaders had thus gained a new freedom to set their agenda and organise their time. The price was an ever-growing G7/G8 bureaucracy at lower levels.

At Birmingham, the leaders could thus have an extended discussion of a few selected items. They appreciated this opportunity and got through their agenda faster than expected, leaving time for bilateral and other contacts. This format however, inevitably focussed attention on the leaders themselves and their personal contribution to the outcome. This was of varied quality. There was substantial discussion among the heads of crime and debt, which led to some advances. But other items, like employability and financial architecture, were treated more summarily. On these the main contribution of the leaders was to give their authority and their impetus to the work being done at lower levels - they added nothing of their own.

The new format also led to the issue of more concise documentation. But though the main G8 communiqué was kept to ten pages or less, the language was dense and it was too long for full quotation. The attitude of the media remained ambivalent and their coverage of summit results was generally superficial and incomplete.

Though Birmingham was the first G8 summit, the Russians contributed little to the substantive outcome on economic issues. Yeltsin sought to make Russia more involved in the G8 by proposing future meetings to be held in Moscow, on crime and on the 'millennium bug'.[18] The main foreign policy issues at Birmingham, India and Indonesia, though suitable for G8 treatment, also did not give salience to Russia. Meanwhile the G7 leaders started the Birmingham summit by meeting without Yeltsin and issued a statement on issues where Russia had nothing to contribute. The G7, at the level of both the heads and their finance ministers, remained vigorous and necessary; it was in fact more active at Birmingham than at Denver the year before. The Russians did not like it, but were obliged to accept it; and the G7 members were not deterred by the risk of Russian displeasure.

The choice of themes for Birmingham identified this as the first summit which would address directly popular anxieties about globalisation: about loss of jobs and job security; about international crime; about panic and instability in the financial markets; and about the world's poorest countries falling further behind. Birmingham therefore concentrated on employability, crime, financial architecture and debt relief for poor countries. References to globalisation were integrated into the summit documents, as they treated the different issues. For example, on jobs the leaders said:

> The challenge is how to reap the benefits of rapid technological change and economic globalisation whilst ensuring that all our citizens share in these benefits…..

On crime:

> Globalisation has been accompanied by a dramatic increase in transnational crime….. Such crimes pose….. a global threat which can undermine the democratic and economic basis of societies.

On financial issues:

> Globalisation has the power to bring immense economic benefits….. But the Asian financial crisis has revealed that there are potential weaknesses and vulnerabilities in the global financial system.

On world poverty:

> One of the most difficulty challenges the world faces [is]: to enable poorer developing countries to….. benefit from the opportunities offered by globalisation.[19]

In these passages the G7 and G8 leaders, while recognising the advances and opportunities created by globalisation, expressed their anxiety about its risks and dangers, especially for poor countries and less privileged members of society.

At Birmingham, Blair got his colleagues to agree that globalisation, while beneficial and inevitable, was not an undiluted good and needed to be managed accordingly.[20]

Despite these successes in procedure and general approach, the content of the specific understandings reached at Birmingham was less substantial than had been hoped. There were no great breakthroughs, but rather a number of small advances across a wide field. Even where the leaders could not agree on everything, as on the response to India, they avoided outright disagreement. On the two main economic items - financial architecture and debt - the results were rather disappointing. The progress on financial architecture proved short-lived, while outstanding disagreements on debt relief were not resolved. But Birmingham laid essential foundations for the more complete agreements on both these subjects reached at Cologne a year later.

Conclusion: The Renewal of the Summit

Birmingham launched a new summit series and provided evidence that a fundamental renewal of the summits was taking place. The main pointers to this renewal were the following:

- The Birmingham summit was hosted by the leader of a new left-leaning government, returning to power after more than 15 years in opposition, at a time when G8 governments generally were moving towards the centre-left. That made Blair and his G8 colleagues ready to innovate, in both summit format and summit agenda.
- Birmingham focused explicitly on globalisation and especially on how to help those who were put at risk by it. The agenda shifted towards social issues, like employability, trans-border crime and the problems of developing countries.
- This was a true G8 summit, with Russia present from the start. Because of Russia's weakness, the main economic work of the summit was done by the G7 and would be for some years ahead. G8 work on social issues like employment and crime was useful in binding in the Russians, though because policies were slow-acting it was hard to show results. But where, as in trade, the main differences arose between Europe and the United States, the presence of Russia could inhibit progress.
- For the first time, the summits showed themselves responsive to pressure from public opinion, especially in the sustained campaign for debt relief. They seemed ready to grant legitimacy to the views of civil society without always being sure whom they represented.

The performance of the Birmingham summit can be briefly judged against the criteria defined in Chapter 1. The summit showed strong *leadership* in its procedural innovations. These gave fresh encouragement to the G8 heads, who could see results from their own efforts. The summit was also fairly *effective* in reconciling international and domestic pressures in its treatment of employment and crime. *Solidarity* was good over India, where the heads avoided friction, but there were weaknesses over debt relief and international trade. The summit took unusual pains to make its conclusions *acceptable* to outside opinion, though with limited success. There was good *consistency* between the different items on the agenda, except for the neglect of trade. Finally, the results on financial architecture and debt relief were not *durable* in themselves, as they needed to be re-done a year later. But the procedural innovations introduced at Birmingham would show high *durability*, with 'heads-only summits' becoming the accepted format for the 2000s.

Notes

1 This chapter is based on Chapter 10 of *Hanging In There* (Bayne 2000). This in turn was drawn from two notes prepared for the University of Toronto G8 Research Group with whom I attended the Birmingham summit, as the *LSE Magazine's* correspondent. For references in this and later chapters, I have drawn on my files of the *Financial Times* and *The Economist*. Budd 2003 adds a valuable perspective from a participant in the sherpa process for Birmingham, Cologne and Okinawa.

2 In organising a 'retreat' for G7 leaders, Blair was following a well-established practice at Commonwealth Heads of Government Meetings (CHOGM). See Bayne 1998 for a comparison of the Birmingham summit and the Edinburgh CHOGM of October 1997, both chaired by Blair.

3 See B. Stokes, 'Winning Combination', *Financial Times*, 14 May 1998.

4 Sergei Kiriyenko took over as Yeltsin's Prime Minister in March 1998. Yevgeny Primakov succeeded him in August 1998, after the Russian default.

5 A paper given by Dr DeAnne Julius at a conference just before Birmingham raised the prospect that the financial crisis was far from over; see Julius 1998.

6 See G. Baker, 'G7 Attempts to Restore Calm to World Finance', *Financial Times*, 31 October 1998. Further references to work on the financial architecture in 1998 are in Chapter 5 below.

7 Suharto stepped down on 21 May, after 32 years in power. See P. Montagnon, 'The Waves from Indonesia', *Financial Times*, 22 May 1998.

8 The tests took place on 11 and 13 May. See A. L. Kazmin and K. Guha, 'Jubilant India Shrugs off World Disapproval' and G. Baker and A. L. Kasmin, 'Defiant Delhi Carries out Two More Nuclear Tests', *Financial Times*, 13 and 14 May 1998.

9 The worst dispute had been over gas supplies to Europe from the Soviet Union at the 1982 Versailles summit - see Chapter 2 above.

10 D. Buchan, 'Moral Pressure Builds up on Tests', *Financial Times*, 12 June 1998. For Pakistan's tests, see 'Pakistan Defiant as its First N-tests Draw Condemnation', *Financial Times*, 29 May 1998.

11 These employment plans developed the type of job-creating measures examined at an LSE conference organised by Professor Richard Layard shortly before Birmingham. See CEP 1998.

12 This meeting took place in October 1999; see *Financial Times* News Digest, 20 October 1999.

13 See G. Brown (British Finance Minister), 'Debt and Development - Time to Act Again', *The Economist*, 21 February 1998.

14 The Jubilee 2000 campaign was strongly backed by the British charity Christian Aid, which had done serious analytical work on poor countries' debt problems.

See Lockwood, Donlan, Joyner and Simms 1998. Oxfam was also deeply involved; see K. Watkins, 'Life and Debt Situation', *Financial Times*, 23 January 1998.

15 The German government was not moved by a massive postcard campaign orchestrated by Christian Aid - see P. Norman, 'Postcards Hit a Nerve in Bonn', *Financial Times*, 2 April 1998. This tactic had more success when the charities began to target Schroeder, leader of the German opposition, as the elections approached.

16 This was widely reported in the British press. See, for example, L. Elliott, 'Fury at G8's Debt Failure', *Guardian*, P. Vallely and others, 'Rich Nations Snub Pleas of the Poor', *Independent* and 'Blair Admits Failure on Debt Relief Package', *The Times*, all on 18 May 1998.

17 The ministerial marked the 50th anniversary of the foundation of the GATT. See '50 Years of the GATT', *The Economist*, 16 May 1998.

18 The millennium bug - now barely remembered - was the fear that many computers would have problems in moving from 1999 to 2000. The fear proved almost groundless.

19 The quotations are from paras. 6, 13 and 18-19 of the G8 communiqué and para. 6 of the G7 statement. Texts of these and all G8 summit documents are available on www.g8.utoronto.ca.

20 Blair had taken a similar line at the Edinburgh Commonwealth Heads of Government Meeting in October 1997; see Maud 1998 and Bayne 1998.

Chapter 4

Debt and the Balkans: Cologne 1999

Gerhard Schroeder, the host for the Cologne summit, had led the German Social Democratic Party (SPD) to victory in September 1998, bringing an end to 16 years of rule by the Christian Democrats (CDU) under Helmut Kohl. The Green Party replaced the Free Democrats (FDP) as the junior coalition partner. Schroeder resembled Blair in many ways.[1] He and his party had come back to power after nearly two decades in opposition. He was keen to establish effective but innovative policies, which would mark a clear break with what had gone before. This made him a natural supporter of the reforms to the summit process brought in at Birmingham the year before. The Germans adopted the new 'heads-only' format without hesitation for the Cologne summit of June 1999.[2]

Schroeder's election as German Chancellor in September 1998 marked a further shift among G7 members away from the political right towards the centre-left. This shift had begun in the previous summit series, as Clinton and Chrétien in North America were followed by Blair in Britain and Lionel Jospin (as Prime Minister under Chirac) in France. This leftward trend was now pursued even more strongly in Europe. In addition to Schroeder in Germany, Massimo d'Alema succeeded Prodi as Italian Prime Minister, and virtually all the other EU member states now had left-leaning governments, with Spain the only major exception. The G7 governments, taken together, were closer to the centre-left than at any time in the summit's history, completely reversing the trend to the right seen in the 1980s and early 1990s. This reflected a move by governments in most G7 countries to capture the middle ground rather than a shift all the way across the ideological spectrum. But it made the leaders on balance more interventionist and concerned with social issues and thus ready for innovation at the summit.

Preparations and Format

The preparations before Cologne were rather more hasty and improvised than the year before. Nothing was done before the German elections, which brought in the new government headed by Chancellor Schroeder. Even then some confusion prevailed, because of tension between Schroeder and his first finance minister, Oskar Lafontaine.[3] But as the summit approached, a pattern emerged under the pressure of continuing financial upheaval and the crisis in Kosovo.

In the twelve months following Birmingham there was intensive work in the G7 finance ministers on financial architecture, while the G8 foreign ministers held important meetings in summer 1998 on South Asian nuclear tests and in spring 1999 on Kosovo. As the summit approached, G8 employment ministers met in Washington and G8 environment ministers in Schwerin, Germany. The pre-summit ministerial meetings were simpler than before Birmingham but less integrated. G8 foreign ministers met near Cologne on 8-10 June. They issued a six-page document on both global and regional issues. But their most important achievement was to agree, together with regional states, on proposals for Kosovo and a Stability Pact for South Eastern Europe (20 pages together). G7 finance ministers met separately, without Russia, on 11-12 June in Frankfurt. They agreed documents on debt relief and on new financial architecture (24 pages), though these were not issued publicly till the summit a week later.

In the year since Birmingham, events had conspired to frustrate the integration of Russia into the economic work of the summit, while reinforcing the political value of the G8. Russia's default in August 1998 showed it was part of the problem affecting the world financial system and could hardly contribute to its solution. The 'Cologne Debt Initiative' was briefly welcomed in the G8 communiqué, but the initiative itself was spelt out in the G7 leaders' statement and the related document from G7 finance ministers. So the main economic results from the summit - on financial architecture and debt - came from the G7 only and the Russians had nothing to contribute. This was in contrast to the central foreign policy issue at Cologne. The key problems on Kosovo could not be resolved without Russian involvement - indeed some of them were of Russia's making.

The Cologne Summit, 18-20 June 1999

The political context for Cologne 1999 was still conducive to harmony among the participants.[4] In the US, despite the success of his economic policies, Clinton remained in political difficulty. Persistent sexual scandals had led to his impeachment early in 1999, though he was acquitted. The European economies continued to recover and the new European currency - the euro - was successfully launched in eleven EU countries on 1 January 1999.[5] This gave a political boost to the Europeans, even though the value of the euro against the dollar was weaker than they had hoped. The new Japanese leader, Keizo Obuchi, was hampered by the persistent sluggishness of Japan's economy. But he was helped by unexpected good news about Japan's economic performance in early 1999.

The leader in greatest difficulty was Yeltsin, who was now in his last year in office. The Russian economy was still struggling to emerge from the rouble crisis of August 1998. Since dismissing Chernomyrdin shortly before Birmingham, Yeltsin had worked through three more prime ministers by Cologne - Sergei Kiriyenko, Yevgeny Primakov and Sergei Stepashin.[6] His health continued to worsen and he had nearly collapsed at the funeral of King Hussein of Jordan in February. The summit would be his first international visit since that occasion. Ostensibly for health reasons but really because of his dispute with the G7 over Kosovo, Yeltsin decided only to come to Cologne on the last day of the summit, sending Stepashin to represent him on the first two days.

G7 Economic Subjects

G7 heads met on the afternoon of 18 June, with no Russians present. They discussed the world economy, new financial architecture and debt relief. They issued a substantial statement (of six pages) supported by reports from the G7 finance ministers on the latter two subjects. At Cologne, unlike Birmingham, the main discussion on debt was in the G7, not the G8.

World Economy

As was now usual, the statement contained brief national recommendations to each G7 member. Obuchi was able to give a good account of the Japanese recovery and the others followed Clinton in regarding this as very hopeful.

New Financial Architecture

Over the months leading up to Cologne there had been intensive work by the G7 finance ministers across a wide front.[7] A new Financial Stability Forum was created, bringing together regulators of financial markets. There were proposals to strengthen or replace the IMF's Interim Committee and arguments about the future of the G22. The IMF was encouraged to develop and apply new standards of economic data required from all its members and new codes of practice in monetary and fiscal policy. The G7 debated how to reduce the risks to the system from offshore financial centres and highly leveraged institutions, like hedge funds, and how to get the private sector to play a more helpful role in financial rescues.

The Cologne summit endorsed a lengthy report from the finance ministers on these and other topics, discussed further in Chapter 5. But, as at Birmingham, the leaders did no more than give their authority to what their ministers had prepared. They did not act to resolve some of the outstanding differences among the G7, for example on the nature and composition of the successor to the G22. They were in no mood for radical action and seemed to have concluded, once again, that the immediate crisis was over and the urgency of the reforms had receded.

Debt Relief

At Birmingham, the previous German government under Kohl had been the main obstacle to progress on debt relief for low-income countries. But this situation was transformed when the government changed. Early in 1999 Chancellor Schroeder announced his intention to make debt relief a centre-piece of the Cologne summit, led by a much more positive German approach.[8] In the summit preparations every G7 member advanced proposals for improving the HIPC programme, with the German plans now being the most generous after the British.[9] These developments gave new encouragement to the charities and other NGOs involved in the Jubilee 2000 Campaign, who organised another massive demonstration in Cologne and handed over a petition to Schroeder.

The G7's 'Cologne Debt Initiative', as agreed at the summit, recommended to the IMF, World Bank and Paris Club major improvements to the design and financing of the HIPC programme. Debt relief should release resources for health, education and other social needs. The relief provided should reduce eligible countries' debt to no more than 150% of exports (instead of 200-250% hitherto) and should become available after three years of observing IMF discipline instead of six. Relief on government debt covered by the Paris Club should go up from 80% to 90% or even more, while any remaining aid debt should be forgiven altogether. Sales of 10 million ounces of IMF gold were recommended to help meet the costs to the IMF, while the G7 would consider further bilateral contributions 'in good faith'. In total these reforms should reduce the debts of eligible countries by more than half - from $130 billion to something over $60 billion.

In some respects, the heads went further than their finance ministers. In particular, they added a recommendation that three-quarters of the countries eligible for the HIPC programme should have debt relief programmes agreed by the end of 2000. They also stressed the importance of involving the private sector. In this way, the heads went a long way towards the demands of the major charities behind the public campaign. However, the charities' response was guarded, since the measures fell short of the complete cancellation they wanted.[10] The weakest G7 commitment was on the financing, but this was resolved at the IMF and World Bank meetings in September. The Cologne Debt Initiative thus clearly ranked as a major summit achievement. The details are analysed in Chapter 5 in a broader account of G7 involvement in debt relief initiatives.

G8 Economic and Social Issues

The main G8 agenda of economic and social issues occupied the heads on 19 June, with Stepashin representing Russia. The results were embodied in the nine-page G8 communiqué.

Economic Help for Russia

The most sensitive issue among the G8 was how to help Russia back to economic health. Fundamental economic mismanagement led to Russian default on its debt in August 1998 and little had been done since then to correct what was wrong. Even so, the G7 had encouraged the IMF and World Bank to reach new agreements with Russia to provide more financing.[11] At Cologne they promised relief on Russia's outstanding debts if these agreements were implemented. They even suggested possible relief on debts taken over by Russia from the former Soviet Union if the economic reforms went far enough, though here the Germans were expected to drive a hard bargain. Beyond this, the G7 leaders promised more intensive technical help to reform the Russian economy, making their sherpas directly responsible. In response to pressure from Stepashin, these commitments appeared in the main G8 communiqué, not in a separate statement on Russia. Even so, Stepashin could not be sure that Yeltsin would endorse them when he arrived.

Employment, Education and Social Protection

G8 employment ministers had met again in the run-up to Cologne. For the summit itself, however, the leaders decided to widen the basis of their discussion and reached agreement in brief but uncontroversial exchanges. One major theme was education, especially lifelong learning. This was identified as a major contribution to employability and to a harmonious society in conditions of globalisation. The summit adopted a separate 'Cologne Charter on Lifelong Learning' and agreed specific projects on educational exchanges among the G8, on raising education standards and on using technology for distance learning. A second theme was the need for social safety nets to protect those left behind by globalisation, so as to 'give globalisation a human face'. The communiqué urged international institutions like the IMF, the World Bank and the International Labour Organisation (ILO) to give attention to this topic, recognising implicitly the damage done to Asian countries in the recent financial crisis from the lack of social protection.

International Crime and Conflict Prevention

Crime was on the agenda again for Cologne. But as the summit approached, the crisis in Kosovo shifted attention away from the dangers of crime in undermining society to the corrosive effect of civil conflict. Cologne began to formulate an approach to 'human security' and crisis prevention, which addressed the root causes of conflict and threats to human rights; these included crime, drug trafficking and terrorism. This approach enabled the G8 to bring together these different aspects of international public order. Though the discussion at Cologne was brief, the heads gave instructions to the G8 foreign ministers. They were charged to work up this subject before their meeting planned for December 1999 and to produce recommendations for the 2000 summit in Okinawa.

Other Economic Issues

Other issues were treated more cursorily:

- *Trade* At Cologne, as at Birmingham, there were short exchanges only on trade, looking forward to the next series of multilateral negotiations, due to be launched at the Seattle WTO meeting in December. The US would still not endorse the European idea of a comprehensive 'Millennium Round' and Clinton would go no further than 'broad-based and ambitious negotiations . . . achieving substantial and manageable results'. The EU's position was undermined by a weak decision on agriculture at the European Council in March.[12] Though Cologne focused on making the WTO more responsive both to civil society and to developing countries, there was no attempt to define the content of a new round or even to resolve the deadlock over the new Director-General of the WTO.[13]

- *Development* Apart from debt and trade, the Cologne summit briefly addressed other measures intended to benefit developing countries. The G8 communiqué contained a commitment to increase the volume of official aid - the first such commitment from the summit for many years.[14] But the prospects of getting aid untied seemed to be pushed off into the future. The Americans' difficulties in getting aid funds out of Congress remained a persistent constraint.
- *Environment* Environmental topics got little attention, except for the new and controversial issue of food safety and genetic modification. There was a prospect of open disagreement between Europeans and North Americans on the treatment of genetically modified organisms (GMOs), on which Chirac proposed a new international institution.[15] The matter was defused by passing it to the OECD, with a promise of a further exchange at Okinawa in 2000.

G8 Foreign Policy Issues

Discussion over dinner on 18 June produced agreement on short statements on the Middle East, Jordan, Nigeria, Kashmir and Cyprus. But the main political issue was Kosovo and the Balkans, which could not be resolved till Yeltsin arrived on 20 June.

Kosovo and the Balkans

The G8 leaders had already used the Birmingham summit the year before to give a warning to Yugoslav President Slobodan Milosevic - Kosovo being one of the few foreign policy issues discussed at head of government level. In the months leading up to Cologne the internal repression by the Belgrade Serbs in Kosovo grew worse and Milosevic proved wholly obstinate. On 24 March 1999 the North Atlantic Treaty Organisation (NATO) began a bombing campaign aimed at crippling Serbian military capacity and obliging Milosevic to admit a NATO-led peace-keeping force to Kosovo and accept a political settlement.

The immediate consequences were shocking for NATO. The Serbs increased their violence to the point where hundreds of thousands of refugees fled from Kosovo, in pitiful conditions. The Russian government, from Yeltsin downwards, denounced NATO's action and threatened to intervene in support of Milosevic. It was the worst dispute between Russia and NATO since the Cold War ended.[16]

In this dangerous situation, the G8 framework proved its worth. The Germans called a G8 foreign ministers meeting in Bonn in early May. This meeting agreed principles for a peace settlement in Kosovo, very close to NATO's original objectives, which were fully endorsed by the Russians.[17] Yeltsin nominated ex-Prime Minister Chernomyrdin as his personal emissary, working together with the EU's representative, President Marti Ahtisaari of Finland. NATO continued and intensified its bombing campaign, which gradually wore down Milosevic's resistance. In early June he accepted the peace plan presented to him by Chernomyrdin and Ahtisaari, requiring the withdrawal of all Serbian troops from

Kosovo, the return of the refugees and the introduction of an international force composed of contingents from NATO forces and Russia.[18]

When G8 foreign ministers met on 8-10 June outside Cologne, they were able to tie up all the details on Kosovo - as they thought. They agreed terms for a UN Security Council resolution, which was adopted unanimously apart from a Chinese abstention. This gave the Kosovo operation the United Nations cover it had not had before. They also moved to address the wider problems of the Balkan region, which had been profoundly shaken by the conflict in Kosovo and the huge flows of refugees. The G8 joined with eight regional governments, the other EU member states, Turkey and many international institutions to draw up a Stability Pact for South Eastern Europe, to reinforce peace and stimulate economic recovery.[19]

Despite all this progress, the position of Russia and of Yeltsin himself remained ambivalent. The Kosovo settlement was very unpopular in Russia and there was always a fear that Yeltsin would disown Chernomyrdin. The peace-keeping arrangements within Kosovo also angered the Russians. Kosovo was divided into five sectors under the responsibility of the US, Britain, France, Germany and Italy - five of the G8 countries. The Russian military wanted a sector of their own. NATO resisted this, fearing that it would become a safe haven in Kosovo for the Serbian troops, which were meant to withdraw totally. On 12 June, less than a week before the summit, a contingent of 200 Russian troops stationed in Bosnia drove across Serbia and into Kosovo to occupy Pristina airport, before any NATO forces were ready to move. This was in flat defiance of the security arrangements worked out in NATO and even took Igor Ivanov, the Russian Foreign Minister, by surprise. But it had the backing of Yeltsin himself.[20]

Intensive negotiations followed in Helsinki between the Russians and Americans to resolve exactly what Russian troops would do in Kosovo. These successfully reached a compromise agreement on 18 June, the day the summit opened. But everything depended on how Yeltsin would behave when he met the other G8 leaders in Cologne. Would he denounce what Ivanov and Stepashin had agreed and produce yet more surprises?

The Meeting with Yeltsin

"I am among my friends now" said Yeltsin, as soon as he met the other heads of government on 20 June.[21] That set the tone for the meeting he attended, lasting only one hour. Yeltsin endorsed the arrangements for Kosovo made at Helsinki and elsewhere, as well as the idea of the new Stability Pact. He also gave his blessing to everything that Stepashin had agreed earlier in the summit. This enabled the G8 leaders to give their collective authority to all the agreements made at lower levels on Kosovo and the Balkans. Schroeder announced a further summit meeting for the G8 with their partners in the new Stability Pact, which took place in Sarajevo on 30 July.[22]

Assessment of the Cologne Summit

Procedurally, the Cologne summit worked very well. Schroeder was not able to organise a 'retreat', as Blair had. But the heads were able to leave their personal mark on the proceedings. The economic discussions focused on debt relief for the poorest, where the G7 leaders were personally engaged, including Schroeder himself. The key political issue was Kosovo, where Yeltsin's involvement was vital. For all their good intentions, however, the length of summit documents began creeping up again. The main communiqué and foreign policy statement were no longer than at Birmingham, but the G7 document was twice as long, and there was an additional 'Charter on Lifelong Learning'.

Cologne continued the explicit focus on the strains generated by globalisation identified at Birmingham, specifically jobs, crime, financial panic and world poverty. It carried forward the work on financial architecture and debt, with especially important results on debt relief. The Cologne summit also expanded the G8's range on the other issues. It added education and social protection to employment and coupled conflict prevention to crime as aspects of international public order. The G8 communiqué put the new topics, like social protection and conflict prevention, into the context of globalisation. On social protection the leaders said:

> As the process of globalisation has gained momentum….. rapid change and integration has left some individuals and groups feeling unable to keep up….. We therefore need to ... give globalisation a "human face"…..

On conflict prevention:

> In many countries, violent conflicts and civil wars continue to be an obstacle to making good use of the opportunities of globalisation.[23]

In the process, however, some traditional summit subjects, such as trade and the environment, got pushed to the edge of the agenda.

Economically, the major achievement of Cologne was agreement on the new debt initiative. This built on the work done at Birmingham the year before to produce a very extensive set of commitments, to which the heads themselves made a personal contribution. Cologne also completed the work begun at Birmingham on the new international financial architecture, though here the heads did no more than add their authority to what their finance ministers had already agreed. These two topics are examined further in the next chapter.

Politically, the Cologne summit proved extremely well timed and demonstrated the value of the G8 grouping, both at foreign minister and head of government level. The summit provided the occasion for bringing Russia back into close cooperation with the leading NATO powers, after the dangerous confrontation over Kosovo. Cologne also illustrated very well the political dynamics that flowed from enlarging G7 to G8.

Full G8 membership meant a lot to Yeltsin. He had worked for it for seven years, from before any of the present Western leaders took office. At the G8 summit he was now visibly operating on equal terms with Clinton and other Western heads of government, maintaining Russia's power and influence despite its economic troubles. It was unlikely that Yeltsin would abandon this privileged position because of Kosovo; but he needed the summit so that he could be seen in company with his peers. Just as calling Denver 'the Summit of the Eight' helped to reconcile Yeltsin to NATO enlargement, so the timing of Cologne helped to reconcile Yeltsin to cooperating with the West over the disciplining of Serbia.

If Yeltsin was committed to the G8, so were the G7 members committed to Russia. Ever since they invited Gorbachev to London in 1991, they had accepted a responsibility to help Russia economically and to prevent it collapsing into chaos, however misguided Russian policies might be. The renewed promises of help for Russia made by the G7 at Cologne reflected this continued responsibility. These G7 promises soon led to results. Despite Russia's very shaky record in economic management since the default of August 1998, the IMF was persuaded by the G7 to agree a standby credit for Russia of $4.5 billion in July 1999.[24] In August the Paris Club agreed to roll over outstanding Russian debt, though they would not accept debt reduction.[25] In some ways the commitments made at Cologne showed no advance on the undertakings made by the G7 to Yeltsin - and even to Gorbachev - in the early 1990s, when the attempts to reform Russia's economy were only just beginning. But from now on Russian economic performance improved steadily, thanks to increased earnings from oil exports.

Conclusion

The Cologne summit confirmed the attachment of the G8 to the 'heads-only' format, with supporting ministers meeting separately. This encouraged uncluttered discussions, with scope for personal contributions by the heads. But the volume of documentation was growing again and the attitude of the media remained sceptical. The most original feature of Cologne was its demonstration of the merits of moving from G7 to G8. This paid political dividends in bringing a settlement to Kosovo and averting a dangerous clash between NATO and Russia. In other respects Cologne 1999 followed closely the example of Birmingham 1998, as follows:

- The G8 heads continued to give priority to managing globalisation and helping those who were put at risk by it. The agenda remained concentrated on social issues, like education and social protection, and on the problems of developing countries. The two-year focus by the heads on debt-relief for the poorest brought real advances.
- The heads divided their attention between issues of domestic concern and issues affecting the international system, especially financial architecture and debt relief. But there were already signs that the international issues were edging the domestic ones off the agenda.
- The summit responded to the sustained public campaign for debt relief and was ready to grant civil society a role in international development. The

NGOs concerned recognised the effort made by the G8, though they were not satisfied.

In terms of the performance criteria, the G8 exercised political *leadership* in striking deals over Kosovo and debt relief. There was some *effective* reconciliation of domestic pressures, eg in education, but interest was waning. *Solidarity* that had been weak at Birmingham was strengthened at Cologne over debt relief, but not over trade, which still revealed a lack of *consistency*. All the results achieved on Kosovo, financial architecture and debt relief, proved *durable* and broadly *acceptable*, especially the first two.

In 2000 the summit would be in Okinawa, the first time the Japanese had held a summit outside Tokyo. In the Japanese political system the head of government had less authority than in Europe or North America. The Japanese hosts would have to handle Clinton in his closing months, as well as the successor to Yeltsin. However, Japan had a good record in chairing successful summits under the old format. The procedures developed for Birmingham and Cologne were now well enough established to give plenty of guidance to the Japanese on how to organise an effective summit in the new style.

Notes

1 On taking office, Blair and Schroeder tried to reconcile their political philosophies - the 'Third Way' and the '*Neue Mitte*' - see M. Wolf, 'Not the Right Way', *Financial Times*, 16 June 1999. But later they drifted apart and Schroeder moved closer to Chirac. While Blair was always active in the G8, Schroeder took relatively little part after Cologne.

2 This chapter is largely based on Chapter 10 of *Hanging In There* (Bayne 2000); supplemented by Budd 2003 and my *Financial Times* and *Economist* collection. Cologne is the only summit covered in this book that I did not attend with the University of Toronto G8 Research Group.

3 Matters improved after Lafontaine resigned in March 1999.

4 As in 1998, a fruitful EU/US summit took place on the margins of the G8 meeting. See G. de Jonquières, 'US and EU promise to make a new start', *Financial Times*, 22 June 1999.

5 Greece also soon joined, to make twelve countries in the Eurozone. But the UK (a G8 member), Denmark and Sweden stayed outside - and are still outside in 2005.

6 Kiriyenko was Yeltsin's Prime Minister at the time of Birmingham in May 1998. Primakov took over in August 1998, after the Russian default. He was replaced by Stepashin shortly before Cologne. Stepashin in turn was succeeded as Prime Minister in August 1999 by Vladimir Putin, who would emerge as Yeltsin's successor as President.

7 The G7 finance ministers' work is well summarised in Kenen, Shafer, Wicks and Wyplosz 2004, pp. 51-54 - Nigel Wicks was UK G7 deputy at the time. For further references, see Chapter 5 below.

8 Schroeder announced this policy change in an article in the *Financial Times*, 21 January 1999.

9 For the different national plans, see R. Chote, 'Better Terms for Poor Proposed' (UK and Germany), N. Dunne, 'Clinton Urges Debt Relief for Poor Nations' (US) and

T. Alden, 'G7 Urged to Ease Debts' (Canada), *Financial Times,* 20 February, 17 and 26 March 1999.

10 As five British charities wrote to the *Guardian* on 19 June 1999, "The proposed $50bn of debt write-off is an impressive figure, but this does not go far enough". See also M. Holman and N. Dunne, 'Debt Relief Plan Painfully Inadequate', *Financial Times,* 16 June 1999.

11 A new IMF loan was agreed in March and the Russians raised the issue of debt relief. See J. Thornhill, 'IMF Promises $4.8bn in New Loans to Bolster Russia' and 'Russia to ask for Soviet debt write-off', *Financial Times,* 30 and 31 March 1999.

12 M. Smith, 'Defeat for Champions of Market Liberalisation', *Financial Times* 27 March 1999.

13 Renato Ruggiero's term as Director-General had expired in April without agreement on his successor. The matter was only resolved in September, with a split term for Mike Moore (New Zealand) and Supachai Panitchpakdi (Thailand).

14 See Chapter 8 below for the summit record on aid flows.

15 See 'Clinton and Chirac Clash over World Food Watchdog', *Financial Times,* 18 June 1999.

16 See 'Kosovo Special - War with Milosevic' and 'A New Cold War?', *The Economist,* 3 and 17 April 1999.

17 R. Atkins and D. Buchan, 'Moscow Endorses Plan for Kosovo', *Financial Times,* 7 May 1999.

18 'Breakthrough in Kosovo?', *The Economist,* 5 June 1999.

19 R. Atkins, 'G8 Talks Secure Deal to Pave Way for Peace in Kosovo' and 'German Stability Pact Set to Win Support', *Financial Times,* 9 and 10 June 1999.

20 J. Thornhill, 'Yeltsin Ordered Surprise Deployment of Troops', *Financial Times,* 14 June 1999.

21 Yeltsin's remark was widely reported by the media, eg *Daily Telegraph, Independent, The Times,* 21 June 1999.

22 The Sarajevo summit, which was preceded by a pledging meeting, agreed that Serbia could not benefit from the Stability Pact while Milosevic remained in power. See P. Norman, 'Donor Conference Pledges Kosovo Aid' and S. Wagstyl and others, 'Milosevic Haunts Sarajevo Summit', *Financial Times,* 29 and 31 July 1999.

23 The quotations are from paras. 19 and 39 of the G8 communiqué. For the full text of the Cologne summit documents, see www.g8.utoronto.ca.

24 J. Thornhill and S. Fidler, 'IMF Approves $4.5bn Credit for Moscow', *Financial Times,* 29 July 1999. Martin Wolf was highly critical of the IMF agreement in 'Price of Forgiveness', *Financial Times,* 11 August 1999. John Odling-Smee, the head of the IMF's Russia programme, defended the Fund in a letter - 'Why IMF is Standing by Russia' - to the *Financial Times* on 23 August 1999. Later, however, he has himself criticised G7 political interference; see A. Jack, 'G7 "Interfered in IMF Bid to Push Russian Reform"', *Financial Times,* 5 October 2004. A much broader attack on the IMF's strategy in Russia is in Stiglitz 2002, pp. 133-165.

25 S. Iskandar and A. Ostrovsky, 'Russia wins Reprieve on Foreign Debt', *Financial Times,* 2 August 1999.

Chapter 5

Summit Performance I: Financial Issues and Debt

Confusion in the international financial system was one of the original motives for creating the G7 summits, so that monetary issues were a standard item on the agenda in the 1970s. This went into abeyance in the 1980s, but financial issues reappeared during the 1990s, driven by the advance of globalisation. Free movement of capital was one of the dominant features of globalisation, being used to underpin rapid growth, especially in East Asia. But the growth in the volume and speed of capital movements outstripped the capacity of governments to control them. A volatile and unpredictable financial system, where money moved on impulse and could penalise prudent as well as imprudent countries, appeared to be one of the greatest dangers of globalisation. A second danger was that very poor countries, held back by unsustainable burdens of debt, would be unable to realise any of the benefits of globalisation and would fall steadily further behind into poverty, misery and disease.

The first two summits of the new G8 sequence, Birmingham 1998 and Cologne 1999, were directly concerned with the response to globalisation and took place while the Asian financial crisis was raging. They were therefore deeply involved with financial issues: new international financial architecture and debt relief for low-income countries. The decisions taken offer a good basis for assessing the performance of these new-style summits in this major area of policy. Financial issues were also treated at later summits in the sequence, though with much less intensity. This chapter will therefore look forward to some of the later summits, anticipating the narratives in the following chapters.[1]

The chapter treats separately each of the two main issues - financial architecture and debt relief. After a brief review of early treatment by the G7 summits, it examines the achievements of Birmingham, Cologne and later summits in greater detail. It then assesses the performance of the G8 summits in each area in the light of the six criteria identified in Chapter 1. These are:

- *Leadership* Did the summit succeed in stimulating innovation and resolving differences, in ways that could not be achieved at lower levels?
- *Effectiveness* Did the summit exercise its talent for reconciling domestic and international pressures, so as to produce agreed results?
- *Solidarity* Were all the summit participants fully committed to the outcome, in the context of collective management?

- *Durability* Did the agreement reached at the summit provide a lasting solution to the problem?
- *Acceptability* Was the agreement reached among the summit leaders readily accepted by the wider international community?
- *Consistency* Did the summit's decisions on international financial issues fit in well with the policies adopted on other subjects?

A third financial issue - abuses of the financial system - was briefly considered by the summit in 2000 and 2001, but was then overtaken by concern about the financing of terrorism. It will therefore be covered in Chapter 12.

International Financial Architecture

Early Summit Treatment

The first summit of all, at Rambouillet in 1975, was dominated by financial issues. The summit reached agreement that the IMF should permit floating exchange rates as a legitimate currency regime, as opposed to a temporary expedient in times of crisis. France had hitherto resisted this. But at Rambouillet Giscard agreed to legitimise floating, in return for undertakings from the United States and the others to intervene to counter short-term currency fluctuations. This agreement was based on meticulous advance preparation between American and French officials. The IMF rapidly introduced amendments to its Articles that embodied the Rambouillet agreement.

When measured against the criteria, the Rambouillet results score highly. The summit showed *leadership*, in resolving the persistent dispute between France and the US, and proved *effective*, thanks to the careful preparation. The Rambouillet agreement was *durable* where it was incorporated into the IMF's Articles, being readily *acceptable* to the wider membership of the IMF and creating no problem of *consistency*. However, the informal arrangement on countering short-term fluctuations did not prove *durable*. *Solidarity* was weak, because of American scepticism, and G7 countries adopted economic policies that were *inconsistent* with currency stability.

The Halifax Reforms

The summit briefly returned to the international monetary system at Versailles in 1982, but the new agreement reached there on stabilising exchange rates broke down within a few hours. Thereafter the summit did not address broad monetary issues (as opposed to debt problems) until the Halifax summit of 1995, following the crisis that overwhelmed Mexico at the end of 1994. The Mexican crisis was marked by the collapse of exchange rates, the haemorrhage of volatile capital and rapid contagion both around the region and further afield. It was checked by an exceptional IMF-led programme, on the record scale of $50 billion, early in 1995.

This Mexican programme provoked sharp disagreement between the US and the Europeans. The 1995 Halifax summit restored harmony and agreed a series of reforms to the international monetary system, as a response to the experience of Mexico.[2]

The G7 leaders agreed a four-point plan, which was rapidly adopted by the IMF and World Bank. The four elements were: stronger IMF surveillance for all countries, based on better data; a new emergency financing mechanism, backed by extra funds; better cooperation between regulators of financial institutions; and exploring procedures for countries comparable to insolvency for firms. Chirac, in a striking image, denounced international speculators as the AIDS virus of the world economy.

The Halifax measures were intended to deter further outbreaks of the disease. In fact they only provided a period of remission, before the crisis broke out worse than before.[3] This was because the implementation of the Halifax programme was tardy and incomplete. The G10 declared 'insolvency' impractical for countries; G7 finance ministers made only limited progress on regulation; and the funds for the new mechanism were committed far too slowly.[4] That left stricter surveillance as the only defence. This on its own was not enough, as countries in difficulty had every incentive to conceal unwelcome data. The Halifax reforms scored highly on *leadership, solidarity* and *acceptability*. But later developments showed that they were neither *effective* nor *durable*. The work of reform had to start again in the light of what happened in Asia two years later.

The G8 Summits and International Financial Architecture

The Asian Financial Crisis

The Asian financial crisis began on 3 July 1997, when the Thai authorities were no longer able to defend the parity of the baht against the dollar. The crisis spread rapidly to the other economies of the region. Thailand, Korea and Indonesia all negotiated programmes to gain drawings from the IMF, but the markets were not satisfied. Further capital outflows and plunges in exchange rates led to another round of IMF rescue packages, associated with debt rescheduling. By early 1998 a total of $115 billion had been committed for the three countries together. All of them, together with most of their neighbours, faced deep and prolonged recession.

There was one crucial difference between this Asian crisis and the earlier Mexican one. The Mexican upheaval happened because of mistakes by the government, which ran up a huge budget deficit financed by short-term borrowing. The three Asian countries were running prudent fiscal policies. Their main mistake, in hindsight, was to fix their national currencies to the US dollar when it was falling. This encouraged irresponsible financial behaviour by both local borrowers and Western lenders, which turned to disaster when the dollar started to strengthen. The extravagance of the private financial sector was encouraged by weak and sometimes corrupt systems of financial supervision.[5]

So the crisis was largely provoked by the private sector and this had two important consequences:

- The IMF applied its usual medicine of fiscal and monetary tightening to restore stability, at an inevitable cost to economic activity. But many observers, including the World Bank, argued that this was the wrong way to curb a crisis provoked by the private sector. The IMF defended itself against criticism, but confidence in it was shaken.[6]
- The private financial sector was held to have got off too lightly. Funds provided by the IMF or G7 were used to pay off debts to Western private creditors, while citizens of the borrowing country suffered severe hardship. The G7 looked for ways of 'bailing in' private creditors in future, rather than bailing them out.

Initial Reforms at Birmingham

In response to the crisis, the G7 finance ministers worked up a package of reforms in the first half of 1998, which was brought together for the leaders at Birmingham.[7] The Birmingham summit endorsed proposals under four headings, picking up elements of the 1995 Halifax programme:

- *Increasing Transparency* This advocated not only better economic data and stricter surveillance but also more openness in national fiscal and monetary policy-making and in the IMF's own activities.
- *Strengthening Financial Systems* The summit recommended 'a system of multilateral surveillance of national financial supervisory and regulatory systems', but did not agree on how this should be organised.
- *Helping Countries Prepare for Global Capital Flows* The summit sought to deter other countries from encouraging irresponsible capital flows, but did not agree on whether capital controls were acceptable or not.
- *Ensuring the Private Sector Takes Responsibility* The aim was to develop a framework for associating private lenders with the resolution of financial crises.

The Birmingham proposals, set out in the G7 communiqué and finance ministers' report, were a work in progress. There was nothing on further financing and only a few hints of future institutional change. It was intended that the finance ministers should settle unresolved issues and complete the programme at the IMF/World Bank meeting in October. But this plan was overtaken by events.

The Crisis Widens

By the time of the Birmingham summit the Asian economies had calmed down. Russia did not look under threat and in July 1998 agreed a new reform programme with the IMF, backed by total financing of $20 billion. But again the markets sensed that this was not enough and Russia's first IMF drawing of $5 billion was exhausted in a single month of massive capital outflows. In mid-August Russia ceased to defend the rouble and defaulted on its government debt.[8] Many Western lenders suffered major losses in the Russian 'meltdown'. In particular, the highly leveraged American hedge fund Long-Term Capital Management revealed that it was insolvent and was only saved by a desperate rescue operation mounted by the Federal Reserve.[9] Simultaneously the Brazilian economy came under attack, with capital flight in advance of the presidential elections. Brazil appealed to the IMF, which assembled a $40 billion support package, but with no participation from the private sector.[10]

Completing the Architecture at Cologne

The G7 finance ministers held crisis meetings in October 1998 and agreed on the outline of a new programme of reforms.[11] These were partly drawn from reports by the G22, an informal group called together by the US and involving Asian and other developing countries affected by the crisis. This programme was elaborated at further G7 meetings and at the IMF/World Bank early in 1999. It formed the basis of the proposals that the G7 heads of government endorsed at Cologne.[12]

The Cologne programme, as set out in the summit documents, had six components, all more elaborate than the 1998 proposals:

- *Strengthening the Institutions* The main innovation was the Financial Stability Forum, to provide multilateral surveillance of financial regulators - see below. The IMF's Interim Committee should become permanent *de jure* rather than *de facto*. An 'informal mechanism among systematically important countries' was proposed, building on the G22 created by the US in 1998. But the Europeans had protested against the G22's Pacific bias and the composition of the new body was not resolved at Cologne.
- *Transparency and Best Practice* Cologne endorsed all the measures proposed at Birmingham. The IMF and World Bank had already brought into effect codes of best practice in policy-making. The G7 called for more transparency in the private sector too.
- *Financial Regulation in Industrial Countries* The new Financial Stability Forum brought together the G7, the Fund and Bank and the international groupings of regulators for banks, insurance and securities.[13] It focused at once on three sensitive issues: risk assessment for banks; highly leveraged institutions, like hedge funds; and offshore financial centres.
- *Financial Systems in Emerging Markets* This admitted the possibility of measures to control capital inflows and discouraged countries from defending fixed exchange rates at all costs.
- *Crisis Prevention and Involving the Private Sector* The key innovation was the new Contingent Credit Line, agreed at the IMF in April 1999, and intended to protect countries following sound policies from the contagion of financial instability. This was strongly promoted by the United States, but some believed that any country drawing on it would automatically become a target

for speculation. There were more elaborate provisions for involving the private sector, but it was unclear they could ever be applied.

- *Social Policies to Protect the Poor* These proposals were mainly focused on the World Bank and the UN, including principles of good practice in social policy.

All these proposals were intended for endorsement and completion at the 1999 annual meeting of the IMF and World Bank. Further progress was made there, for example in agreeing the composition of the new G20, the successor to the G22, and choosing Paul Martin of Canada as its first chairman.[14] The IMF Interim Committee formally became the International Monetary and Financial Committee (IMFC). But the involvement of private lenders in financial rescue operations remained controversial.[15]

Developments after Cologne

From Cologne 1999 onwards, the heads were not called upon to take any substantive decisions on monetary reform. The Okinawa summit in 2000 reviewed progress in the Cologne programme, but added nothing new. At Genoa in 2001 and Kananaskis in 2002 the heads expressed concern about developments in Latin America (Argentina and Brazil) but took no action at the summit. The financial collapse of Argentina late in 2001 prompted active discussion among the G7 finance ministers, both on how best to help Argentina itself and on how to involve the private sector in financial rescues, which was still unresolved. But these topics never reached the heads of government.

Though none of these measures agreed at Birmingham and Cologne were really radical, they amounted to an extensive overhaul of the machinery for preventing and responding to financial crises.[16] Their short-term impact was good, in that they restored calm to the system. Without the pressure of crisis conditions, implementation of the measures inevitably slowed down and some of the more difficult issues, like involving the private sector in financial rescues, remained unsettled.[17] There was a sense that the reform process was incomplete, so that new ideas kept surfacing, especially from the United States.[18]

Nevertheless, the system survived well the strains imposed upon it in the early 2000s by the slowdown in the US economy, the persistent weakness in Japan and the terrorist attacks of 11 September 2001. The G7 finance ministers and the IMF could not save Argentina from financial collapse and default, which brought them renewed criticism. But there was little contagion from Argentina's debacle, while IMF support programmes successfully rescued Turkey and Brazil from dangerous crises.[19] The most serious challenge to the IMF and World Bank came from increasingly virulent attacks on its underlying policies, especially from groups of NGOs that mounted hostile demonstrations against meetings in Washington and Prague.[20] Both Fund and Bank sought to develop a dialogue with their more responsible critics and brought in some changes in policy as a result. But here again the G8 heads were not involved.

Assessment under the Criteria

On the international financial architecture, the G8 summits get a generally favourable assessment:

- At Birmingham 1998 and Cologne 1999 the heads of government showed *leadership.* They directly addressed the issue causing the greatest disturbance in the international economic system. They provided the focus for their finance ministers' work and a stimulus to them to reach agreement. They gave essential authority to agreements once reached, to ensure wider acceptance. The conclusions on financial architecture were key achievements of these two summits. However, the leaders did not themselves contribute elements of policy, nor did they resolve disputes at the summit itself. This was in contrast to their personal involvement with debt relief.
- Birmingham and Cologne, taken together, were *effective* in reconciling domestic and external pressures. After the Asian crisis, the heads were concerned not to make the same mistake as Halifax, where agreed measures were not followed up. In practice the agreed G7 measures were largely put into effect, though once calm returned, implementation tended to slacken off. The key was thorough and detailed preparation, carried through by the G7 finance ministers and their officials.
- *Solidarity* was in general good. During the preparations of the measures, there were often deep divisions between G7 members, which could take a long time to resolve. The US especially took some initiatives, like creating the G22, without waiting for approval by its partners. But once the new architecture was agreed by all, collective management worked well.
- Initial reactions to the new architecture were guarded, with fears that it was inadequate either to prevent or to treat new crises. But in practice it proved robust and *durable* enough to withstand the strains caused by the slowing US and Japanese economies, together with the shock of the terrorist attacks. While it could not save Argentina, it prevented the sort of contagion that had followed the Mexican and Asian crises. Some elements, however, like the Contingent Credit Line, did not endure, while debate continued on others, like involving the private sector.[21]
- All the reform proposals emerging from the summits proved widely *acceptable* in the IMF and World Bank. The G7 did not leave this to chance, but took care to involve other parts of the membership in the reform process. This was initially done through the G22, which had brought in some of the key Asian emerging markets. The new G20, forecast at Cologne 1999 and confirmed at the next IMF Annual Meeting, put this wider consultation on a permanent footing and proved very valuable.[22] However, IMF and World Bank policies based on the new architecture steadily lost their *acceptability* with non-state opinion, both in academic circles and civil society, during the early 2000s.

- The judgement on *consistency* is less positive. While the summits of the late 1990s had good reasons for focusing on financial architecture, this led them to neglect other parts of the international economic system, notably the trade regime. The new financial architecture also responded mainly to the needs of the advanced economies, like the G7, and the 'systemically significant' countries that sat on the G20. Some parts of the new system looked very complex and demanding for small and poor countries. It was only with the summits of the early 2000s (Okinawa and Genoa, considered in Chapters 6-8 below) that the G8 turned its full attention to the problems of developing countries, especially the poorest.

Debt Relief for Low-Income Countries

Early Summit Treatment

The G7 summit gave very little attention to the debt crisis that broke in August 1982, though major debtors were threatening to default on their borrowings from commercial banks. Default on this scale could lead to a systemic collapse, but the Reagan Administration only once brought debt issues to the summit, at London in 1984. This changed at once, however, when President George Bush senior and his Treasury Secretary Nicholas Brady took office. The 'Brady Plan' introduced the radical concept of debt reduction, ie that debts need not be repaid in full. When the IMF meetings in spring 1989 could not agree on it, Bush and Brady raised the issue to summit level. The Brady Plan was endorsed by the Paris summit of July 1989 and accepted at the IMF Annual Meeting in September. So the summits from 1982 to 1988 score badly against the criteria, while Paris 1989 scores very well.

The Brady Plan solved the problem of debts owed mainly to banks by middle-income developing countries. It did not deal with poor countries' debts, owed mainly to governments. These debts were much smaller in total and thus did not threaten the financial system, but they were a heavier burden on the countries concerned. The first moves to help poor debtor countries came from the Toronto G7 summit of 1988 and were called 'Toronto terms'. They provided that the major creditor governments, meeting in the Paris Club, would grant relief equal to one-third of their debts to low-income countries eligible for rescheduling, subject to these countries following economic programmes agreed with the IMF.[23]

This got the process started, but Toronto terms soon proved inadequate. When the Commonwealth Finance Ministers met in Trinidad in 1990, John Major, then British Finance Minister, proposed that relief go up to half of the eligible debt owed to the Paris Club. This took advantage of the concept of debt reduction, as endorsed in the Brady Plan, and was agreed by the G7 at the London III summit in 1991. The scale of relief was further raised to two-thirds of eligible debt by the Naples summit of 1994; what had begun as Toronto terms became Naples terms.

The Heavily Indebted Poor Countries (HIPC) Programme

Naples terms would still not suffice for many poor countries, because they only covered their debts to governments. They did not touch the large proportion owed to the IMF and World Bank themselves, who had never allowed relief on their loans for fear that their high credit rating would suffer. When Commonwealth Finance Ministers met at Valletta in 1994, just after the Naples summit, the British minister, Kenneth Clarke, proposed a further set of measures to help poor debtor countries observing IMF discipline. These formed the basis of the proposals agreed by the 1996 Lyon summit, where the heads of the IMF and World Bank joined the leaders. The main points were: all aid loans should be converted to grants; relief on debt owed to the Paris Club should go up to 80%; and the IMF and World Bank should offer special loans on softer terms to offset earlier lending. (The original British idea that the rates of these loans should be subsidised through the sale of IMF gold could not be agreed at Lyon.) The entire IMF and World Bank then adopted these proposals as the Heavily Indebted Poor Countries (HIPC) initiative.

The summit performance on low-income debt was much better than on middle-income debt. The G7 heads had shown *leadership* in moving forward a neglected international problem and had been fairly *effective* in overcoming resistance from their bureaucracies and the institutions. Once agreed by the G7, the proposals proved *acceptable* elsewhere. But *solidarity* among the G7 was weak; the UK, France and Canada were keen, but Germany and Japan were unenthusiastic, as was the United States at first. This affected the *durability* of the agreements - the G7 had to keep coming back to improve them.

The G8 Summits and Debt Relief

Birmingham and the HIPC Programme

The Heavily Indebted Poor Countries (HIPC) were those states that were eligible for soft loans from the International Development Association (IDA) and whose external debts were more than twice their annual export earnings. 41 countries met these criteria, most being in Africa. The benefits of the HIPC programme looked substantial, since it aimed to reduce each country's debt to a sustainable level, which could be serviced without compromising development goals. But the conditions were demanding. Each eligible country must meet the targets of an IMF reform programme for three consecutive years. This should lead to a 'decision point', after which a debt relief programme would be drawn up and agreed by the IMF, World Bank, Paris Club and other creditors. The agreed relief took effect from 'completion point', reached within three years of the decision point, while IMF discipline continued. The UK, France and Canada urged that the process should move through as fast as the rules allowed, but Germany, Japan and the US tended to slow things down.

Between the Lyon and Birmingham summits, progress was slow. By May 1998, one country alone, Uganda, had reached completion point, while seven others had passed decision point. All the other eligible countries were further behind and 13 had yet to start the process at all. Many in this last group were victims of civil conflict, like Angola and Rwanda. Major international charities and NGOs were now concerned at the human deprivation that the debt burden caused for poor countries.[24] They launched the Jubilee 2000 campaign, with the public slogan 'Break the Chains of Debt', calling for full debt relief for poor countries by 2000.[25] At Birmingham, Jubilee 2000 organised a human chain of 50,000 people, six miles long, to encircle the convention centre where the G8 formal meetings were held.

At the Commonwealth Finance Ministers' meeting in September 1997, British Finance Minister Gordon Brown had launched another initiative, called the 'Mauritius Mandate', aimed at using the deadline of 2000 as pressure for faster progress. This called for all HIPC countries to have embarked on the process of sustainable exit from their debt problems by the year 2000; and to have firm decisions on debt relief for at least three-quarters of them by the same date. Blair's objective at Birmingham was to get the G8 to endorse as much as possible of the Mauritius Mandate.[26]

In the event, the heads endorsed the target of getting all eligible countries into the system by 2000. But there was no commitment to having debt packages agreed for 75% of them by that date. There was instead a less precise undertaking 'to ensure that when they qualify countries get the relief they need', with the additional prospect of 'interim relief measures where necessary'. The G8 introduced a new concept of helping 'poor post-conflict countries' to get emergency debt relief.[27] In general, the G8 members were precise about what they expected the debtor countries to do, but vaguer and more conditional on what they would do themselves.

The Cologne Debt Initiative

The Birmingham results were dismissed with deep disappointment by the charities and other NGOs, but they continued to press for more rapid and radical debt relief. They argued that, even when countries fulfilled all their obligations to the IMF, the amount of debt relief received was negligible. They insisted that low-income countries could never escape poverty unless they could shift more resources from debt repayment into education and health. Jubilee 2000 planned another massive demonstration for the Cologne summit, backed by a petition with two million signatures.

A fundamental change in the German position gave them strong encouragement. In January 1999 Chancellor Schroeder announced his intention to make debt relief for the poorest a central issue for the Cologne summit. He called for deeper and faster debt relief, for the complete forgiveness of aid debt and for more generous financing, hinting at German agreement to IMF gold sales.[28] Schroeder's announcement stimulated all the other G7 countries to put in their own proposals for improving the HIPC programme and other approaches to debt relief.

The greatest hesitation now came from France, an early advocate of debt relief, because it still had a high level of aid debt, and from Japan, which had problems with the concept of forgiving government debt.

The Cologne Debt Initiative was set out in the G7 statement by the leaders and a supporting report by G7 finance ministers. It preserved the basic approach to debt relief in the HIPC programme but recommended a complete overhaul of the terms and conditions. There were six main elements:

- *Poverty Reduction* The funds saved through debt relief must be channelled into basic social programmes, such as health and education. The G7 asked the World Bank and IMF to ensure that this happened. These provisions aimed to satisfy both the charities and the opponents of debt relief, who argued that the money saved was often diverted into unproductive uses.
- *Faster Debt Relief* The Cologne initiative still distinguished between 'decision point' and 'completion point', but allowed for relief to start much quicker after 'decision point'. The leaders added a provision, not in the finance ministers' report, aiming to get three-quarters of eligible countries to their decision point by 2000. This key provision of the 'Mauritius mandate', denied at Birmingham, was thus endorsed at Cologne.
- *Deeper Debt Relief* The HIPC programme aimed to reduce poor countries' debt to 'sustainable levels', defined at 200-250% of exports. This ratio had proved too high and Cologne lowered it to 150%. For debts owed to national governments covered by the Paris Club, the proportion of relief was raised from 80% to 90%, going up to 100% if needed. All aid debts not already converted to grants should be forgiven.
- *Total Value of Debt Relief* The G7 estimated that these measures would more than double the debt relief available under the HIPC programme, to $50 billion in nominal terms. A further $20 billion (nominal) would come from forgiving aid debt. The G7 calculated that this would reduce by more than half the stock of debt, totalling $130 billion, that was owed by HIPC countries and not already covered by debt relief schemes.
- *Financing* Much of the sluggishness in the HIPC programme had been due to the reluctance of G7 members to finance it, though James Wolfensohn, the World Bank President, insisted the Bank would need extra funds.[29] Cologne recognised more finance would be needed, but the provisions were imprecise. Though the G7 finally agreed that the IMF should use the interest on the proceeds from selling 10 million ounces of its gold, there were fears this would depress the world gold price.[30] On bilateral contributions, especially to the World Bank, the G7 would only 'consider [them] in good faith'.

The Cologne summit proposals on debt, like those on financial architecture, required endorsement from the full membership of the IMF and World Bank. This was given at the Annual Meeting in September 1999 and further progress was made in mobilising the necessary finance. The IMF decided to revalue its gold internally, rather than selling it, and this was endorsed by the US Congress, which had opposed outright sales. G7 members and others pledged bilateral contributions totalling $2.5 billion to the trust fund created by the World Bank.[31]

The Cologne Debt Initiative was thus a major advance.[32] It showed up how little had actually been achieved at Birmingham. But the exchanges at Birmingham were necessary to open up discussion of the subject and reveal the strength of public concern. Without Birmingham, Cologne would not have gone so far. Cologne did not satisfy the Jubilee campaigners who wanted forgiveness of all debt. But the G7 judged this would do more harm than good.

Developments after Cologne

After this good start, however, the Enhanced HIPC programme moved much more slowly than expected. This was partly because of the time needed for each debtor to negotiate a new Poverty Reduction Strategy Paper (PRSP) with the Fund and Bank, to ensure the money saved on debt relief was used to promote development. By the time of the Okinawa summit in 2000 - the target year for the Jubilee 2000 Campaign - only nine countries had reached 'decision point'. Thanks to intense efforts by the Fund and Bank and the release of necessary funds by the US Congress, the total was brought up to 23 by Genoa in 2001. By then all the G7 governments had also moved to provide 100% relief on their bilateral debt.[33]

Yet not only the pace but also the content of the Enhanced HIPC programme attracted renewed criticism from the campaigning NGOs. Their main arguments were that, even after implementation of all available relief, many countries' debts were not sustainable. Often these countries were dependent on export earnings from primary commodities, whose prices were declining, and they could not diversify their exports because of trade barriers maintained by rich countries. The NGOs were also highly critical of the policies being recommended to poor countries by the Fund and Bank, as part of their wider attacks on the institutions, noted above. The campaigners argued that events had justified their original contention that only 100% relief on all debt, including debt to the IMF and World Bank, would produce a lasting solution, while the institutions' finances would not be harmed by such a move.[34]

The IMF and World Bank admitted the force of some of these criticisms, but the summit did little to respond to them.[35] The G7 finance ministers urged other Paris Club members to follow their example. They considered ways of helping countries emerging from conflict to benefit from the programme. At later summits, such as Kananaskis in 2002 and Sea Island in 2004, the heads acted to ensure that the Enhanced HIPC programme did not run out of funds and extended its life, so that all eligible countries could take advantage of it. But during the first G8 sequence neither the finance ministers nor the heads proved able to improve the basic terms and conditions of the HIPC programme as laid down at Cologne, despite increasing worries about debt sustainability in many beneficiary countries. They resisted pressure from African leaders to move towards the more generous debt relief advocated in NEPAD - see Chapter 12. Although by October 2004 the US and the UK were advancing plans to give 100% relief on all multilateral debt, they differed among themselves and had not convinced their G8 colleagues.[36]

Assessment under the Criteria

The review of the summit's performance against most of the criteria on this issue yields a broadly positive judgement:

- The summit consistently showed *leadership* in pursuing this issue, from back in 1988 up to 1999. If the heads of government themselves had not pushed for action on debt relief for the poorest, nothing would have happened at all. The initial proposals were not adequate for the scale of the problem. But the G7 leaders remained engaged and kept coming back to improve them. Birmingham was disappointing, but laid the foundations for the success of Cologne. The heads were personally engaged, going further than their finance ministers were prepared to go.
- The summit did have problems of *effectiveness* in reconciling domestic and external pressures. These measures to help the poorest were not provoked by any systemic crisis or major threats to the G7's economic interests, but were driven by a clear ethical motivation. For a long time, this was not strong enough to ensure sufficiently generous terms of debt relief or adequate financing. In particular the US had persistent difficulty with Congress, which did not release adequate funds till 2000.
- The summit also overcame serious problems of *solidarity*. The UK and Canada were keen from the start, working together in the Commonwealth, and so was France. But the US, Germany and Japan were reluctant participants and held up progress. The US position softened after Clinton took office, while the change of government in 1998 converted the Germans from deep scepticism to eager support. Japan was not prepared to hold things up on its own, so that major progress became possible at Cologne.
- At the outset the summit found it hard to agree on a *durable* debt-relief programme. Every year or so they had to come back and adapt it. But this reflected determination to come up with a programme that would really achieve its objectives. Cologne finally appeared to have achieved *durability*, in the sense that the Enhanced HIPC programme agreed there was widely implemented. But later summits were unable to agree modifications to the programme in order to improve the results to be gained from it.
- Successive debt relief programmes emerging from the summits had no real difficulty in winning *acceptance* internationally, from other governments. Each programme was endorsed by the full membership of the IMF and World Bank and any problems arose within the G7 itself. The summit also faced the harder test of *acceptability* from the charities and other NGOs that made up the Jubilee 2000 Campaign for complete debt forgiveness. The campaigners recognised the advance made by the heads at Cologne, but hoped that would lead on to even more generous relief. The absence of improvement in the terms of the HIPC programme after Cologne turned the NGOs against the summit, so that they became highly critical.

- The judgement on *consistency* showed some improvement by the G8 summits, after rather poor performance earlier in the 1990s. Debt relief was for many years the only area where the G7 summits directly addressed the problems of the poorest countries. In other fields of concern to these countries, notably aid policy and trade access, the summits of the 1990s did much less. But after their concentration on debt relief in 1998 and 1999, the summit participants realised that a wider involvement in development issues was essential to complement the debt relief measures. This was taken further in preparing for Okinawa 2000 and Genoa 2001, as the next chapters will show.

Lessons from the Summit Record on Finance and Debt

It is now possible to draw some lessons from the G8 summit record in handling issues concerned with the international financial system in the 1990s and early 2000s. These conclusions look at their performance under the six criteria.

Leadership

The heads of government successfully provided leadership, to drive forward agreement and resolve differences that had persisted at lower levels. On the new architecture the heads moved to address the worst financial upheaval since the debt crisis of 1982. They did not resolve issues at the summit itself, but they ensured that their finance ministers came to agreement and gave authority to their work. On debt relief for the poorest, the heads were personally active and intervened directly to make progress in a neglected area. This enabled Cologne 1999 to achieve results that had not been possible at Birmingham 1998 and for the heads to go beyond what had been agreed among finance ministers.

Effectiveness

The effectiveness of these summits was due to careful advance preparation, to limit the items requiring attention at the summit itself. Without proper preparation, the leaders could not reach clear decisions, so that the summit did not lead to effective follow-up action. The results from Halifax on financial reform and from Lyon on debt relief had been undermined by this. But the G7 heads followed up the rather unsatisfactory results from Birmingham, on both financial subjects, with further preparatory work that produced good results at Cologne.

Solidarity

In both subjects, the summits managed to overcome the divisions between them and generate successful collective management. In financial architecture, the G7 framework was able to discipline the tendency of the United States to take initiatives without adequate advance consultation. In debt relief, the iterative treatment of the subject, together with positive changes of government in the United States and Germany, served to bring about convergence between the enthusiasts and the sceptics. In particular the United States, though never in the lead, became firmly committed to the process.

Durability

On both international finance and debt relief the results from Birmingham and Cologne proved durable, in that they are still in operation over five years later. There was, however, a difference between them. The financial architecture, to which the heads made little personal contribution, proved more effective than had been expected at the time. There have been financial crises since then, especially in Argentina, but they have been limited in number and non-contagious. Debt relief, where the heads were innovative and interventionist, became more contested. The Enhanced HIPC programme was clearly a great advance, but the heads have failed to respond to some well-founded criticisms.

Acceptability

The demands made on the summit under this criterion had grown over the years. The G7 or G8 needed to give a lead from the summit - that was expected of them. But they could not expect others to follow blindly. They had to explain their proposals persuasively within the global institutions, such as the IMF, responding to the concerns of others. For example, the new G20 forum helped to associate major developing countries with the reform of the financial architecture.

The G8 also had to respond to a wider public. Charities and other NGOs, grouped under the banner of civil society, were keen to correct what they saw as the dangers of globalisation, for example for the poorest countries. The summit leaders had to be ready to explain and defend their decisions before this audience too. On both the financial issues covered, criticism of the summit by civil society intensified in the 2000s. Despite this criticism, the G8 welcomed the involvement of private business and civil society in the implementation of summit decisions wherever possible. The Poverty Reduction Strategies linked to the Enhanced HIPC programme provided an example of this. Involving private lenders in financial rescues proved more difficult.

Consistency

The analysis suggests that consistency is a hard criterion for the summit to satisfy. Those summits that gave close attention to financial matters neglected international trade. The G8 paid a heavy price for this neglect, which contributed to the spectacular failure of the WTO Ministerial at Seattle to launch a new round of trade negotiations in December 1999. The summits' attention to debt relief during the 1990s showed up how little the G8 was doing otherwise to help the poorest countries. The complexity of the new financial architecture likewise risked creating new burdens and problems for small and poor countries. The Okinawa 2000 and Genoa 2001 summits showed a first recognition of these underlying inconsistencies and sought to go beyond debt relief to address wider problems of world poverty.

Conclusion

In the sixth summit series, since Birmingham 1998, the G8 heads were directly responding to anxieties about what was perceived as the dark side of globalisation. There were worries about financial panic, where the herd instincts of the market penalised prudent and imprudent alike and the poor and weak were most likely to suffer. There were concerns about world poverty, where low-income countries, especially in Africa, were falling ever further behind. Measures to make the financial system stronger and more equitable addressed these anxieties directly. The summits showed leadership and solidarity in these areas and produced some broadly effective, durable and acceptable results. More clearly needed to be done, especially to integrate the summits' financial proposals into a wider economic and social context. But the summits after Cologne turned to this broader agenda.

Notes

1 This chapter is based on Chapter 11 of *Hanging In There* (Bayne 2000) combined with Bayne 2002. It speaks mainly of G7, not G8, as Russia contributed little.
2 For a review of monetary issues before Halifax, see Cooper 1995.
3 Initial assessments of the Halifax programme had been generally satisfied with the progress and did not expect a new crisis to break out. See Kenen 1996.
4 The G10 is a group of eleven countries that subscribe to the IMF's General Arrangements to Borrow and cooperate on other Fund issues - see Kenen, Shafer, Wicks and Wyplosz 2004, pp. 20-22, for a list of such groups. As for the new financing mechanism, Congress did not agree to release the US share till October 1998; see 'A Deal at Last', *The Economist,* 17 October 1998.
5 An early review of the state of the affected economies is in the 'East Asia Survey' in *The Economist,* 7 March 1998. Haggard 2000 contains an extended scholarly analysis of the Asian crisis.
6 Critics included Martin Wolf and Jeffrey Sachs (*Financial Times,* 9 and 11 December 1997), Martin Feldstein (Feldstein 1998) and Joseph Stiglitz, Chief Economist of the World Bank, ('Sick Patients, Warring Doctors', *The Economist,* 18 September 1999 and note 20 below). Stanley Fischer replied for the Fund - see 'Lessons from a Crisis', *The Economist,* 3 October 1998) and Fischer 1998. Camdessus and Wolfensohn 1998, in a volume prepared for the Birmingham summit, gave a joint defence on behalf of both the Fund and the Bank.
7 Work 'to strengthen the international monetary system' began at the G7 finance ministers meeting in February - see R. Chote and W. Munchau, 'G7 Ministers See Little Need to Sound Alarm over Asia', *Financial Times,* 23 February 1998 and 'New Financial Architecture' *The Economist,* 11 April 1998. There was parallel work in the G22 (G7 plus Australia and 14 emerging markets) called together by the US; see Kenen and others 2004, pp. 15-16.

8 The *Financial Times* followed the Russian crisis closely. See J. Thornhill, 'Russia's New Deal', N. Dunne, 'Russia claims Policy Victory as IMF Releases $4.8bn loan' and J. Thornhill and S. Fidler, 'Russia Ends Rouble-Dollar Peg', *Financial Times,* 15 and 22 July and 18 August 1998.

9 'UBS Writes Off £405m in LTCM', *Financial Times,* 25 September 1998.

10 S. Fidler and G. Dyer, 'Brazil Obtains $41bn Rescue Package', *Financial Times,* 14 November 1998. The first package ran into problems and had to be re-done in March 1999 - 'First Steps to Safety', *The Economist,* 13 March 1999.

11 The main points are in 'Resolve to Put New Rules in Place', *Financial Times,* 31 October 1998. For early comment, see M. Wolf, 'Currency Vacuum' and J. Sachs, 'Stop Preaching', *Financial Times,* 2 and 5 November 1998.

12 A timetable was agreed at the G7 finance ministers meeting in February, R. Chote, 'Forum to Help Prevent Crises Agreed' *Financial Times,* 22 February 1999. See also the 'Global Finance Survey' in *The Economist,* 30 January 1999. Kenen and others 2004, pp. 51-53, note: 'This intense activity is perhaps the most fully developed case of the G7 providing a leadership role'.

13 The main regulators were the Bank for International Settlements (BIS), the International Association of Insurance Supervisors (IAIS) and the International Organisation of Securities Commissions (IOSCO), while non-G8 monetary authorities were also added: Kenen and others 2004, pp. 71-73. The Financial Stability Forum held its first meeting in April, see H. Davies, 'A Forum for Stability', *Financial Times,* 14 April 1999.

14 A. Beattie, 'New Forum to Supplement G7 Work', *Financial Times,* 27 September 1999. See also A. Beattie and H. Simonian, 'Lively Debate at First G20 Talks', *Financial Times,* 17 December 1999.

15 S. Fidler, 'IMF Proposals to Ease Debt Crises May Founder', *Financial Times,* 29 September 1999.

16 An immediate assessment is in the *Financial Times* Economic Survey, 24 September 1999, pp. I-VI. For early scholarly analyses see Eichengreen 1999, Evans 2000 and Kenen and Svoboda 2000. More mature judgements are in Kenen 2001, Armijo 2002 and Vines and Gilbert 2004.

17 Argentina's default stimulated new work on this issue in the IMF early in 2002, including a proposed Sovereign Debt Rescheduling Mechanism, but this ran into the sand a year later. See A. Beattie, 'IMF Outlines New Plan for Bankrupt Countries to Restructure Debts' and 'US Set to Block "Sovereign Chapter 11" Proposals', *Financial Times,* 2 April 2002 and 31 March 2003. The ideas are summarised in Kenen and others 2004, pp. 47-49.

18 US Treasury Secretary Larry Summers was already advocating more reforms later in 1999 - see E. Crooks, 'Summers Urges IMF to Focus on Preventing Crises', *Financial Times,* 15 December 1999. An American commission chaired by Allan Meltzer produced in early 2000 a report calling for the IMF to lend only to countries meeting strict conditions in advance and for the World Bank to provide grants not loans (Meltzer 2000). The latter idea was taken up by the new Bush Administration in 2001. For more recent ideas, see Rogoff 2004.

19 On Argentina's collapse, see Teunissen and Akkerman 2003. On Turkey's recovery, see M. Wolf, 'Turkey Must Not Take its Turnround for Granted', *Financial Times,* 20 October 2004.

20 Some of the sharpest attacks on the IMF came from Joseph Stiglitz after he had ceased to be Chief Economist of the World Bank, see Stiglitz 2002.

21 A. Beattie, 'IMF Ready to Abandon Unused Panic Credit Facility', *Financial Times,* 18 November 2003.

22 For an early analysis of the G20, see Kirton 2001. Paul Martin of Canada, the first G20 chair, joined the G8 heads in 2004 - see Chapter 11 below. A recent reflection on the G20's performance is in Kirton 2005a.

23 Evans 1999 gives an insider's account of how the summits came to focus on debt relief for the poorest and how agreements were reached. For France's role in the early initiatives, see Attali 1995, pp. 42-51.

24 See Dent and Peters 1999 for the origins of this movement.

25 Jubilee 2000's main campaign was reinforced by more detailed proposals to speed up the HIPC process, widen its eligibility, increase the relief given and give special treatment to countries suffering civil conflict. See Lockwood and others 1998.

26 The role of the Commonwealth in debt relief is examined in Bayne 1998.

27 The quotations are from the G8 communiqué, accessible on www.g8.utoronto.ca.

28 The German position was first set out in Chancellor Schroeder's article in *Financial Times,* 21 January 1999. See also 'For Debt Relief, Some Thanks', *The Economist,* 20 March 1999.

29 Wolfensohn's position is reported in R. Chote, 'G7 Urged to Find Extra Cash for Debt Deal', *Financial Times,* 29 April 1999.

30 M. Holman, 'Poor Countries Will Not Gain from Gold Sale', *Financial Times,* 18 June 1999.

31 On the use of gold, see S. Fidler, 'IMF to Revalue Gold Stocks to Finance Debt Relief Scheme' and D. McGregor, 'US Deal Clears IMF Debt Relief Plan, *Financial Times,* 24 September and 17 November 1999. On the World Bank Trust Fund, see A. Beattie, 'Poorest Countries' Debt Relief Initiative Agreed', *Financial Times,* 28 September 1999.

32 For an immediate assessment, see 'How to Make Aid Work', *The Economist,* 26 June 1999. For later scholarly analyses, see Birdsall and Williamson 2002 and Addison, Hansen and Tarp 2004.

33 The movement was started by the UK in December 1999, with the aim of setting an example - See C. Adams, 'Brown Unveils Details of Debt Relief Package', *Financial Times,* 22 December 1999. For other G7 countries, see Chapter 6, note 12.

34 See J. Sachs, 'The Charade of Debt Sustainability' and S. Fidler, 'Financial Institutions Urged to Cancel Debt', *Financial Times,* 26 September 2000 and 11 April 2001.

35 See A. Beattie, 'Debt Relief Plan Missing Targets, Says IMF Study', *Financial Times,* 6 September 2002.

36 The United States favoured converting all loans to HIPC countries to grants, but without providing extra money for the Fund and Bank. The United Kingdom was convinced that extra funds would be needed and offered to contribute ten percent of the total. See A. Balls and A. Beattie, 'Differences Between US and UK to Stall Debt Relief Deal', *Financial Times,* 30 September 2004, and Chapter 12 below.

Chapter 6

Targeting Development: Okinawa 2000

By the time of the Okinawa summit in July 2000, some of the novelty had worn off the 'heads-only' format established at Birmingham in 1998. The sense of crisis had left the international financial system and calm had returned to the markets. In contrast, the multilateral trading system was in turmoil, after the failure of the WTO ministerial meeting held in Seattle in December 1999 to launch a new round of negotiations. Much of the blame for Seattle's collapse was laid at the door of the Americans and of Clinton personally. But at Okinawa he had only six months left in office. New American initiatives, in trade or other matters, seemed unlikely until the US presidential elections were over. Even so, the Japanese Prime Minister, Keizo Obuchi, was determined to leave his personal imprint on the summit he would host, the first summit of the new millennium.[1] His ideas determined the summit agenda, the choice of site and the start of major G8 outreach.[2]

Preparations: Agenda, Site and Outreach

Obuchi wanted the summit to focus on issues of development and in this area the Japanese conducted the preparations with great thoroughness, especially as regards information and communications technology (IT). But instead of concentrating the agenda, as Blair and Schroeder had done, Obuchi identified three broad themes - prosperity, peace of mind and stability. Such a wide formulation made it hard for the Japanese to keep the agenda under control, because almost any economic topic could be raised under 'prosperity' and any political one under 'stability'.

Obuchi also decided that the summit should be held in Okinawa, with the finance and foreign ministers also meeting in Western Japan, at Fukuoka and Miyazaki. This was the first time Japan had hosted the summit outside Tokyo, but it proved a mixed blessing. The facilities provided were unusually lavish, apparently costing about $750 million in total. This included substantial public works conducted under the summit label, as well as the extra costs of security, supplies and transport in a remote location. The amount spent attracted hostile comment from NGOs and media, who also gave wide coverage to local protests against the massive US military presence in Okinawa.[3]

By developing outreach from the summit, the Japanese introduced modifications to the format that would have a lasting effect. They made great efforts to involve non-G8 countries, both in pre-summit consultations and in meetings with the ministers and heads.[4] An early proposal by Obuchi to associate Asian leaders with the summit process gained the backing of the rest of the G8 but failed because of the resistance of China.[5] But his successor Yoshiro Mori invited five other G8 leaders (Clinton, Schroeder and Putin could not be there) to meet a group of non-G8 heads of government in Tokyo on their way to Okinawa. The guests were chosen for their status as representing different groupings. There were three African Presidents - Obasanjo (Nigeria) for the G77, Mbeki (South Africa) for the Non-Aligned Movement and Bouteflika (Algeria) for the Organisation of African Unity. The Prime Minister of Thailand was invited as chair of the Association of South-East Asian Nations (ASEAN) and of the UN Conference on Trade and Development (UNCTAD) held in Bangkok earlier in 2000.

After the massive demonstrations at Seattle and subsequent international meetings, the Japanese hosts paid particular attention to NGOs. The Japanese sherpa visited London early in 2000 to meet NGO representatives; this became a standard part of summit preparations. At Okinawa itself the Japanese hosts provided official facilities for NGOs, with an NGO centre, for the first time at a summit. The NGO presence was, however, constrained by Okinawa's remoteness. In consequence, apart from some mass demonstrations against the US military presence, the Japanese were spared the upheavals that afflicted international meetings in Washington, Prague and Nice during 2000.[6]

These modifications increased the transparency of the summit process, though initially the change was more in the form than the substance. In 2000 the content of the meetings with both non-G8 leaders and NGO representatives was limited. But Okinawa laid the foundation for a much more significant meeting with African leaders at Genoa a year later.

The summit preparations illustrated the extent of the G8 apparatus below the level of the heads. During the early part of 2000 there were meetings of G8 employment and environment ministers, as had become customary, as well as a meeting of education ministers, as provided in the Cologne communiqué. Following the pattern set at Birmingham, the G7 finance ministers met at Fukuoka ten days before the summit. They issued substantial reports on international financial architecture and on IT, with a short release on money-laundering. Two more reports were held over to the summit. The G8 foreign ministers met at Miyazaki a week before the summit. Their main declaration featured conflict prevention and covered a substantial report on detailed aspects of this topic, including small arms trade and the illicit traffic in diamonds. This reflected work done since their meeting dedicated to conflict prevention at Berlin in December 1999.[7] Their declaration also dealt with terrorism, UN issues, crime, environment and 11 regional issues, most of which did not need attention by the G8 leaders.

The Okinawa Summit, 21-23 July 2000

Most of the heads of government that gathered at Okinawa were summit veterans and knew each other well - including Prodi, now attending as President of the European Commission rather than Italian Prime Minister. But sadly Obuchi had died two months before the summit itself and it was hard for his successor, Yoshiro

Mori, to step into his shoes. Mori could present Japan's position fairly well, but found his role in the chair more difficult.

Of the others, Chirac, Blair and Chrétien took a full part. Schroeder was active on involving Russia and Prodi on trade and food safety. Giuliano Amato of Italy, a newcomer, spoke seldom but always to the point and was already preparing for the summit hosted by Italy in 2001 - though he would not survive in power to chair it. While the other Europeans and Chrétien were reasonably secure in office, Clinton was constrained because he had only a few months remaining. He was preoccupied by the Middle East talks in Washington; he had had to leave them at a critical stage and they finally ended in stalemate.[8] The local hostility to the US bases in Okinawa was also unsettling for him.

Okinawa was the first appearance of Vladimir Putin as the new President of Russia. The G7 leaders needed to come to terms with Yeltsin's successor, to convince him of the merits of G8 summit membership and of the obligations it carried. They would use this to support democracy and sound economic management in Russia and to encourage responsible Russian foreign policy. In practice, the transition went smoothly. Unlike the unpredictable Yeltsin, Putin proved a skilful summit operator from his first appearance. He put across his arguments effectively but knew when not to push his luck and formed a special rapport with Schroeder.

G7 Economic Issues

Financial Architecture and Abuses of the Financial System

The G7 leaders met openly for two hours on the afternoon of 21 July before Putin arrived. They issued a statement which covered two reports from their finance ministers on 'Debt Relief and Poverty Reduction' and 'Actions Against Abuse of the Global Financial System', which included money-laundering.

There was a predictable exchange on world economic prospects. Everyone was very confident, apart from some worries over oil prices, and no one forecast the bursting of the 'dot.com bubble' later in the year. On financial architecture, the leaders endorsed the finance ministers' document from Fukuoka, adding nothing of their own. The report was essentially a progress report on action to implement the measures agreed at Cologne, especially in reform of the IMF and the multilateral development banks. There was little new in the G7 statement except a positive reference to regional arrangements - a nod towards recent moves by Japan.[9]

On money-laundering and other financial abuses, the leaders again endorsed the finance ministers' report issued at the summit, adding nothing themselves. This report was more original, as it picked up the work done by the Financial Action Task Force (FATF) on money-laundering, by the OECD on harmful tax competition and by the Financial Stability Forum on offshore financial centres.[10] In each area delinquent countries, whose internal regulations were inadequate, had been identified and named. The G7 offered to help them mend their ways, identifying eight areas of improvement, but hinted at sanctions if they did not reform.[11]

Debt Relief and Development

Debt relief for the poorest countries was the most serious subject for the G7 heads - as at Cologne, the Russians were not involved. Blair led off the discussion, stressing the extent of public feeling on the topic. He had had 150,000 postcards and 100,000 e-mail messages on it during the last three months. But the problem for the G7 was that, despite considerable efforts, their major initiative from Cologne in 1999 was falling behind schedule. Bilaterally the G7 had in fact gone beyond their Cologne commitments, since all had agreed to give 100% reduction of bilateral debt, instead of the 90% reduction promised a year before.[12] But the multilateral aspects were creating obstacles. The requirement for beneficiary countries to conclude 'Poverty Reduction Strategies' was slowing things down. There was doubt whether financial pledges made to compensate the World Bank would be met, especially by the United States, where funds were held up in Congress. Many eligible countries in Africa were being undermined by conflict, either internal or external, so that they could not meet the conditions required.[13]

As a result, the Cologne target of getting three quarters of the 41 eligible countries to their 'decision point' by the end of 2000 would not be met. (This target had been added by the heads of government themselves). Only nine countries had qualified so far, and eleven more were expected to make it by the end of the year. The G7 leaders were clearly frustrated by this and made clear their anxiety about conflict in Africa. But they could not offer any radical measures to speed things up. For this they were denounced by Jubilee 2000, the civil society grouping campaigning for total debt relief by the end of the year, who said they were "totally dismayed" by the G7 statement.[14] This was a setback, since the leaders had engaged their personal reputations in the debt relief measures, which had been the summits' main contribution so far to helping the poorest countries.

G8 Political Issues

The working dinner on the first evening, as usual, focused on political issues. Korea, the Middle East peace process and former Yugoslavia were the main topics discussed by the leaders. This dinner was Putin's first G8 appearance and he was an active participant, leading on Korea and taking part on Yugoslavia too. He had travelled to Okinawa via Pyongyang and Beijing, which allowed him to make a unique contribution to the Korean discussions. This was a risky strategy for a newcomer, but Putin carried it off. After breakfasting with Putin next day, Schroeder floated the idea that the G7 need no longer meet without the Russians present. This was not agreed, however, and Clinton said in public that the G7 was still needed. Putin bid to host the summit of 2003 in Russia, but this bid was left on the table.

The G8 issued separate statements on Korea, welcoming the reconciliation between North and South, and on regional issues (South Asia, Middle East, the Balkans, Africa, Cyprus).[15] Other political issues featured in the G8 communiqué, under the heading 'Greater World Stability'. The provisions on conflict prevention included agreement on a conference on the diamonds trade and its role in conflict in Africa.[16] On disarmament the G8 set the goal of 'an international financing plan for plutonium management'.[17] There was apparently no discussion of China, which was not mentioned in the G8 documents except in the context of its accession to the WTO.

G8 Economic and Global Issues

The main G8 agenda was covered in two sessions on 22 July. The morning session covered economic issues, under the title 'Greater Prosperity'; the afternoon dealt with the environment and related topics, labelled 'Deeper Peace of Mind'. These sessions provided the basis for the G8 communiqué, which set out aspirations for the 21st century and a wide-ranging response to the demands of globalisation.

Information and Communications Technology (IT)

IT was the most substantial subject covered. Work on this topic provided a major focus for the summit preparations, including a conference with leading private sector figures, which the Japanese had organised just before the summit.[18] Though the heads' discussion was fairly general, they were able to issue an extensive document, the Okinawa Charter on Global Information Society. The Charter offered a vision of 'an information society that better enables people to fulfil their potential and realise their aspirations'.

The document fell into three parts:

- *Digital Opportunities* focused on economic activities and their regulation in developed countries. There was a balance between the 'leading role' of the private sector and the responsibility of government 'to create a predictable, transparent, and non-discriminatory policy and regulatory framework'. A long set of principles began with recognisable US objectives, such as keeping electronic commerce duty-free, but ended with European concerns about consumer trust and privacy.
- *Digital Divide* dealt with social policies in developed countries, including wider network access and education.
- *Global Participation* focused on IT for developing countries. After welcoming contributions from other institutions and the private sector, it created a 'Digital Opportunity Taskforce' (DOT-Force), with a wide range of tasks, to report to the Genoa summit in 2001.

The first two parts of the Charter represented a fair synthesis of current discussion of the role of IT in richer countries. The Charter was most innovative in asserting that developing countries could benefit from IT, even the poorest. But many aspects were left unresolved. The Charter recognised the 'gaps in terms of basic economic and social infrastructures' in poor countries, such as no electricity, no telephones and low education. But it did not say much about how these gaps could be filled. The resources required and available were not identified, though Japan pledged $15 billion over five years. So the initial public reaction was sceptical.[19]

Development

There was a wide-ranging discussion of development issues among the heads. Blair and Chirac returned to the issue of debt relief, urging greater efforts to show that the summit leaders cared about the poorest countries. They and other leaders also covered increased aid volumes, better trade access and education, especially for women.

The G7 finance ministers' report on debt relief and poverty reduction, issued at the summit, claimed to help developing countries to 'benefit from the forces of globalisation'. But though full of exhortation and good intentions, it lacked clear commitments either on increased aid or improved trade access. The long development section of the G8 communiqué offered an advance on the finance ministers' document. It recognised the scale of the problems - 'still 1.2 billion people living on less than one dollar a day' - and the inadequacy of earlier G7 and G8 measures. But it fell short of a satisfactory response.

The Okinawa communiqué contained the usual provisions on aid effectiveness. But, unlike Cologne, it made no commitment to increase aid volume. After a failure to agree on untying aid for least-developed countries in the OECD in June, the G8 set a more limited target.[20] The leaders were unable to add anything substantial on debt relief. The communiqué largely repeated the G7 statement, while aiming to get a total of 20 countries to 'decision point' by the end of the year. (This objective was met, though it was below the target set at Cologne.)[21] The G8 also expressed support for the target of universal primary education set at the Dakar Conference, but without any precise commitments.[22]

Infectious Diseases

The heads also focused on the fight against the infectious diseases that held back poor countries. Mori pledged $3 billion over three years in aid, plus a fund to support NGOs. Clinton spoke of US action to subsidise the cost of drugs for poor countries. The leaders committed themselves to a partnership to deliver three targets set by the UN and the WHO for reducing AIDS, tuberculosis and malaria.[23] They called for a strategy conference later in 2000 and a UN conference on AIDS in 2001. The aims of the partnership included 'mobilising additional resources', access to drugs and vaccines and stimulating research. But there were no details on how these aims could be met.

Trade and the WTO

There were divided views among the leaders on whether, after the disaster of Seattle, the G8 should call for a new trade round in the WTO by the end of the year. Mori, in summing up the discussion, said that all could agree the round should start 'by the end of the year, if possible'. The communiqué duly said the G8 would 'try together with other WTO members to launch such a round during the course of this year'. The round should have 'an ambitious, balanced and inclusive agenda', including market access, WTO rules, support for developing countries and making trade compatible with social and environmental policies. This looked like a slight move towards the EU/Japanese preference for a 'comprehensive' round. But it was not clear that the G8 had resolved their internal differences or worked out how they could persuade developing countries to agree to the non-trade items that had proved so divisive at Seattle.

The incentives offered to the poorest countries were disappointing. The US had finally adopted, in May 2000, the Africa Growth and Opportunity Act giving trade concessions to Africa, the Caribbean and Central America. But this had taken years to get through Congress, so that Clinton could not offer more. The G8 members admitted that their earlier offers on market access and capacity building were not good enough: 'We recognise the need to go further with greater urgency in this area - and we will do so'. But a long passage on capacity-building building contained only rhetorical commitments, while nothing more was said in the communiqué about better market access at all.[24]

Russian Economy

During the G8 discussions, Putin explained his economic reform programme, hoping it would produce results and gain support. From G7 briefings the night before it was clear that if Putin had asked for debt reduction, he would not have got it. The Russian economy had recovered over the past year. It was now thought strong enough to pay its debts in full, though rescheduling could be offered in the Paris Club if Russia agreed an IMF programme. Although Russian Prime Minister Mikhail Kasyanov had argued publicly that the G8 should consider debt reduction, Putin wisely did not raise debt at all.[25] There was nothing on Russia's economy in the summit documents.

Global Issues

During their afternoon session, the leaders focused on crime, food safety and the environment. Ageing, earlier featured by the Japanese hosts, was not discussed. The exchanges were lively but fairly inconclusive:

- *Crime* The discussion on crime and drug-smuggling concentrated on various international events, such as the UN Convention on Organised Crime and another conference on high-tech crime, to be hosted by Japan. These points were reflected in the communiqué, which also envisaged another meeting of G8 interior and justice ministers.

- *Food Safety* This had been raised at Cologne, without substantive agreement. At Okinawa views were divided between those who would rely on scientific evidence (Clinton, Chrétien and Blair) and those advocating the precautionary principle (the other Europeans). The matter was not resolved and the communiqué contained language giving comfort to both camps. A compromise proposal to create 'an independent international panel' was only noted, not adopted, because of differing views about its composition.[26]
- *Environment* The heads discussed bringing into force the Kyoto Protocol on climate change, without resolving transatlantic differences, and forest management, including illegal logging. These topics featured in the communiqué, though without much advance on known positions. On two more topics the leaders called for action before the Genoa summit in 2001. They created a task force to encourage the use of renewable energy in developing countries - a British proposal. They agreed to support environmental guidelines on export credit, promoted by the Americans.[27]

Assessment of the Okinawa Summit

This was an ambitious and hard-working set of meetings - taking the summit and ministerial meetings together. They produced a large number of commitments, but many of these were high on rhetoric and low on precise measures and identifiable resources. So the initial impression fell short of the expectations created by all the preparatory work and left much open for future implementation.

The Japanese kept to the letter of the procedure introduced at Birmingham, but allowed both summit agenda and documentation to get overloaded again. The Okinawa communiqué, at 16 pages, was over 70% longer than Cologne's.[28] This showed that if the summits should revert to open-ended agendas and long documents, going far beyond what the leaders actually discussed, they would lose the benefits of the reforms introduced at Birmingham.

On the substance, the political side of the proceedings went well, with an easy transition from Yeltsin to Putin. There was a timely consensus on Korea and some innovative work on conflict prevention, which would need to be followed up, especially at the UN. There was a sense of purpose over the financing of plutonium management lacking from the issues concerned with developing countries. But political issues were not central to this summit.

There was general satisfaction with the performance of the G7's own economies. Even Japan seemed to be recovering and the imminent setback to growth in the US was not foreseen. The G8 therefore concluded that domestic worries about globalisation, for example over jobs, no longer needed attention. There were few contentious issues between the G8 themselves that had to be resolved at Okinawa. On IT the divergent approaches of Americans and Europeans were skilfully reconciled. The report on financial architecture was largely work in progress; the report on money-laundering was based on work done elsewhere. There were differences on food safety and the environment, but in the absence of operational pressures the G8 could safely agree to differ.

So the main focus of Okinawa was on economic subjects of concern to developing countries. Ever since Lyon 1996, the summits had shown increasing concern that the poorest countries were being left behind by globalisation. But they had found it hard to match their good intentions with effective measures except on debt relief. NGOs were becoming more vocal in their claims that poor countries were being neglected. The failed WTO meeting at Seattle showed the extent of the dissatisfaction of the developing countries, as well as the ability of NGOs to mobilise. The Okinawa summit was an opportunity for the G8 to regain the initiative and to show themselves responsive to the needs and concerns of developing countries, especially the poorest. The topics chosen - trade, debt relief, infectious diseases and IT - were, in principle, very suitable for this purpose. But the treatment of them, though often full of detail, was not always satisfactory.

In two new subjects, IT and infectious diseases, Okinawa adopted an original approach and laid out programmes that would be highly beneficial, if properly implemented. But this would depend on the G8 recognising the scale of the measures needed to help the poorest countries and making precise commitments of the necessary funds. There was a welcome readiness to involve the private sector, but this could not be a substitute for government action. So the results of Okinawa could only be judged in the light of the achievements of the DOT-Force and the follow-on action planned for infectious diseases. In fact, thanks to the joint efforts of the Japanese and Italian G8 Presidencies, implementation in both areas was very effective. This will be considered further in the next two chapters.

In traditional development subjects, however, like debt relief, trade and aid flows, Okinawa was a disappointment. The Cologne *debt* initiative, which should have been a major asset, had clearly run into problems. Though there were some good reasons for the slow progress, the failure to meet the Cologne timetable undermined confidence in summit commitments. Offers of *trade access* for poor countries were recognised as being inadequate, but the summit did not agree on new ones. The commitment to start the new WTO trade round in 2000 looked insecure - and proved to be so. In the absence of any commitment to increase *aid volumes*, the various promises of assistance scattered throughout the documents lacked conviction.

Conclusion

The Okinawa summit provided some good examples of innovative *leadership,* in outreach, IT and infectious diseases. But it was not very *effective* where hard domestic decisions were required, as in trade and aid flows. *Solidarity* among the G8 was good but limited in scope. The initiatives in IT and infectious diseases proved both *durable* and *acceptable*, after initial scepticism. But the failure to do more on debt undermined G8 *acceptability* with NGO campaigners. The summit was *consistent* in its aims, but not in its execution of them. Despite some clear achievements, Okinawa was not as successful as Birmingham or Cologne.

Above all, the Okinawa summit showed that the G8 needed to improve their communications with developing countries, with NGOs and with public opinion generally. The advance of globalisation meant there were far more active players in the system, who had to be convinced of the merits of the G8's decisions. Okinawa made some important advances in outreach to non-G8 governments, private firms and NGOs and later summits would build upon them. The G8 communiqué went further and said: 'We must engage in a new partnership with non-G8 countries, particularly developing countries, international organisations and civil society'. This was the first time the summit had suggested such a partnership and its nature was not otherwise defined. It would not be easy to achieve such a partnership in a way that preserved the direct, informal nature of the summit circle. Its success would depend on the G8 having a convincing message to put across to its 'new partners', by whatever methods were chosen to convey it.

Notes

1 For Obuchi's summit ambitions, see M. Nakamoto and G. Tett, 'Setting the Agenda for the Next 25 Years', *Financial Times* Survey of Kyushu/Okinawa, 23 June 2000.

2 The account of the Okinawa summit in this chapter is largely derived from Bayne 2001 and Bayne 2002a. See also Budd 2003.

3 On the cost, see G. Tett, 'Dispute over High Cost of Hosting G8', *Financial Times*, 27 July 2000. On the demonstrations, see M. Nakamoto, 'Okinawa Demonstrators Protest over US Military', *Financial Times*, 21 July 2000.

4 An earlier attempt by President Mitterrand of France to have a meeting between the G7 and other heads of government at the 1989 Paris summit failed because of resistance from the other G7 members, especially the Americans; see Attali 1995, pp. 277-285. But by 2000 this resistance had disappeared.

5 See G. Tett and others, 'Beijing May Have Seat at July Summit', *Financial Times*, 14 February 2000 and 'Japan Plays the Wrong China Card', *The Economist*, 19 February 2000. An analysis of China's links with the summit is in Kirton 2001a.

6 For immediate comment on the wave of demonstrations, see 'NGOs - Sins of the Secular Missionaries' and 'Anti-Capitalist Protests', *The Economist*, 27 January and 23 September 2000. Hajnal 2002 examines the developing relationship between the G8 and civil society.

7 A report of the Berlin meeting, which also covered the situation in Chechnya, is in D. Buchan and others, 'Moscow's G8 Partners Urge Grozny Truce', *Financial Times*, 18 December 1999.

8 See 'The Ballad of Camp David' and 'After Camp David', *The Economist*, 22 and 29 July 2000.

9 Japan had agreed a network of currency swaps with other Asian countries in May. See P. Montagnon, 'Asia Agrees Plan to Prevent Repeat of Economic Crisis', *Financial Times*, 8 May 2000.

10 The Financial Action Task Force had been founded by the 1989 Paris summit to fight the laundering of the proceeds of the drugs trade and had since extended its remit to all earnings from criminal activity - see Chapter 12 below for its role in terrorist finance. The Financial Stability Forum was part of the new financial architecture - see Chapter 5 above.

11 For the background on money-laundering and tax evasion, see leader, 'Role of Shame' and M. Peel and C. Adams, 'Nowhere to Hide', *Financial Times,* 23 and 26 June 2000.

12 The UK had already acted in 1999. They were followed by France (M. Huband, 'France to Ready to Write off $7bn in Debt'), Japan (M. Nakamoto, 'Japan Decides to Forgive Debts of Poorest Nations') and Germany (A. Beattie, 'Germany Plans Debt Write-Off'), *Financial Times,* 5, 11 and 14 April 2000.

13 S. Fidler and A. Beattie, 'Debt Initiative Leaves Poor Nations Short-Changed', *Financial Times,* 3 April 2000.

14 Quoted in S. Fidler, B. Groom and G. Tett, 'Charities in Attack on "Obscene" G8 Spending', *Financial Times,* 22 July 2000. Jubilee 2000 had earlier claimed the industrialised countries were "reneging on promises of debt relief" - A. Beattie, *Financial Times,* 3 July 2000.

15 On reconciliation in Korea, see 'The Two Koreas', *The Economist,* 15 April 2000.

16 The civil war in Sierra Leone had drawn attention to this problem - see D. Buchan and M. Holman, 'A Warlord's Best Friend', *Financial Times,* 20 May 2000. The planned conference took place in London in October.

17 This later mutated into the 'Global Partnership' agreed at the Kananaskis summit in 2002 - see Chapter 9.

18 Japan's objectives were set out in M. Nakamoto, 'Mori Joins the IT Generation', *Financial Times* Survey of Kyushu/Okinawa, 23 June 2000.

19 *The Economist* shared this scepticism - see 'A Raw Deal' and 'On Top of the World', 22 and 29 July 2000.

20 For the OECD discussions, see A. Beattie, 'Tied Aid Plan at Risk' and 'OECD Meeting Fails to End Tied Aid', *Financial Times,* 19 and 23 June 2000. Agreement was finally reached in the OECD, after more setbacks, early in 2002.

21 A. Beattie, 'Debt Relief for 20 Nations Expected This Year', *Financial Times,* 19 December 2000.

22 See Budd 2003, p. 145. The Dakar Conference in April had renewed targets set ten years previously, despite a drop both in aid and national spending on primary education meanwhile - W. Wallis 'Gulf Remains Between Rhetoric and Reality in Education', *Financial Times,* 1 May 2000.

23 The damage done by these diseases had been the subject of recent conferences in Africa on malaria (W. Wallis, 'Malaria Has Cost Africa up to $62bn') and AIDS (D. Pilling, 'Talk That Saves Lives'), *Financial Times,* 25 April and 8 July 2000.

24 On the Africa Growth and Opportunity Act giving trade concessions to Africa, the Caribbean and Central America, see D. McGregor, 'Way Clear for US-Africa Trade Bill', *Financial Times,* 4 May 2000. In September 2000 the European Commission announced its 'Everything but Arms' initiative, aimed at giving duty-and quota-free access to all civilian imports from least-developed countries - M. Smith, 'EU May End Duty for Poor Nations' *Financial Times,* 21 September 2000. See Chapters 7 and 8 below.

25 See M. Kasyanov, 'A Financial End to the Cold War', *Financial Times,* 20 July 2000. G7 briefing is reflected in G. Tett, 'G7 to Deflect Russia's Call for Cut in Debt', *Financial Times,* 21 July 2000.

26 The idea had been raised at an OECD conference at Edinburgh - M. Wrong, 'G8 May Set Up Advisory Body', *Financial Times,* 1 March 2000.

27 See Budd 2003, pp. 141-142. Neither proposal proved durable. The report on renewable energy was not endorsed by the G8 at Genoa, see Chapters 7 and 8 below. The OECD discussions on export credit failed to reach agreement.

28 By contrast, the last summit held in Japan - Tokyo III 1993 - was content with an economic declaration of only six pages, though that summit was crucial in bringing the Uruguay Round to a conclusion.

Chapter 7

Transcending the Riots: Genoa 2001

The Genoa summit was the target of violent riots, which left one dead, over 200 injured and an estimated $40 million of damage. The riots obsessed the media, who claimed the G8 leaders themselves achieved little and that summits in this form could not survive. But though preoccupied with the causes and consequences of the riots, the leaders in fact launched some important initiatives, though Genoa's impact would depend on how far they were fully implemented.[1]

Summit Preparations

Italian Prime Minister Amato, like Obuchi before Okinawa, took an active, personal part in the summit preparations.[2] The Italians, as hosts, strove to maintain continuity with the Okinawa summit. They kept up the focus on development issues like IT and infectious diseases, which were topical after the adoption of the Millennium Development Goals by the UN.[3] They brought the summit agenda back to three precise themes - poverty reduction, global environment and conflict prevention.[4] This enabled the documents issued by the leaders to be kept commendably short: G8 communiqué of 3,300 words on five pages; G7 statement of 1,800 words on six pages; and four more statements of a page apiece.[5] The full summit documentation, however, was much more copious: three reports from G7 finance ministers; four statements from G8 foreign ministers; texts on the new Global Fund to fight AIDS, tuberculosis and malaria; and reports from the task-forces on IT (the DOT-Force) and renewable energy.

The Italians maintained the heads-only format introduced at Birmingham and extended the moves towards greater outreach begun at Okinawa. Earlier in 2001 there were meetings of G8 ministers of employment, environment and (jointly) interior and justice. Nearer the summit, G7 finance ministers met in Rome on 7 July. They completed work on three reports sent forward to the summit, on development banks, financial abuses and debt relief. They also briefed the press in surprisingly optimistic terms on world economic prospects. G8 foreign ministers met also in Rome on 18-19 July. They issued conclusions covering the Middle East and eleven other regional issues. On conflict prevention, they endorsed progress reports on small arms, diamonds, children in conflict, civilian policing and conflict and development. They added two new items to this agenda - women in conflict and the private sector. In a long statement on disarmament they avoided open disagreement on missile defence, while Colin Powell (US) and Igor Ivanov (Russia) were at pains to show how well they could work together on other things.[6]

The Genoa Summit, 20-22 July 2001

By the time of the summit, Amato had left office, after the electoral defeat of the 'Olive Tree' coalition that had governed Italy since 1996. The new Italian Prime Minister, Sergio Berlusconi, only arrived in June and wisely kept on the sherpa team that had been responsible for the preparations under his predecessor. Berlusconi had chaired a summit before - at Naples in 1994 - but he seemed ill at ease with the new format.

This was the first G8 summit for US President George W. Bush. The arrival of Bush and Berlusconi marked the reversal of a long movement towards left-of-centre governments in the G8 countries that had begun with Clinton and Chrétien back in 1993. Though he clashed with Chirac at times, Bush found the summit a useful platform for putting his views across, probably more useful than he had expected. His frank and open manner seemed to go over well. This was also the first summit for Japanese Prime Minister Junichiro Koizumi, who proved a livelier summit participant than most Japanese leaders.

Apart from these three newcomers (and Guy Verhofstadt of Belgium for the EU Presidency), all the heads were familiar with the summit process and each other. Blair and Chrétien had both been recently re-elected. Blair was very active, especially on Africa, and worked well with Bush. Chirac was outspoken and individualistic, as usual, though Schroeder made little obvious impact. Chrétien attracted interest because of what Canada would be doing at next year's summit, while Prodi seemed in shock because of the riots.

The Summit Timetable

The G7 leaders met on the afternoon of 20 July and issued a statement. They were then joined by Putin and UN Secretary General Kofi Annan for the announcement of the Global Fund. At dinner the G8 met leaders from developing countries, mainly from Africa, and heads of international institutions. The main G8 agenda occupied the second day, 21 July, with political items taken over lunch and future summit organisation over dinner. The usual communiqué was issued on 22 July.

The Violent Demonstrations

The policy discussions at the summit were inevitably distracted by the riots in the streets. Genoa was an awkward city for security. The G8 delegations and media were isolated in the 'Red Zone' round the port, many being lodged on board ship. A wider 'Yellow Zone' was meant to keep protesters at a safe distance. A massive police presence, ugly physical barriers, deserted streets and boarded-up shops made Genoa look like a city under siege, even before the riots began.[7]

Large crowds of demonstrators - estimated at anything up to 300,000 - descended on Genoa and were lodged in tented camps around the city.[8] The great majority were peaceful demonstrators, lobbying on issues like debt forgiveness, action on AIDS or protecting the environment. But there were substantial groups of obstructive protesters, trying to break police cordons by force of numbers, and of destructive activists, seeking violent confrontation with the authorities. On the first day, one protester was killed during ugly clashes with the police. Confrontation continued in central Genoa on the second day, with cars burnt and shops sacked and looted, though elsewhere some mass demonstrations passed off peacefully. At midnight that day the police raided, without a warrant, the headquarters of the Global Social Forum, the Italian umbrella body for peaceful protest groups. Though they claimed to have found members of the anarchist 'Black Bloc' being sheltered there, well as illegal arms, police actions attracted strong censure both inside and outside Italy.[9]

The violence was roundly condemned, however, by responsible international NGOs, like Drop the Debt and Médecins Sans Frontières. They realised that confrontational protests could never influence G8 decisions in the way the orderly marches of Jubilee 2000 had done at Birmingham 1998 and Cologne 1999. Many of them cancelled their peaceful demonstrations for fear they would get taken over by the violent minority or moved their events outside the centre of Genoa.[10]

The G8 heads were shocked by the violence and issued a statement regretting the death. They closed ranks in insisting that such riots must not prevent them from meeting, though some, including Berlusconi, were uneasy at leaders of rich countries being isolated in an ivory tower. The heads spent much time, especially over dinner on 21 July, in discussing ideas to make the summits more acceptable and less a focus for protest. These ideas included:

- *Choosing more suitable sites for summits* Chrétien said the 2002 summit would be at Kananaskis, a small resort in the Canadian Rockies.
- *Reducing the size of delegations* The US had brought 900 people to Genoa, the UK only 27. Chrétien said that next year accommodation at Kananaskis would limit national delegations to 30.
- *Greater efforts to consult civil society groups* During the summit preparatory process, the Italians had started well in consulting international NGOs, but got sidetracked into dealing with Italian groups only.
- *More systematic involvement of non-G8 countries* The G8 foreign ministers in Rome spoke of creating a 'forum' for regular contact with developing countries.

In fact, non-G8 countries and NGOs were already becoming deeply involved in summit preparations and follow-up.

G7 Economic Issues

The G7 heads, before Putin arrived, discussed the world economy, as usual, and Africa, in preparation for their meeting with African leaders over dinner. The G7 statement covered economic prospects, a new trade round, strengthening the financial system and debt relief, plus a sentence welcoming the closure of the

Chernobyl nuclear power plant. Some of these issues, however, were not actually discussed among the heads until the G8 met the following day.

Economic Prospects

Since the finance ministers' upbeat briefing on 7 July, Greenspan had said the US economy had touched bottom, but was not yet recovering, while the crisis had deepened in Argentina.[11] Even so, the leaders expressed confidence in a future recovery and support for Koizumi's strategy in Japan. Berlusconi had received a letter from President Fernando de la Rua of Argentina about the measures being taken there. Both he and Chirac said publicly that a reply was sent promising that the G8 would provide more help if these measures did not work. However, the wording of the G7 statement was more guarded. In the event, the G7 finance ministers backed a new IMF package later in 2001, but this could not prevent Argentina's economic collapse at the end of the year.[12]

Trade and the WTO

The G7 statement contained a strong passage committing the heads to 'engage personally and jointly in the launch of a new ambitious Round' in the WTO. The statement responded well to the concerns of developing countries, while avoiding any impression of the G7 dictating to them. There was no reference to contentious agenda items like labour standards or anti-dumping, which were left for future negotiation in Geneva. The statement helpfully associated Japan and Canada with the US-EU agreement achieved at the Gothenburg European Council in June.[13] Unlike previous summits' treatment of a new trade round, Genoa reflected a genuine transatlantic rapport, achieved between EU Commissioner Pascal Lamy and US Trade Representative Bob Zoellick. This commitment on a new WTO Round was one of the most positive results of the summit.

Strengthening the Financial System

In their statement, the G7 heads endorsed two reports prepared by the finance ministers, one on the multilateral development banks (MDBs) and the other on abuses of the financial system. The key points were:

- The report on MDBs wanted the banks to focus on poverty reduction - not defined in detail - and to tighten up their management procedures. The tone was rather paternalistic towards developing countries. The report did not endorse Bush's late proposal for converting World Bank loans into grants, made after the G7 finance ministers had met.[14] The heads' statement made a non-committal reference to this, but the other G7 members had considerable reservations.
- The report on financial abuses recorded action taken in money-laundering, offshore financial centres and tax havens since the G7 meetings in Japan the year before. There had been progress on money-laundering since the

Financial Action Task Force (FATF) had identified 15 'non-cooperating' jurisdictions in June 2000. Four of these had been taken off the list and eight others had improved significantly. But three countries, including Russia, remained vulnerable to counter-measures later in the year; and six new countries had come onto the list. The message on tax havens was much weaker than a year before, partly because of protests from the targeted countries but mainly because of pressure from the new US administration.[15]

Debt Relief

The G7 statement endorsed the findings of the third finance ministers' report, called 'Debt Relief and Beyond'. This gave an update on the Enhanced HIPC Programme over the last year, noting that 23 countries had now reached 'decision point' (as against only nine by Okinawa), leading to overall debt relief of $53 billion. It then addressed some unfinished business: getting the best use of resources saved by debt relief; helping conflict countries to get into the programme; ensuring debt relief was sustained, leading to a 'lasting exit'; and getting other creditors to match what the G7 had done. But there was no improvement in the terms of debt relief, so that campaigners for complete debt forgiveness or the reduction of IMF/World Bank debt (like Drop the Debt) were clearly disappointed, as they had been at Okinawa.[16]

The Global Fund to Fight AIDS, Tuberculosis and Malaria

Berlusconi and Annan, in the presence of the other G8 leaders, announced the formation of a Global Fund to fight AIDS, tuberculosis and malaria, with pledges from the G8 countries of $1.3 billion (plus $0.5 billion from other sources). Annan welcomed this initiative, as 'a very good beginning', though he added that 'much, much more is needed' and recalled the UN estimate of $7-10 billion extra spending per year. Though Annan spoke only of AIDS and implied UN ownership of the Global Fund, earlier tensions between UN and G8 plans were eased at Genoa, so that the two approaches were combined.[17]

The G8, as their communiqué later made clear, intended the Global Fund to cover not only AIDS, but also tuberculosis and malaria, as forecast at Okinawa. They envisaged management by a board of donor and beneficiary countries and 'specialised organisations', which would involve the WHO and World Bank as well as the UN. The G8 were actively seeking contributions from the private sector and the involvement of NGOs at local level. Private firms and non-profit bodies would also take part in the Fund's management as non-voting members of the board. The sensitive issues of pharmaceutical patents and prices for drugs were addressed by seeking the cooperation of firms in the industry and by invoking the flexibility provided in the WTO's TRIPS agreement.

Most comment from NGOs criticised the amounts committed to the Global Fund as too small in light of the size of the AIDS epidemic.[18] However, the Fund was not designed to meet all the needs of the AIDS crisis. It would provide extra financing to be integrated into national health plans, for which recipient countries remained responsible. There would be limits to the amount of extra money the target countries could absorb early on. The aim was also to tie the Fund's spending to clear output targets. The main weakness in the G8 position at Genoa was that their pledges looked like one-time contributions, without any assurance of continuity of funding. But Bush and Blair, among others, indicated that they would be ready to provide more once the Global Fund was in operation.

The Outreach Dinner and the Genoa Plan for Africa

The G8 heads had a working dinner on 20 July with five African Presidents (Algeria, Mali, Nigeria, Senegal and South Africa), representatives from El Salvador and Bangladesh and the heads of the UN, FAO, WHO, WTO and World Bank. In part, the choice of non-G8 participants reflected the summit's focus on poverty reduction. But Bouteflika (Algeria), Mbeki (South Africa) and Obasanjo (Nigeria) had also been at the dinner before Okinawa.

The discussion concentrated on Africa and especially the G8 response to the plan for the revival of Africa expounded by the African leaders present. This plan, called the New African Initiative, represented a fusion of the Millennium Africa Plan, promoted by Mbeki of South Africa, with the Omega Plan launched by Wade of Senegal, together with ideas from the UN Economic Commission for Africa. The essential feature of this plan was its focus on the responsibility of the African countries to put their own house in order, if they hoped to attract support from the G8 and other sources of outside help. The New African Initiative later became the New Partnership for Africa's Development (NEPAD).[19]

The exchanges led to the issue next day of a short statement on a 'Genoa Plan for Africa'. This was a spontaneous initiative by the heads, which arose from the direct contacts of the G8 with the African leaders and went much further than expected. It welcomed the African commitments as 'the basis for a new intensive partnership between Africa and the developed world'. It promised help from the G8 both in conflict prevention and in a wide range of development activities, including health, education, IT, private investment and international trade. Each G8 member would designate a personal representative to prepare an Action Plan, under Canadian leadership, for approval at the summit in 2002. Blair publicly called it a 'Marshall Plan for Africa'.[20]

This initiative confronted the problems in the continent that risked becoming marginalised as globalisation advanced. It linked in well with other parts of the G8 agenda, both under poverty reduction and conflict prevention. It was an example of the summit finding synergy between the economic and political strands of its agenda, which it had rarely done before. It reflected the new interest of the G8 leaders in outreach, as suitable for a globalising world and a response to criticisms of exclusiveness. However, as always, the test of this initiative would lie in the implementation, on both the G8 and the African side. There was much exhortation to international institutions. But the G8 made no new commitments, for example of aid funds or trade access. The G8 had also added another wing to the G8 bureaucratic architecture.

G8 Economic Issues

The greater part of the G8 heads' discussion on 21 July was devoted to the theme of poverty reduction, supported by the report from the G7 finance ministers, 'Debt Relief and Beyond'. Their communiqué covered trade, investment, health and education, following the lines of the preparatory document of the Italian Presidency. But except where the communiqué confirmed commitments already made, for example in infectious diseases, its content was rather disappointing.

Trade and the Poorest Countries

Two brief paragraphs in the G8 communiqué, on trade access and capacity building, reflected fuller treatment in the finance ministers' report. The finance ministers admitted that the poorest countries had lost market share, especially because they faced high tariffs for their main exports. As compared with the promises made at Okinawa, however, the actual commitments on market access were uneven. The EU's 'Anything But Arms' initiative, in operation since March 2001, was a real advance.[21] But the Americans had not moved beyond the Africa Growth and Opportunity Act, while Canadian measures introduced in September 2000 omitted many products of greatest interest to the poorest countries. Pledges to do better in future thus rang rather hollow. Similarly, the passages on capacity building were short on commitments on what more the G8 would do themselves, as opposed to coordinating existing actions and encouraging others.

Primary Education

Education promised to be the subject with the greatest substance. The G8 renewed earlier commitments to help countries to meet international targets in primary education.[22] But they could not find an obvious focus for their actions, in the way that they had in health. They therefore created a task-force of officials to work on this over the next year. Chrétien announced his wish to focus on education at the 2002 summit. There was also a useful cross-reference to the DOT-Force report (see below) and an acceptance (by the finance ministers) that 'additional resources should be provided' for education.

Aid

There was some discussion among the heads of expanding aid volumes, with Berlusconi and Prodi invoking the target of giving 0.7% of GNP in aid. But this did not feature in the communiqué, which only spoke of 'strengthening and enhancing effectiveness' of aid.

IT and the DOT-Force

The most impressive document issued at the summit was the first report of the Digital Opportunity Task-Force (DOT-Force) established at Okinawa to help poor countries benefit from IT. This was remarkable both for process and substance. It was produced by a group combining governments of both G8 and developing countries, international institutions, private firms and NGOs. Many of the members came to Genoa to present the report and conveyed an impressive sense of common purpose.

The report laid out a strategy and an action plan for IT in developing countries. It recommended that all countries should develop 'eStrategies' (with help to make them internationally compatible), develop IT access and entrepreneurship and build up capacity in education and health. No estimates were given of the resources needed. The DOT-Force members justified this by saying that their task was to devise the policy environment, within which resources could be deployed. But the World Bank described their current IT-related lending; and the Canadian chair of the DOT-Force for the next year stressed that their report in 2002 would focus on implementation.

This report was a considerable achievement, in the face of great initial scepticism. The G8 communiqué endorsed the report and renewed the DOT-Force's mandate, while the leaders commented favourably on it during their discussions. Few of them, however, drew public attention to the DOT-Force and its work in press briefings.

Renewable Energy

The Task-Force on Renewable Energy had a similarly wide composition to the DOT-Force and its report (which was circulated, but not presented) had the same objective of creating the right policy environment. However, the communiqué did no more than thank the participants for their work, without taking a position on it, and remitted any further action to G8 energy ministers. The report recommended that renewable energy should be subsidised in developed markets, so as to create a market large enough to stimulate cost-saving technologies. But the United States and Canada were not prepared to discriminate against their large oil and gas firms and the new US administration claimed this would inhibit their national energy strategy.

Environment

The main issue was climate change, in the light of Bush's rejection of the Kyoto Protocol earlier in the year.[23] Given the wide transatlantic gap, the G8 looked for points to which all could subscribe. Everyone could agree, including Bush, on the need to reduce greenhouse gas emissions and to take action to bring this about. References in the communiqué to flexibility of policy and cooperation on research looked like gestures towards the US position. In return, the Americans indicated that they were working on alternative approaches to the Kyoto Protocol, but these would not be ready till later in the year. The communiqué implied the Americans would be ready to involve others in this process, but in fact nothing came of it. Discussions on the margins of the summit, however, were useful in persuading Japan, Canada and Russia that they should ratify the Kyoto Protocol so that it could enter into force, even though the Americans stood aside from the process.[24]

Biotechnology and Food Safety

A brief discussion produced the usual uneasy truce between those who relied on scientific evidence and the partisans of the precautionary principle. Blair said the former view prevailed, Prodi said the latter did; in fact both views were well recorded in the communiqué. There was a slight advance as compared with Okinawa, in that France and other Europeans were readier to give weight to scientific evidence; but the US remained sceptical about the precautionary approach. An earlier passage in the communiqué noted the potential value of biotechnology for agriculture in poor countries.

G8 Political Issues

Outside Africa, political issues had low priority at the summit. They did not feature in the main G8 communiqué, but were dealt with in separate statements on the Middle East and Regional Issues. On the Middle East, the heads briefly confirmed the foreign ministers' unanimous view that the Mitchell Plan was the only way forward and that outside monitoring, as proposed by the EU, could be helpful.[25] The short G8 Statement on Regional Issues covered Macedonia and the Korean peninsula, seeking peace and reconciliation in both.

Conflict Prevention and Disarmament

Conflict prevention was a lead subject for the Italian presidency. After the progress made by G8 foreign ministers at Berlin in December 1999 and at Miyazaki in July 2000, the Italians sought agreement to extend the process and bring the issue back to the heads. However, the other heads and their foreign ministers seemed more interested in specific cases of conflict, especially in Africa, than in the general concept of conflict prevention, which was not discussed at the summit itself. The Italians had to be satisfied with the strong conflict prevention component of the Genoa Plan for Africa.

Putin (against his officials' advice) decided not to raise disarmament among the G8 leaders, so that the subject was not mentioned in their documents. Instead, Putin used the summit as the occasion for a fruitful bilateral with Bush, which suggested a deal might be struck linking missile defence with the reduction of nuclear weapons.[26]

Assessment of the Genoa Summit

Most of the media comment from Genoa reacted to the riots by advocating changes in the style and organisation of summitry.[27] But in fact summits would always be judged by the quality of the agreements reached and that in turn depended on the efficiency of the G8 process.

There was a striking contrast between the full involvement of many NGOs in the G8's work and the violent riots on the streets. Genoa demonstrated how far the G8 had moved in the last two years to involve both private firms and non-profit bodies in summit preparation and follow-up. This was most vivid in the Global Fund and in the reports from the DOT-Force and the renewable energy task-force. But in almost every other economic topic the greater participation of civil society was now sought. This also applied in the political agenda, for example in the two new topics, women and the private sector, added to conflict prevention.

The G8 leaders had started to accommodate these new actors after they began meeting on their own at Birmingham in 1998. But at the same time the official apparatus of G8 ministerial and official bodies continued to grow. Genoa added new official groups on Africa and education, a meeting of energy ministers and a conference on climate change. This gave an impression of a proliferating bureaucracy stifling the summit, so that some of the leaders were hankering once again after a much simpler format. In fact, the leaders needed to give the same freedom of action to the subordinate groups as they had taken for themselves, only giving personal attention to key initiatives like the DOT-Force.

In substance, the Genoa summit, like Okinawa in 2000, concentrated on issues relating to developing countries, especially the poorest. This focus on poor developing countries was fully justified, in particular since the adoption of the UN's Millennium Development Goals. The most intractable problems of globalisation, as well as the worst suffering from conflict and natural disasters, arose among the poorest countries, especially in Africa. The Italian choice of topics, concentrating on poverty reduction and conflict prevention, also allowed good continuity between the Japanese and Italian presidencies. Two of the main achievements of Genoa - the Global Fund to fight AIDS, tuberculosis and malaria and the DOT-Force report - built on foundations laid at Okinawa the year before.

The Genoa Plan for Africa was the greatest innovation from the summit. This was the first time the G8 had entered into a specific partnership with a group of non-G8 countries; the only parallel was the G7's involvement with Russia in the early 1990s. It provided an opportunity to integrate the political and the economic agenda, where the summits had seldom managed to achieve their potential. It included conflict prevention, an Italian priority. There were strong links with many other topics handled by the G8 under poverty reduction, including debt relief, trade access, IT, health and education. Blair's comparison with the Marshall Plan was apt, since the African states, like the post-war European countries, were prepared to take 'ownership' of their efforts to achieve political and economic revival.

The G8 agreed in Genoa on some major initiatives designed to help poor countries, focusing on health and Africa. They also reached a vital and very welcome consensus on a new trade round, which resolved differences among themselves, as well as showing sensitivity towards developing countries. This good progress on innovative subjects like the Global Fund, however, contrasted with less satisfactory results in mainstream development issues, like trade access for poor countries, financial flows and debt relief. In general, the Genoa documents set out clear diagnoses of the development problems the G8 addressed. But instead of taking new policy measures or providing new resources, the G8's prescription was usually to intensify existing actions or to coordinate them better. In other areas, for example in climate change, renewable energy or food safety, Genoa did not have much success in resolving internal G8 divergences. The Italians made little progress on their second agenda item, the environment. Overall, the Genoa summit provided a good example of the strengths and weaknesses of the G8 process as a response to advancing globalisation.

Conclusion

Thanks to good preparation by the Italians, Genoa recaptured the spirit of the Birmingham reforms, which had weakened at Okinawa. There were good examples of *leadership,* on Africa and the Global Fund, and the action taken there proved *durable*. Genoa was also *effective* in overcoming domestic obstacles on trade policy, but not on many of the other development and environment items. *Solidarity* was thus finally restored on trade and proved strong on Africa, but was weak on climate change and renewable energy. As with Okinawa, there was more *consistency* in the agenda than in the results achieved.

The most important test for Genoa, which would determine its *acceptability*, was whether the promises made were honoured. The recent record showed that the leaders were good innovators but poor implementers. But the G8 now worked much more closely with other governments, private business and civil society - that was one consequence of advancing globalisation. As a result its performance record came under closer scrutiny. It was when the G8 failed to keep its promises that serious campaigning NGOs became most frustrated and obstructive protestors gained support.

In this context, however, the immediate results from Genoa were promising. The Doha WTO meeting in November successfully launched a new trade round. The Global Fund to fight AIDS, tuberculosis and malaria became operational in April 2002 and began committing funds in support of specific projects. Thanks to good cooperation between the Italian and Canadian Presidencies, the procedural Genoa Plan for Africa was converted into a G8 Africa Action Plan by the time of the next summit, while parallel momentum was maintained among the Africans. These results were achieved despite the terrorist attacks that shocked the world two months after Genoa, on 11 September 2001.

Notes

1 This account of the Genoa summit closely follows Bayne 2002b. For an alternative assessment, see Zupi 2001.
2 For example, he spoke by video link to a London conference, promising G8 action on poverty - A. Beattie, 'Trying Times in the War on Poverty', *Financial Times*, 27 February 2001.
3 See M. Littlejohns and others, 'UN Wins Vote of Confidence in World Grown Wary of Ideals', *Financial Times*, 9 September 2000, and Chapter 8 below.
4 The Italian preparatory paper on Poverty Reduction was published electronically on www.esteri.it/g8/docum.htm together with a 'fact file' on Conflict Prevention. The Italian Presidency also sponsored a book on the G8 summit, Sherifis and Astraldi 2001.
5 The G8 communiqué from Genoa was only one-third the length of the one from Okinawa in 2000.
6 Bush's decision to withdraw from the Anti-Ballistic Missile Treaty had aroused strong Russian protests. See 'George Bush's Arms Control Revolution', *The Economist*, 5 May 2000.
7 Genoa had been chosen to be the site by Prime Minister Massimo d'Alema, as a Northern industrial city needing more public attention. The choice was made during 1999, before the wave of hostile demonstrations that began at Seattle. The original intention had been simply to seal off the port area - the Red Zone. But a wider Yellow Zone was then added following the experience at the Summit of the Americas at Quebec City in April 2001, when tear gas drifted back into the meeting-place - E. Alden and others, 'Protests Erupt at Quebec Summit', *Financial Times*, 21 April 2000.
8 J. Harding and A. Beattie, 'To the Barricades', *Financial Times*, 19 July 2000.
9 This account is based on the detailed analysis in della Porta and Reiter 2002. See also Hajnal 2002.
10 A. Beattie, 'Violence May Lead Aid Groups to Avoid G8 Talks', *Financial Times*, 16 July 2000.
11 On Greenspan's comments, see 'US Diagnosis', *Financial Times* leader, 19 July 2001.
12 See E. Alden, 'IMF to Offer Argentina $8bn Aid' and T. Catan, 'Argentina in $155bn debt default', *Financial Times*, 22 August and 24 December 2001.
13 G. de Jonquières, 'Bush and EU Leaders Agree to Launch New Round', *Financial Times*, 15 June 2001.
14 R. Wolffe and A. Beattie, 'Bush Seeks Overhaul of World Bank Loans Policy', *Financial Times*, 18 July 2001.
15 Wechsler 2001 gives a good account of work over the year under all three headings. See also E. Alden, 'Blacklist Leaves Mark on Money-Laundering', *Financial Times*, 5 December 2000.
16 Adrian Lovett, Director of Drop the Debt, commented: "This is the sort of thing that gets the summit a bad name." See A. Beattie and S. Fidler, 'G8 Claims of Advances at Summit Disputed', *Financial Times*, 23 July 2001.
17 For the first public launch of this idea, see W. Wallis, 'Annan Proposes Global Fund to Fight AIDS', *Financial Times*, 27 April 2001. The debate over the nature and target of the new fund is reviewed in A. Beattie and D. Pilling, 'A Fund of High Hopes and Huge Obstacles', *Financial Times*, 21 June 2001. See also note 18 below.
18 S. Fidler and A. Beattie, 'G8 Fund to Fight AIDS "Inadequate"', *Financial Times*, 21 July 2001. This article gives the quotations from Annan referred to in an earlier paragraph - see note 17.

19 An early comment is in 'Africa's Millennium Action Plan', *The Economist,* 7 July 2001, while a good scholarly account of the origins of NEPAD is in de Waal 2002. For more references, see Chapter 12 below.

20 I heard Blair say this at his final press conference, though the media did not appear to pick it up at the time. The comparison later became widely used; see Hamill 2002 and Bayne 2003.

21 P. Norman, 'EU to End All Curbs on Trade with Poor Nations', *Financial Times,* 27 February 2001. See Chapter 6, note 24 and Chapter 8 below.

22 One of the Millennium Development Goals adopted by the UN in September 2000 was to get all children into primary school by 2015. See also Chapter 6, note 22 above.

23 Bush announced his decision in March, rejecting expert advice. This was strongly contested by European countries, which introduced a note of contention at the EU/US summit in Gothenburg. See N. Dunne, 'White House Split as Bush Rejects Kyoto' and P. Norman and J. Dempsey, 'Big Split Remains Over Kyoto Protocol', *Financial Times,* 30 March and 15 June 2001.

24 Japan ratified later in 2001, after changes had been agreed in the operation of the Protocol. Canada ratified in December 2002, but Russia delayed till October 2004.

25 This plan for resolving the confrontation between Israel and the Palestinians that had broken out in 2000 was developed by former US Senator Mitchell, with American, European and Russian support. See 'Israel and the Palestinians', *The Economist,* 26 May 2001. The Mitchell Plan lapsed after further clashes between Israel and the Palestinians and was superseded by the 'Road Map' prepared in late 2002.

26 S. Fidler, 'US and Russia Move a Step closer on Defence', *Financial Times,* 23 July 2001. In fact such a deal did not materialise.

27 For example, Q. Peel and A. Beattie, 'An End to Fireside Chats', *Financial Times,* 21 July 2001.

Chapter 8

Summit Performance II: Trade Issues and Development

The summits treated international finance issues at intervals, as Chapter 5 showed. But international trade was on their agenda almost every year. Trade, just as much as finance, raised issues that required the intervention of heads of government. In the second half of the 20th century, the share of each G7 economy exposed to international competition steadily expanded. This gave greater scope for conflicts between international and domestic policies, which could not be resolved by internal arbitration by presidents and prime ministers within their own governments but also involved external partners. So trade was an obvious subject for the summits, where the heads of government could appreciate their international responsibilities at first hand and reflect them in the decisions they took at home. But trade was also an awkward subject for the summits to handle, because of the division of responsibility between the European Commission and the G7 European members.[1]

The advance of globalisation increased the potential for conflict. Trade policy no longer operated at the border, but penetrated deeply into domestic policy-making. This was the consequence of many of the agreements concluded during the Uruguay Round, which also created the new World Trade Organization (WTO), with much stronger powers to settle disputes. But the failure of the WTO, at its ministerial meeting at Seattle in December 1999, to launch a new negotiating round, revealed how far developing countries had become alienated from the world trading system. This obliged the G8 summits to shift their attention from finance to trade, with special concern for the problems faced by developing countries. This move matched the decision taken by the summits from Okinawa 2000 onwards no longer to concentrate on debt relief, but to respond across a broader development agenda to the danger that the poorest countries were being left behind by globalisation. The G8's greater concern with these issues was stimulated by the adoption of the Millennium Development Goals by the UN General Assembly in September 2000.

This chapter therefore assesses the contribution made by the G8 Summits both in international trade and in international development issues. It focuses particularly on the results achieved at Okinawa 2000 and Genoa 2001, together with the summits that followed. Like Chapter 5, it will anticipate some of the narratives in subsequent chapters. The two issues - trade and development - will be examined separately, beginning with a review of their treatment by earlier summits before concentrating on the achievements of the G8 sequence.

The summits' performance in each area will then be assessed under the six criteria defined in Chapter 1, namely:

- Leadership;
- Effectiveness;
- Solidarity;
- Durability;
- Acceptability;
- Consistency.

Finally, the chapter draws some lessons from the summit's performance.[2]

International Trade: Early Summit Treatment

The Tokyo Round

The G7 summits began after the GATT had launched the Tokyo Round of multilateral trade negotiations, but the round had not got far. At Rambouillet in 1975 the heads declared their firm resistance to protectionism and fixed a deadline of the end of 1977 for completing the Tokyo Round. By identifying themselves with the success of the negotiations, the leaders could invoke their international obligations to counter domestic demands for protection. At London I in 1977, the heads had to extend the deadline, but they set the next year's summit as the target for major progress. Just before the Bonn I summit in July 1978, a 'framework of understanding' was reached in Geneva and the G7 trade negotiators continued work on the margins of the summit. This enabled the heads to promise completion of the GATT negotiations by 15 December 1978 and this deadline was substantially met.[3]

Between the Rounds

The recession provoked by the second oil crisis and prolonged by tight macro-economic policies greatly strengthened protectionist pressures. These persisted in the United States, even after growth revived, because of the widening external deficit. Though the summits continued to condemn protectionism, trade barriers were raised on both sides of the Atlantic, while Japan's large surpluses were a further source of tension. From the 1981 Ottawa Summit onwards, the United States, with growing support from Japan, pressed for a new trade round to keep protectionist demands in check. The Europeans resisted at first, essentially because of French refusal to negotiate on agriculture. At Bonn II in 1985, France prevented the summit from agreeing that a new round should begin the following year. But at Tokyo II 1986 the leaders could endorse the call for a new round after minimal discussion and had a useful debate on agriculture, helping to fix it firmly on the agenda.[4]

The Uruguay Round

Trade generally got little summit attention in the early years of the Uruguay Round. But the Houston Summit of 1990 was obliged to give it priority, as the round was due to end in December of that year. Houston agreed on stronger machinery for dispute settlement, a possible new institution to replace the GATT, (which later became the World Trade Organization) and a fragile compromise on the agriculture negotiations. The heads undertook to complete the Uruguay Round on time by the end of the year. However, the agricultural compromise collapsed, so that the Uruguay Round failed to conclude in 1990. The next two summits - London III 1991 and Munich 1992 - again set targets to complete the round by the end of that year, but both times they failed, because of persistent differences between the United States and the European Union over agriculture.

Later in 1992, however, after the Europeans had embarked on an internal reform of the Common Agriculture Policy (CAP), an initial deal was struck between the US and the EU on agriculture. The trade ministers of the Quad were brought to meet in Tokyo just before the summit of 1993, to work out the tariff deal still missing from the Uruguay Round agreements. All this gave conviction to the G7's latest end-of-year deadline, set at the Tokyo III summit, so that the round finally concluded in December 1993. GATT trade ministers signed an ambitious range of agreements at Marrakesh in April 1994 and created the new World Trade Organization with extensive legal powers.[5]

From Marrakesh to Seattle

After 1995, when the WTO was in operation and holding regular ministerial meetings, there seemed less need for summit attention. But dissatisfaction with the world trading system was growing, for several reasons:

- WTO agreements and dispute rulings penetrated deeper into domestic policy and aroused new demands for protection;
- Many developing countries concluded that the round had brought far more benefit to the richer economies than to themselves;
- The United States and the European Union were distracted by a series of bilateral trade disputes;
- There were no wide-ranging negotiations in progress to keep these adverse trends in check.

Aware of these problems, Leon Brittan, the EU Trade Commissioner, promoted the idea of a new 'Millennium Round', with a comprehensive agenda, to start in 2000. The Americans, however, wanted a limited agenda, giving priority to the non-trade issues of labour and environmental standards. The first G8 summits - Birmingham 1998 and Cologne 1999 - made a serious error in neglecting trade. The heads had brief exchanges on launching a new round, but failed to reconcile the differences between them. They did not recognise the mounting discontent with the Uruguay Round regime among developing countries. They did not realise how far the WTO had become the focus of anti-globalisation agitation. The consequence was that the Seattle WTO ministerial of December 1999 ended in disaster, with no agreement to launch a new round.[6]

G7 Summit Performance on Trade

The assessment of the G7 summits (and the first two G8 summits) shows that they gave their strongest performance when international trade negotiations were in progress, as follows:

- The summits showed convincing *leadership* when, as at Bonn I 1978 and Tokyo III 1993, the heads mobilised their trade negotiators to ensure that deadlines were successfully met. Their attempts to maintain the momentum of negotiations were more successful in the Tokyo Round than the Uruguay Round, when they missed three deadlines in a row. But that was preferable to the disagreements of the mid 1980s or the neglect of the late 1990s.
- The summits were *effective* when they were prepared to resist firmly domestic pressures for protectionism. They did this during the Tokyo Round and again during the Uruguay Round on most subjects, though not on agriculture. But in the early 1980s, when no multilateral negotiations were in progress, the G7 raised trade barriers under pressure from the second oil crisis. After 1995 transatlantic disputes allowed domestic pressures for protection to regain lost ground.
- On general support for the trading system, there was good *solidarity* among the G7 members, with the EU becoming steadily more committed to multilateralism. The great exception was agriculture, which deeply divided the US and Canada from the EU and Japan and often frustrated agreement on broader issues.
- The G7 heads produced *durable* results from the Tokyo Round and eventually from the Uruguay Round, though the missed deadlines damaged their reputation.
- The final results of the Tokyo and Uruguay Rounds were judged broadly *acceptable*, but there was dissatisfaction among the developing countries. After the end of the Uruguay Round, that dissatisfaction gathered strength and was the main obstacle to agreement at Seattle. The WTO became identified with the negative aspects of globalisation, especially by NGOs concerned with social, development and environmental causes.
- Summit commitments on trade could be reinforced by *consistent* policies in other economic areas, as at Bonn I in 1978, or undermined by *inconsistent* ones, as with European support for agriculture in the 1980s. Weak commitments on trade could also frustrate summit efforts elsewhere.

After Seattle: Trade at the G8 Summits

The G8 summits from 2000 onwards faced the challenge of restoring confidence in the multilateral trading system and making it acceptable to developing countries. This required action on two fronts. The first was the successful launch and pursuit of a new negotiating round in the WTO, to redeem the failure at Seattle. The second was agreement among the G8 on specific trade policy measures that they and other rich countries could take in order to help poor developing countries.[7] These two aspects are treated separately below.

Re-launching the WTO

Okinawa in 2000 showed some recognition of past failures, but its message was still inconclusive. It gave no clear sign that European advocacy of a 'comprehensive round' and US preference for a limited agenda had been reconciled. It continued to press for non-trade items like labour standards and the environment, though these were clearly anathema to the developing countries. The heads made only a weak commitment to launching a new round before the end of the year. They implicitly recognised the difficulty of doing this during a US presidential campaign, which gave Clinton no flexibility. As a result, a new round remained in abeyance in 2000.

Preparing for Doha

The arrival of the Bush Administration in the United States brought a profound change. Bob Zoellick, the new USTR, was a close friend of Pascal Lamy, the EU Trade Commissioner, whom he had got to know through the G7 summit process in the early 1990s.[8] Lamy and Zoellick acted to ensure that the persistent US/EU bilateral trade disputes on bananas, beef hormones and tax treatment of American exports did not undermine broader cooperation in multilateral contexts. Zoellick announced the US intention of seeking 'fast-track' negotiating authority from Congress (now renamed 'trade promotion authority') for a new WTO round, as well as for bilateral and regional trade agreements.[9] The United States and European Union reached agreement on their approach to a new WTO round and made this clear both at the OECD and at a EU/US summit linked to the European Council at Gothenburg in June 2001.[10] The Genoa summit a month later provided the opportunity to broaden this into a G8 consensus and to give the authority of the heads to a genuinely collective approach to the WTO ministerial meeting due in Doha, Qatar, in November.

The passage on trade in the Genoa G7 statement was short and general. But it contained a personal commitment by the heads to launching a new round that would respond to the needs and aspirations of developing countries, especially the poorest. It made no attempt to prescribe the agenda, omitting any reference to items that had proved contentious in the past. As the WTO ministerial approached, this flexible and sensitive approach was reflected in the specific positions adopted by both the United States and the European Union. In the documents issued at the Doha meeting that successfully launched a new round:

- The US abandoned its pressure on labour standards, which were barely mentioned;
- The US and EU scaled back their demands on the environment, which also took a minor place;
- The US agreed to include anti-dumping measures, which it had always resisted before;
- The EU accepted language that implied the ultimate abolition of agricultural export subsidies;
- While the EU still sought the inclusion of investment, competition, government procurement and trade facilitation, it accepted that negotiations would not start till after a further decision in 2003.

While moderating their own demands, the G8 members agreed to the inclusion of many provisions favouring the developing countries, starting with the designation of the new round as the 'Doha Development Agenda'.

Many other factors contributed to the success of the WTO ministerial in Doha. Preparations in Geneva were handled with great skill by Stuart Harbinson, the representative of Hong Kong (China), as chair of the WTO Council. Developing countries, both large ones like Brazil and smaller ones from Africa, took an active and constructive part. While at Seattle there had been tension between NGOs and developing countries, at Doha they began forming alliances. They did so very effectively over the negotiation of a declaration allowing developing countries to override patent protection for essential drugs, as prescribed by the TRIPS agreement, in the case of health emergencies.[11] Most of all, the governments present at Doha closed ranks after the terrorist attacks on the United States of 11 September 2001, wanting to show that the international system would not be derailed by terrorism. Nevertheless, without a coherent approach by the G8, the new round would never have got started.[12]

Negotiating the Doha Development Agenda

After this successful launch, however, the Doha Development Agenda soon ran into trouble. Zoellick obtained 'trade promotion authority' in July 2002 after a long struggle with Congress. But this was only achieved at the cost of buying off special domestic interests with increased steel tariffs (later declared illegal by the WTO) and a new Farm Bill that raised agricultural subsidies, though still within internationally permitted limits.[13] Even so, Zoellick was now able to launch ambitious proposals in agriculture and manufactures, though the US still held up an essential provision from the TRIPS Declaration.[14] Meanwhile, the Europeans dragged their feet over agriculture, as reform of the CAP met strong resistance.[15] As the WTO approached its next ministerial in Cancun, Mexico, in September 2003, all its negotiating plans were behind schedule. The Evian summit of June 2003 could have been the occasion for a US/EU deal to break the twin deadlocks on agriculture and TRIPS. But this chance was not taken and the G8 heads simply undertook to work for a successful outcome of the Cancun meeting.

The EU had promised to agree its position on agriculture by the end of June 2003 and in fact did so. The EU and US then developed joint procedural proposals on negotiating agriculture, at the request of the other WTO members. Just before Cancun, the US accepted the extension of the TRIPS Declaration.[16] But these moves did not impress the developing countries. They came much too late and looked like attempts to dictate the future course of the negotiations. Developing countries came to Cancun in two combinations: a G20 of larger countries, led by Brazil, China, India, and South Africa, that negotiated fairly cohesively; and a much looser G90 of poor countries, many of whom relied on advice from NGOs. After confused contacts between the EU, US, other rich countries (Japan and Korea) and these two groupings, the meeting ended in failure.[17]

Despite this setback, it soon emerged that none of the countries concerned wanted the negotiations themselves to fail. Detailed procedural exchanges developed in Geneva, seeking to agree modalities that would allow the round to start again. Both the US and the EU were active, with the European Commission going further than before in offering to end agricultural export subsidies and shelving its ambitions in investment and competition. The Sea Island summit was held in June 2004, as the WTO approached the deadline of end-July it had set for restarting negotiations. Though the summit took the deadline seriously, it did not endorse the Commission move on agriculture, because of French resistance, and did not look any further than seven weeks ahead. Although the Doha negotiations were successfully re-launched from Geneva at the end of July 2004, the summit contributed little to this outcome.[18]

Trade Measures to Help Poor Countries

Alongside the efforts to re-launch the WTO, the summits of Okinawa, Genoa and later years considered specific policies that the G8 could take to ensure poor countries derived more benefit from trade and the world trading system. Such measures were overdue. Some large low-income countries, especially China and India, had increasingly benefited from international trade. But smaller countries, especially in Africa, had being going backwards for 20 years, both in their share of world trade and in the proportion of their national income derived from trade. The measures considered by the G8 were essentially of two sorts: improvements in market access; and help with 'capacity-building', so that poor countries could get more out of the world trading system.

Market Access

The summit documents from Okinawa, Genoa and later summits accepted the need to do more to help poor countries to gain from trade. Sometimes the approach of a summit stimulated national measures. But the joint actions actually taken by the G8 were not very impressive.

Renato Ruggiero, the WTO Director-General, who was invited to the 1996 Lyon summit, had proposed there that G7 countries should admit the products of the poorest countries free of duties and quotas.[19] The US response was the Africa Growth and Opportunity Act, which also provided concessions to Central America and the Caribbean.[20] This was the first significant new trade legislation since 1994, but did not get through Congress till 2000 and was less generous in some respects than what the EU already offered its African, Caribbean and Pacific (ACP) associates. After the Okinawa summit the EU undertook to act and in March 2001 duly introduced its 'Everything But Arms' initiative. This gave duty and quota free access to all civilian imports from least-developed countries, except for rice, sugar and bananas, where transitional arrangements applied.[21] Canada too introduced its version of the initiative in June 2002, after the Kananaskis summit, covering all imports except eggs, poultry and dairy products. While these were welcome moves, they hardly amounted to collective G8 action.

Meanwhile, G8 countries continued to maintain trade barriers in industry, agriculture and services that weighed heavily on poor countries, not all of which counted as 'least-developed'.[22] The EU's Common Agricultural Policy (CAP) was biased against imports and distorted international markets by the use of export subsidies. While domestic production subsidies were being phased out, they were still high for some products, like sugar.[23] The United States retained high subsidies for cotton, sugar and citrus products.[24] Japan still protected rice by high tariffs and Canada did the same for dairy products. All the G8, and especially the United States, maintained high tariffs on processed foodstuffs and basic manufactures like textiles, clothing and footwear, where poor countries could best compete, while tariffs on advanced manufactures traded between rich countries were low or even zero.[25] In services, the G8 severely restricted the movement of labour, where again poor countries could have competitive advantage. All of these issues were on the table in the Doha Development Agenda, so that a successful outcome could produce major improvements for developing countries. But G8 countries resisted moves to open their markets earlier on specific products.

Capacity-Building

Poor countries required a variety of assistance to enable them to get more out of the trading system. They needed help domestically, to create a government and business environment that could encourage and benefit from external competition. They needed help internationally, to keep up with the complexities of trade negotiations in the WTO and elsewhere, since many small countries could not maintain a permanent delegation in Geneva.

This need was recognised in the summit documents from Okinawa onwards, but did not produce a collective response. The G8 encouraged whatever was going on, but offered nothing new. In practice, many G8 members ran generous technical assistance programmes themselves and supported wider action by the WTO, the World Bank or the Commonwealth.[26] But these did not satisfy many poor countries, who turned to NGOs to help them, often entrusting them with actual negotiations, as at Cancun. The results were not always positive.

The NGOs could be dedicated and well-informed advocates, but they were not practised negotiators and were not always committed to reaching agreement.[27]

Assessment under the Criteria

The Genoa summit of 2001 contributed to the successful launch of the Doha Development Round. But in other respects the performance of the G8 summits in trade was disappointing in terms of the criteria, as follows:

- Genoa showed *leadership* in producing a collective G8 approach to a new trade round, which had been missing before. Zoellick and Lamy took advantage of their familiarity with the summit process. But later summits, like Evian and Sea Island, passed up the opportunity to exercise leadership and revitalise the Doha negotiations. None of the G8 summits agreed on collective trade policy measures to help poor countries.
- Genoa was likewise *effective* in contributing to the launch of the Doha Development Agenda, by restraining domestic demands for protection that could have prevented it. But this restraint proved short-lived. Domestic pressures in the EU, the US and Japan all helped to slow down progress in the WTO and inhibited the removal of barriers to poor countries' products. The G8 heads did not act to resist these pressures.
- The close cooperation between Zoellick and Lamy produced a good example of transatlantic *solidarity* during a difficult period. This had a positive effect on trade discussions at the G8 summits from Genoa onwards. But their efforts to promote collective management were frustrated by the operation of domestic interests in all the G8 members.
- The Doha Development Agenda was successfully launched and proved *durable* despite the setback of Cancun. But after its revival in mid-2004 it was a year behind schedule and the content of the final agreements was still unclear. The G8 summit had contributed little to the negotiating process or to measures of lasting benefit for poor countries.
- Genoa helped to ensure that the new round was launched at Doha on terms *acceptable* to developing countries. But thereafter the slow progress and the lack of commitments from the G8 members weakened their position. Groups of developing countries moved to assert their own demands in the negotiations. NGOs entered the debates on the side of developing countries, especially poor ones, which sometimes made agreement more difficult.
- With the aim of a *consistent* approach, the G8 summits agreed a range of non-trade measures to help poor countries, including debt relief and other initiatives considered later in this chapter. These were generally rendered less useful by the weakness of the G8 position on trade, especially market access.

Development Issues: Early Summit Treatment

In contrast to trade, the treatment of development and 'North-South' issues by the G7 summits was insubstantial, even though at the outset these were standard items on the agenda. The early summits coincided with the zenith of the 'New International Economic Order'. They several times reached useful tactical agreements on how to operate in areas of the North-South debate, such as the Conference on International Economic Cooperation, the Cancun North-South summit of 1981 and 'Global Negotiations' in the UN. But all these activities proved to be inconclusive.[28]

Summit interest in development revived with debt relief for poor countries in the late 1980s. The G7 soon realised that their review of institutions in the light of advancing globalisation, begun in 1994, would have an impact on developing countries. Lyon 1996 was the first summit to make development its principal theme, but except for debt relief and the HIPC initiative the commitments made were very general. Clinton sought to maintain continuity by making Africa a major theme at Denver 1997, aiming to advance his domestic legislation. The Europeans, Canada and Japan, who were already active in Africa, were content to let the Americans catch up without themselves doing more. Meanwhile the attention given to poor countries weakened during the 1990s, as developed economies cut back their aid for budgetary reasons or diverted it to Central and Eastern Europe. In 1999 the World Bank and OECD reported that official aid was no higher in real terms than in 1981, while as a share of national income it was the lowest on record.[29]

The G8 Summits and Development

The Birmingham summit of 1998 focused the G8 on how to counter the fears generated by globalisation. One of these was the steady marginalisation of poor countries, especially in Africa. Birmingham and Cologne gave priority to debt relief, but the summits from Okinawa onwards broadened the agenda, in line with the work being done in the United Nations, culminating in the UN Millennium Summit of September 2000. This brought together a number of targets, most of them formulated during the 1990s, into a consolidated list of Millennium Development Goals, which should be achieved by 2015. The eight goals were:

- Eradicate extreme poverty and hunger;
- Achieve universal primary education;
- Promote gender equality and empower women;
- Reduce child mortality;
- Improve maternal health;
- Combat AIDS, malaria and other diseases;
- Ensure environmental sustainability;
- Develop a global partnership for development.[30]

Most of the development initiatives of the summits of the 2000s were linked to one of these goals. The most innovative moves by the Okinawa and Genoa summits were in IT (covered in goal no. 8), infectious diseases, renewable energy (an aspect of environmental sustainability, goal no. 7) and primary education. Later proposals covered clean water (also part of goal no. 7) and famine. These will be analysed more fully below.

The partnership prescribed in the eighth and final goal also covered trade access, debt relief and aid flows. The summits from 2000 onwards tried to cover these mainstream development issues, as well as the more specific goals. Their performance in debt relief has been assessed in Chapter 5 and in trade access earlier in this chapter. Aid volume and effectiveness was regularly discussed at the summit, but seldom led to clear G8 commitments. A promise at Cologne in 1999 to increase aid volumes was not repeated. The World Bank concluded in December 2001 that annual aid flows needed to double, from about $50 billion to about $100 billion, in order to meet the Millennium Development Goals. Gordon Brown, the British Finance Minister, gave strong backing to this aim and proposed a new International Finance Facility to achieve the necessary doubling.[31] But during the first G8 sequence the summit did not agree to support it. Measures to improve aid effectiveness had little better success. An undertaking to end the tying of aid to purchases in the donor country was first made at Birmingham in 1998 but was not finally achieved till early in 2002.[32]

At the Monterrey conference on UN Financing for Development, in March 2002, the United States pledged to increase its official aid by $5 billion per year for five years. Parallel pledges were made by the European Union (worth about $7 billion per year) and by Canada.[33] But this could not be called a joint G8 commitment, as the US announcement had taken everyone by surprise and Japan's aid was falling sharply.[34] The closest the G8 members have come to a joint aid commitment was at the Kananaskis summit in June 2002 when they agreed that one-half of the aid increases they had promised at Monterrey should go to Africa - see Chapters 9 and 12 below.

IT and the Digital Divide - the DOT-Force

The G7 had begun considering issues raised by information and communications technology (IT) in the mid-1990s. A special G7 ministerial conference on the 'Global Information Society' was held in Brussels in 1995 and a follow-up meeting, with wider participation, in South Africa a year later.[35] Discussions were also pursued actively in the context of the OECD. The debate mainly focused on the international regime for electronic commerce (pressed by the United States) and issues of privacy and data protection (a concern of the Europeans). While often controversial, these exchanges had led to a broad consensus, reflected in the first two sections of the Charter on Global Information Society adopted by the Okinawa summit. But much less had been done to address the 'global digital divide', which postulated that poor countries' lack of access to IT would penalise their development. The Japanese hosts for the summit decided to give priority to this aspect and to engage the private sector - business firms and NGOs - who were already involved in the debate in the OECD and elsewhere.[36]

Japan organised detailed preparations for Okinawa on this issue, culminating in a conference in Tokyo in the week before the summit attended by leading international IT firms, such as Cisco Industries.[37] The conclusions of this conference were largely incorporated in the Okinawa Charter. The main G8 decision was to set up the Digital Opportunity Task-Force, with wide participation, to report to next year's Genoa summit on how IT could best contribute to development.

The composition of the DOT-Force was highly original, as compared with G8 follow-up as practiced hitherto. Instead of relying on government sources, it deliberately developed a 'multi-stakeholder' approach. Though the chair was held by a government official (first from Italy, then from Canada), the G8 government representatives were joined by delegates from non-G8 countries (Bolivia, Brazil, Egypt, India, Indonesia, Senegal, South Africa and Tanzania), major IT firms (including Accenture, Hewlett Packard and Siemens), NGOs and international institutions (including the World Bank and UNDP, who provided the secretariat). The full involvement of business and civil society groups enabled the DOT-Force to engage the innovative capacities of the private sector and overcome the initial scepticism of many NGOs on how IT could help poor countries.[38]

The first DOT-Force Report, to the Genoa summit, laid out a strategy and an action plan for IT in developing countries.[39] It focused on a set of well-defined action points, which covered:

- Countries should develop national 'eStrategies', with help to make them internationally compatible;
- Access to IT should be made easier and cheaper;
- IT should be used in education at all levels, as well as in health care and the fight against AIDS;
- IT business activity should be encouraged;
- There should be special efforts to help the poorest countries and encourage local applications.

The DOT-Force did not recommend at Genoa the level of resources needed, though it recorded the projects being financed by the World Bank and others. But it identified a number of areas where projects would be developed by the time of the next summit at Kananaskis.

At Kananaskis 2002 the DOT-Force issued a final report and wound itself up.[40] The final 'report card' set out a range of projects which it had developed, with requests for financing for some of them. All of the projects had strong private sector involvement, which led to a practical, down-to-earth approach, avoiding unrealistic expectations. Most of the projects were to be pursued under the aegis of the UN ICT Task Force, which became the institutional home of the DOT-Force concept.[41] The G8 itself showed no wish to continue its involvement. After the initial impetus from Okinawa, the heads were content to welcome what the DOT-Force did but gave it little of their personal attention.

Infectious Diseases

Health had never been a major issue at a G7 or G8 summit before Okinawa 2000. But the Japanese hosts perceived that the time was ripe for the G8 to recognise that health problems, and especially the major epidemic diseases of AIDS, tuberculosis and malaria, were a major obstacle to countries seeking to escape from poverty. Japan built on mounting concern both among governments and NGOs at the spread of AIDS and its consequences, but they did not wish to ignore more traditional diseases like malaria. Their initiative found ready support among the rest of the G8 and built on interest already generated at Birmingham in 1998.[42]

The G8 decision at Okinawa was in fairly general terms. But it was enough both to stimulate active follow-up among G8 members and to encourage other institutions to move forward, especially the UN. The Italian Presidency maintained infectious diseases as a priority issue for Genoa, with the aim of having concrete decisions there to follow up the general commitments at Okinawa. During the spring of 2001 there were active discussions in United Nations contexts, focusing wholly on AIDS. This led up to the special UN General Assembly on HIV/AIDS in June, which called for the urgent establishment of a 'global HIV/AIDS and health fund'. But the G8 did not want other epidemic diseases to be neglected. By the Genoa summit in July it was agreed that the new Global Fund should cover AIDS, tuberculosis and malaria, the three diseases singled out at Okinawa.[43]

The Genoa summit established the Global Fund to fight AIDS, Tuberculosis and Malaria, with the G8 countries subscribing $1.2 billion out of its initial $1.7 billion endowment. The G8 also agreed that the Global Fund should adopt the same multi-stakeholder approach as the DOT-Force and this was reflected in the composition of its board. This was made up not only of governments and international institutions but also of private firms, charitable foundations and NGOs from both rich and poor countries. Financial support for the fund was sought not only from governments, but also from private corporate and individual donors.[44]

The Global Fund got under way very fast and in April 2002 was ready to make its first financial commitments. It received bids totalling six times more than it had expected and allocated funds totalling $0.6 billion over two years. Though pledges had risen by then to $2 billion, it was clear that the Global Fund's resources were being rapidly depleted, since many of the projects it accepted would require funding over five years or more. But at the Kananaskis summit in June 2002 the G8 did not take the opportunity to replenish the Global Fund. By March 2003 it had to start its own fund-raising campaign, called 'Fund the Fund'.[45]

In January 2003 Bush announced the US Emergency Plan for AIDS Relief, with $10 billion of new funding, making a total US commitment of $15 billion over five years. This included another $1 billion for the Global Fund, provided that other donors to the Fund would match it with $2 billion. This stimulated

Chirac, supported by Blair, to promise at the Evian summit in June 2003 that the Europeans would pledge a second $1 billion over the next year, in the hope that Japan, Canada and other countries would put up a third $1 billion to release the American total. This programme did not work out exactly as planned. It turned out that the US pledge was only for $1 billion spread over five years, while the European Union did not accept a formal $1 billion target either.[46] Nevertheless, many G8, European and other countries increased their pledges or joined the contributors for the first time, so that by mid-2004 total commitments to the Global Fund stood at almost $5.5 billion.

As with the DOT-Force, the G8's attention was moving away from the Global Fund to other aspects of AIDS and infectious diseases. At Kananaskis 2002 the G8 pledged new funding to wipe out polio in Africa and followed this up with a further worldwide pledge at Sea Island 2004. At the Sea Island summit the Americans also persuaded the rest of the G8 to give an international umbrella to their plans to discover, test and diffuse an HIV/AIDS vaccine.

Renewable Energy

Okinawa set up a second task-force, on renewable energy. This was a British initiative, which originated in the NGO community, and was intended both to improve poor countries access to energy and to protect the environment by reducing emissions of greenhouse gases.[47] This again adopted the multi-stakeholder approach, with a composition closely matching the DOT-Force - G8 and non-G8 countries, business firms, NGOs and international institutions. It went further in having co-chairmanship from the public and private sector, by a senior Italian official, Corrado Clini, and a chairman of Shell, Mark Moody-Stuart.

The task-force found that renewable energy, like solar power, was little used in poor countries because it cost too much. It concluded that the cost was high because the total world market for renewable energy was too small, so that there was insufficient incentive for firms to develop low-cost technologies in this area. This would only be corrected if renewable energy was more widely used in large, rich countries. The task-force therefore recommended that G8 and other industrial countries should subsidise renewable energy, so as to make it more competitive against conventional energy sources like oil and gas.[48]

These findings were backed by all the private sector members of the task-force, including the American ones, and by the European and Japanese governments. But the new Bush Administration in the US was not prepared to agree to such interventionist policies, that could put their strong oil companies at a disadvantage. Canada supported the US, for the same reason. At the Genoa summit the G8 took no position on the task-force report, beyond remitting it to their energy ministers. The energy ministers took no further action. Moody-Stuart, on behalf of a new grouping of private firms, sought to revive this approach at the World Summit on Sustainable Development (WSSD) in September 2002, but with no better success.[49]

Primary Education

After the success of their initiatives on IT and infectious diseases, which began at Okinawa and bore fruit at Genoa, the G8 looked for another subject covered by the Millennium Development Goals. They chose primary education and set up a task-force at Genoa to report at Kananaskis one year later. The task-force worked closely with the World Bank, which was seeking to identify and encourage those policies that would enable poor countries to benefit from outside help in improving their primary education systems.[50] But this time the G8 did not adopt the 'multi-stakeholder approach', so that the task-force was composed of officials only.

By the time of Kananaskis, the World Bank had identified a group of poor countries whose sound domestic policies in primary education made them deserving of 'fast-track assistance'.[51] This should enable these countries to meet the millennium goal of having all children completing primary education by 2015. The task-force report endorsed the education policies recommended by the World Bank and regarded them as worthy of G8 support. But the G8 summit did no more than promise increased priority to education in bilateral aid programmes. It made no collective commitment to help all or any of the World Bank's 'fast-track' countries. Though some G8 countries later earned praise for their support, the World Bank was unable to get the funding for the programme that it hoped.[52]

Clean Water and Famine

The later summits, Evian 2003 and Sea Island 2004 sought to stimulate progress on two more Millennium Development Goals, as follows:

- *Clean Water* Chirac had wanted water to be a priority subject at the Evian summit. But the action plan adopted there had few precise commitments and a European Commission initiative came to nothing. Sea Island in 2004 did not return to this topic.
- *Famine and Food Security* The United States pressed for an action plan on this subject at Evian and kept it on the agenda for Sea Island. But at both summits the G8 could not go beyond general statements and support for existing programmes. This was partly because of underlying differences between Europe and the United States on the use of food aid and on GMOs.

As with primary education, it is not clear that the summit has had any lasting impact on these issues.

Transparency and the Private Sector

Two other issues treated by the later summits were not derived from the millennium goals, but reflected the interest of the US and other G8 countries in improving governance and reducing corruption in developing countries, as well as making the private sector contribute more to development. These were:

- *Transparency in Government and Energy Exploitation* At Evian and Sea Island the G8 adopted a range of proposals aimed at improving standards of public administration in developing countries. The most innovative of these began at Evian by advocating greater transparency in exploiting energy and mining resources, to ensure that the proceeds really contributed to development. This 'Extractive Industries Transparency Initiative' gathered support over the next twelve months.[53] At Sea Island the approach was broadened to cover transparency in government operations generally.
- *Mobilising the Private Sector for Development* The summits had often commended the contribution that foreign direct investment (FDI) could make to development. But in practice poor countries attracted little FDI. Sea Island, for the first time, focused on domestic capital formation and endorsed a number of measures, which included making more use of foreign remittances to developing countries, estimated at between $100 and $150 billion a year.

These G8 decisions reflected a much closer interest in the process of development within countries, as opposed to the external contribution of trade, aid flows or foreign investment. But it was hard for the summit to exert a decisive influence while still leaving developing countries 'ownership' of their domestic policy process.

Assessment under the Criteria

The G8 summits showed a mixed performance in development issues, as follows:

- The G8 showed *leadership* in launching a number of highly innovative programmes in development. There were initiatives in IT, infectious diseases, renewable energy and primary education from Okinawa and Genoa, as well as more from later summits. But not all these initiatives were successfully followed through and even with successful programmes the G8 was prone to lose interest once they had been launched. There was no G8 leadership in the broad field of aid volume.
- The G8 was *effective* in carrying through its proposals on IT and the Global Fund. In both areas it pioneered a 'multi-stakeholder approach' to engage the private sector. But in renewable energy it was not effective, because the United States and Canada allowed the domestic interests of their oil and gas industry to stifle progress. The poor results in aid flows reflected the reluctance of many G8 countries to give aid sufficient priority in domestic budgetary debates.
- The G8 showed good *solidarity*, with clear support for collective management, in IT and infectious diseases. But such solidarity was often lacking in other areas. In addition to budgetary pressures in all G8 countries, the new US Administration was reluctant to take collective financial commitments, preferring to act bilaterally even where it was mobilising very large amounts.

This inhibited a joint G8 commitment on primary education and led to confusion over the Global Fund.

- The Global Fund proved a *durable* addition to the international machinery for dealing with infectious diseases. The DOT-Force brought about a lasting change in attitudes to the use of IT in development, though its institutional future was less assured. In other areas - renewable energy, primary education, water - the G8 raised expectations which it later failed to satisfy.
- The 'multi-stakeholder approach' developed by the G8 was designed to make its programmes more *acceptable* both to non-G8 countries and to the private sector. It was intended as an answer to the growing criticism of the G8 as an exclusive body, which gathered strength after Seattle and was reflected in the Genoa demonstrations. This approach helped to tie in a number of influential and responsible firms and NGOs, but others remained hostile, especially when the G8 failed to follow up some of its major initiatives.
- The G8 sought to give *consistent* attention to development from Okinawa onwards. The summits moved from IT, health and renewable energy to Africa and primary education. But this faltered when some initiatives were not completed and the momentum was not regained at later summits, except as regards Africa (see Chapter 12 below). Some worthwhile initiatives in specific subjects, like IT and health, had to be set against limited progress in aid, in trade and in improving the terms of debt relief after 1999.

Lessons from the G8 Summits in Trade and Development

The experience of the G8 summits in treating trade and development issues, especially from Okinawa onwards, reveals a number of lessons about the strengths and weaknesses of the summit process in the early 2000s. These can be considered under the familiar six criteria.

Leadership

The G8 members deserved credit for giving priority to the problems of poor countries. They had recognised that special measures were needed from rich countries to ensure that small, poor ones could benefit from globalisation. But their performance did not always meet their aspirations; they often willed the ends without willing the means. The summits were highly innovative in certain specific aspects of development and they successfully helped to launch the Doha Development Round. But in broader fields, like aid volume, trade access for poor countries and debt relief after Cologne, they did not give a strong lead and opportunities were missed.

Effectiveness

There were worrying signs of G8 weakness in *effectiveness*. In several areas the summits were broadly ineffective in overcoming domestic pressures. The most serious was in trade, where the G8 members contributed to the slow progress of the Doha Development Agenda and the mounting frustration of developing countries. Renewable energy was another victim of domestic interests, while there was a general reluctance to make firm financial commitments in a G8 context, except for the Global Fund to fight AIDS, tuberculosis and malaria.

Solidarity

The G8 dealt rather better with international pressures (on solidarity) than with domestic ones (on effectiveness). The summit showed strong attachment to collective management both on trade, with Zoellick and Lamy working together to overcome earlier divisions, and on development initiatives like IT and infectious diseases. But solidarity was weaker in other aspects of development. For example, there were lapses on renewable energy and famine, which suffered from transatlantic differences on environmental issues and food safety.

Durability

The Japanese, Italian and Canadian G8 Presidencies tried to promote durability by ensuring good continuity between the summits from 2000 onwards. This helped the summits to produce durable results through the Global Fund and - to a lesser extent - the DOT-Force. Launching the Doha Development Agenda was also durable, in the sense that the round is still in being, despite its slow progress. But there were few examples of the summits coming back to a subject to improve the outcome, as they did with debt relief in the 1990s. Subjects were launched and then left to fare as best they could - and a number of summit initiatives did not endure.

Acceptability

The Okinawa and Genoa summits made great advances in the search for greater acceptability, both by extending outreach to non-G8 countries and by developing the 'multi-stakeholder approach' to engage private firms and NGOs. This had some success, though perhaps less than it deserved. Some firms and NGOs became deeply involved in G8 work. But civil society in general became more hostile, in part because of disappointing results on aid commitments and trade. The G8 itself became less attached to the multi-stakeholder approach in later summits, though it was used in the Middle Eastern initiative at Sea Island in 2004.

Consistency

As already indicated, the greatest weaknesses of the G8 were in its restriction of trade access for poor countries and its reluctance to make financial commitments. These tended to undermine the value of the G8's innovative measures in specific development topics, since there was no confidence that the G8 would either fund them or enable poor countries to take full advantage of them.

Conclusion

Genoa 2001, with its focus on world poverty, was the last of the sixth summit series, where the G8 agenda had been predominantly economic (apart from Kosovo). The terrorist attacks of 11 September 2001 switched the G8 towards political issues related to terrorism. But the development agenda survived in the treatment of Africa, under the G8 Action Plan agreed at Kananaskis 2002 and followed through at the two subsequent summits. There was recognition that the fight against terrorism involved economic instruments, to reduce the incentives to political extremism. So the performance of these later summits, to be assessed in Chapter 12, still involved a large economic component.

Notes

1 The awkwardness was increased when Russia joined the summit. Trade issues were always discussed among the G8, even though Russia was not a member of the WTO.

2 The trade part of this chapter draws on Bayne 2001. The development section is new.

3 For accounts of trade discussions at these first four summits, see Putnam and Bayne 1987, pp. 25-47 and 62-94, and de Menil and Solomon 1983, pp. 22-26. For a scholarly analysis, see Cohn 2002, pp. 83-121.

4 The Uruguay Round was formally launched in September 1986, three months after the summit. Accounts of trade discussions at the summits from 1979 to 1986 are in Putnam and Bayne 1987, pp. 110-144 and 170-226. Cohn 2002, pp. 123-165, analyses the Quad (created at Ottawa in 1981) and Wolfe 1998, especially pp. 79-80, examines agriculture.

5 For trade at the summits of 1988 to 1993, see Bayne 2000a, pp. 59-74 and Cohn 2002, pp. 167-230. Assessments of the Uruguay Round results and the new WTO are in Schott 1994, Preeg 1995 and Jackson 1998 and a complete history in Croome 1995.

6 For trade discussions at the summits from 1994 to 1999, see Bayne 2000, pp. 113-132 and 151-167, and Bayne 2001. An account of Seattle is in 'The Battle in Seattle' and 'The WTO After Seattle', *The Economist,* 27 November and 11 December 1999. For scholarly assessments, see Bhagwati 2000 and Bayne 2000b.

7 For a review of the issues facing the world trading system between Seattle and Doha, see Hoekman and Kostecki 2001, especially pp. 385-485.

8 Lamy was sherpa to Jacques Delors, President of the European Commission, from 1984 to 1993. Zoellick was sherpa to George Bush (senior) in 1991-1992.

9 See E. Alden, 'Zoellick Warns on World Trade Talks' and 'Bush Trade Agenda Will Take All Year in Congress', *Financial Times,* 31 January and 20 April 2001. Fast-track authority enabled the Administration to present the results of a trade negotiation to Congress for simple approval or rejection; Congress could not amend the terms.

10 G. de Jonquières, in 'US Promises New Trade Talks', *Financial Times,* 17 May 2001, records Zoellick and Lamy agreeing on a broad-based agenda at the OECD ministerial meeting. See also Chapter 7, note 13.

11 This issue had become increasingly controversial during 2001; see M. Wolf, 'The Price of Saving Lives' and F. Williams, 'Declaration on Patent Rules Cheers Developing Nations', *Financial Times,* 20 June and 15 November 2001. A good scholarly analysis is in Abbott 2002.

12 For an account of the Doha meeting, see 'Doha Round - Seeds of Future Growth', *The Economist,* 17 November 2001. An assessment of the outcome is in Laird 2002.

13 On steel tariffs and the Farm Bill, see 'Special Report - Trade Disputes', *The Economist,* 11 May 2002, and E. Alden and D. McGregor, 'A Cash Crop', *Financial Times,* 10 May 2002. On trade promotion authority, see leader, 'A Good Deal', *Financial Times,* 29 July 2002 and 'Fast Track to Doha', *The Economist,* 3 August 2002
14 Bob Zoellick set out his ideas in 'Bringing Down the Barriers', *Financial Times,* 26 July, and 'Unleashing the Trade Winds', *The Economist,* 7 December 2002.
15 See 'EU Farm Policy: Reform - Forget It', *The Economist,* 5 October, and G. de Jonquières, 'EU's Inertia Over Farm Trade Puts Doha at Risk', *Financial Times,* 27 November 2002.
16 For CAP reform, see T. Buck, 'EU Farm Deal Lifts Trade Talks Hopes'; for TRIPS and drugs, F. Williams, 'WTO Deal on Cheap Drugs Ends Months of Wrangling', *Financial Times,* 27 June and 28 August 2003.
17 A good account of the issues on the table in Cancun, especially for developing countries, is in Mbirimi and others 2003. For the meeting itself, see 'Cancun's Charming Outcome' and 'The WTO Under Fire', *The Economist,* 20 September 2003. Bhagwati 2004a makes clear the failure was not a tragedy.
18 On the deal to restart the Doha Development Agenda, see 'World Trade - Now Harvest It', *The Economist,* 7 August 2004.
19 For Ruggiero's proposal, see G. de Jonquières and R. Chote, Tariff Plea to Aid Poor Countries', *Financial Times,* 1 July 1996.
20 See M. Suzman, 'Senate Passes Africa Bill' *Financial Times,* 5 November 1999 and D. McGregor, 'Way Clear for US-Africa Trade Bill', *Financial Times,* 4 May 2000.
21 P. Norman, 'EU to End All Curbs on Trade with Poor Countries', *Financial Times,* 27 February 2001. This earned praise from Kofi Annan, 'A Route out of Poverty', *Financial Times,* 5 March 2001.
22 For a strong critique of rich countries' trade policies, see Wolf 2004, pp. 212-219.
23 A new reform of the Common Agricultural Policy was begun in 2001; see F. Fischler (EU Agriculture Commissioner), 'A Three-Pronged Reform', *Financial Times,* 8 May 2001. But progress was painfully slow - see notes 15 and 16 above.
24 Four African countries tried in vain at Cancun to persuade the United States to remove its domestic subsidies for cotton production. See F. Williams and G. de Jonquières, 'US Fights Plea by Africans Over Cotton', *Financial Times,* 11 September 2003.
25 This is documented for the United States in Gresser 2002.
26 The United Kingdom, for example, devoted aid resources to capacity-building, in line with policy set out in two White Papers, DFID 2000 and DTI 2004.
27 Oxfam became active in trade policy and produced several influential reports. See A. Beattie, 'Raw Deal for Poor Nations Limits Backing for Free Trade' and M. Wolf, 'Doing More Harm Than Good', *Financial Times,* 12 April and 8 May 2002.
28 The discussions in the summits up to Williamsburg 1983 were chronicled in the first edition of *Hanging Together* (Putnam and Bayne 1984) - see under 'developing countries' in the Index. But they amounted to so little that they were left out of the second edition (Putnam and Bayne 1987).
29 For OECD report that aid from OECD countries in 1997 was only 0.22% of GNP, see R. Chote, 'Aid for Poor Nations Sinks to Record Low', *Financial Times,* 9 February 1999. For World Bank report that aid is lowest in real terms since 1981, see R. Chote, 'Aid to Poor Nations Falls to 18-Year Low', *Financial Times,* 8 April 1999. See also note 34.
30 The goals and associated material are accessible on www.un.org/millenniumgoals/.
31 See A. Beattie, 'World Bank Warns on Push to Cut Poverty', *Financial Times,* 12 November 2001. Brown's proposals are set out in B. Groom, 'Chancellor Calls for

$50bn Fund to Beat Poverty', and C. Adams and A. Beattie, 'Brown in Plea on Development', *Financial Times,* 16 November 2001 and 13 December 2002.

32 It involved long and tense discussions in OECD; see G. de Jonquières, 'Donors Praised for Untying Aid Projects', *Financial Times,* 23 April 2004.

33 A. Beattie, 'US Wakes Up from 20 Year Slumber in Development Field', *Financial Times,* 25 March 2002 and 'A Feast of Giving', *The Economist,* 23 March 2002.

34 Japan's aid fell sharply from about $14 billion in 2000 to $10 billion in 2001. This caused total aid from OECD countries to drop from $54 billion to $51 billion. See 'Japan - We're Number Two', *The Economist,* 18 May 2002, and S. Daneshku, 'Richest Nations' Aid Falls to $51bn', *Financial Times,* 14 May 2002.

35 See Hajnal 1999, p. 38.

36 Much of this discussion of IT is based on a valuable paper by Jeffrey Hart (Hart 2005).

37 For Japan's early preparations, see A. Parker, 'US Group [Cisco] to Advise on Third World IT Project', *Financial Times,* 28 March 2000.

38 Jeffrey Sachs - see Sachs 2000 - was already advocating the greater use of technology in development. See also A. Beattie, 'New Risk to Poor in Digital Divide', *Financial Times,* Survey 2001 and Beyond, 25 January 2001.

39 *Digital Opportunities for All* (DOT-Force 2001).

40 *Report Card* (DOT-Force 2002).

41 For an assessment of the effectiveness of the DOT-Force and a list of the follow-on projects, see Hart 2005, including Appendix 2.

42 British preparations for Okinawa, which were stimulated by an article by Jeffrey Sachs (Sachs 1999), also identified health as a major threat to development. See Budd 2003, pp. 142-143.

43 For the origins of the Global Fund, see the account accessible on www.theglobalfund.org/en/about/road/history/default.asp. This makes clear that the process began at the Okinawa summit. See also Chapter 7, with notes 17 and 18.

44 Global Fund pledges are in www.theglobalfund.org/en/files/pledges&contributions.xls.

45 See F. Williams, 'New Fund to Fight Disease Finds Winners and Losers', and D. Firn, 'Battle with Malaria Losing Ground as AIDS Drains Funding', *Financial Times,* 26 April and 5 November 2002.

46 J. Blitz, 'Blair, Chirac Urge EU Cash for AIDS Fund', J. Dempsey and A. Beattie, 'EU Leaders Back Away from AIDS Pledge' and J. Sachs, 'A Miserly Response to a Global Emergency', *Financial Times,* 18 and 21 June and 17 July 2003.

47 See Budd 2003, pp. 141-142.

48 This account is partly based on a talk by Mark Moody-Stuart at Chatham House in November 2001. See also D. Buchan and A. Taylor, 'Renewable Energy Lobby to Target G8 Genoa Summit', *Financial Times,* 14 July 2001.

49 G. Lean, 'Summit Agreement is Struck, But US Blocks Deal on Clean Energy', *Independent,* 3 September 2002.

50 The World Bank recommended an increase in aid of $2.5 billion per year to enable poor countries to meet the Millennium Development Goal. See A. Beattie, 'Half of All Countries Need "Urgent Help" on Education', *Financial Times,* 27 March 2002.

51 The World Bank was working with Oxfam to bring this programme to the attention of the G7, who were asked to make an immediate commitment of $4 billion dollars. See A. Beattie, 'New World Bank Funding Initiative', *Financial Times,* 13 June 2002.

52 A. Balls, 'Donors Fail on Education Funding', *Financial Times,* 29 March 2004.

53 See 'Oil and Development', *The Economist,* 25 May and C. Hoyos, 'Africans to disclose Details of Oil Deals', *Financial Times,* 19 June 2003.

Chapter 9

New Directions: Kananaskis 2002

The international context for the G8 summit was changed profoundly by the terrorist attacks on the United States of 11 September 2001. American policy became wholly concentrated on the fight against terrorism and the United States expected the same dedication from its allies. At first, however, this campaign was broadly defined to include the roots as well as the manifestations of terrorism, so that the military operations in Afghanistan were combined with economic and political measures worldwide. The rationale was well expressed by Republican Senator Chuck Hagel:

> The root causes of instability in most regions of the world are economic and social . . . Unless we start to recognise that, we will never really get to the core of stopping terrorism.[1]

This enabled the Canadian hosts to choose an agenda that not only matched the new demands of the fight against terrorism but also provided continuity with earlier summit decisions, especially from Genoa 2001, and maintained the G8's focus on responding to globalisation. At an early stage Chrétien chose a three-part agenda - terrorism, Africa and strengthening economic growth - and stuck to it, resisting additions.[2]

Preparations, Site and Civil Society

Kananaskis, a resort in the Rockies, had originally been chosen as the summit site because it was secluded and intimate, out of range of any violent demonstrations such as had upset Genoa. But it also made it easier to provide the greatly increased security needed against any terrorist threat. The security operations, however, were estimated to have added around $250-350 million to the cost.[3] Kananaskis was a small resort, with limited accommodation. The size of delegations had to be kept down and everyone was lodged close together. This encouraged an informal and spontaneous atmosphere, with Blair and Bush meeting by chance in the gym at 6.30 am. But the leaders were cut off from the world at large. In particular, civil society and most of the media were kept in Calgary, 56 miles (90km) away - among the leaders, only Chirac, Koizumi and José Maria Aznar (Spanish EU Presidency) visited the media centre.

Mercifully, the Kananaskis summit attracted no violent protests. No windows were broken; only two demonstrators were arrested; and the security forces were never put under pressure. Marches and rallies in Calgary attracted no more than 2000 people at a time; the police handled them gently and they passed off peacefully. This contrast with Genoa was due partly to the inaccessibility of the summit site but partly also to the reaction against anti-globalisation rioting that had followed 11 September 2001.[4]

An 'alternative summit', the G6 Billion, was held in Calgary in the run-up to the summit. The Canadian foreign minister attended its final session and transmitted its conclusions to the G8 heads, as had been promised. This event, however, took a wholly negative attitude to the G8.[5] The Canadian government had put a lot of effort into outreach to civil society, but were frustrated that this only seemed to generate more strident criticism, especially on Africa. Leading charities like Oxfam and Médecins sans Frontières followed the actual summit proceedings closely. Their comments were also critical, but usually from a more constructive basis, and influenced the media because the heads themselves were less accessible.

As usual, a number of G8 ministerial groups met in the run-up to the summit - environment ministers, employment ministers, energy ministers (in Detroit rather than Canada) and interior and justice ministers (with special emphasis on terrorism). These groups had by now developed a life of their own and their work had little direct impact on the summit itself. The meetings of the G8 foreign ministers and G7 finance ministers in mid-June were more clearly linked to the summit. The foreign ministers focused on terrorism, conflict prevention and selected regional issues - Afghanistan, India/Pakistan, the Middle East and the Balkans. The finance ministers declared their confidence in the economic recovery. They agreed on an allocation between grants and loans for IDA financing and discussed the problem of replenishing the HIPC Trust Fund in the World Bank.[6]

The Kananaskis Summit, 26-27 June 2002

There was unusual continuity with the Genoa summit among the G8 leaders, with Aznar (EU Presidency) the only newcomer. Chrétien, in the chair, was the doyen among the leaders and had already hosted a successful summit at Halifax in 1995. Chirac had just been re-elected and the French government had changed from centre-left (headed by Lionel Jospin) to centre-right (with Pierre Raffarin as Prime Minister). This nudged the balance among the leaders a little further to the right. Bush, Blair, Berlusconi and Putin were all electorally secure. Schroeder (who faced elections in October), Koizumi and Chrétien were less certain of reappearing, but in fact all survived to meet again at the 2003 summit.

The seclusion of the summit made it hard to judge the personal performance of the heads. Blair and Chirac were active and effective players, as always. Bush was an energetic participant, though his style (as Chirac commented to the press) was rather different from the others. Putin held his own on the issues of concern to him and the Bush/Putin chemistry seemed good. Koizumi had skilfully disarmed in advance any criticism of the Japanese economy. Schroeder clearly had a hand in the decision on Russia hosting the summit (see below), as Germany had to delay its turn. Aznar spoke up for Latin America. It was less easy to discern where

Berlusconi or Prodi contributed to the outcome. As chairman, Chrétien had the satisfaction of seeing the summit work out as he had planned it, but he seemed ill at ease in his public appearances.

The same four African leaders as had been at Genoa - Mbeki (South Africa), Obasanjo (Nigeria), Wade (Senegal) and Bouteflika (Algeria) - together with UN Secretary General Annan, had a joint meeting with the G8 heads on the Africa Action Plan. The Africans were more than guests, as they had been at Tokyo and Genoa; they were participants in the summit itself. Among the Africans, Mbeki and Obasanjo were articulate and assured, while Annan made clear that his interest in the summit went beyond Africa.

Summit Organisation and Timetable

For maximum efficiency, the duration of the summit was cut back to a day and a half. There was no G7 statement and no agreed G8 communiqué. Instead, Chrétien issued a 'chair's summary' of just over two pages, covering only points raised by the heads themselves. The summit, however, issued a number of other, more substantial, documents. These covered: the Africa Action Plan; the 'Global Partnership' against the spread of weapons of mass destruction; cooperative action on transport security; and Russia's role in the G8. The heads also endorsed the report of the G8 Task-Force on Primary Education and put their names to a statement on the HIPC initiative, which had clearly been prepared by their finance ministers.

In the summit programme, the first day began with a G7 meeting. After Putin joined them, the G8 heads started their discussion of terrorism. This item included cleaning up nuclear and chemical weapons and installations in Russia, which took up a lot of time. Economic growth was taken later in the afternoon and regional political issues over dinner. The second day was wholly devoted to Africa. The G8 heads first met on their own and were then joined by the African leaders and Annan. The analysis that follows starts with political issues - Russia and the G8, terrorism and regional problems - and then moves on to Africa and economic issues.

Political Issues

Russia and the G8

The first issue tackled in the G8 meeting was Russia's place at the summit. The heads agreed that Russia could host a G8 summit for the first time in 2006, fitting into the sequence between Britain and Germany. This decision was taken by the heads themselves, without any advance preparation - even the sherpas were taken by surprise. It was expected that G7 meetings at the heads' level would cease. The G8 heads also laid out the cycle of summit hosts up to 2010, making clear they expected the summit to persist in its present form and with its current members up till then.

Terrorism and Weapons of Mass Destruction

The heads used the summit to take stock of existing measures against terrorism, including terrorist financing, and added two new instruments to the existing armoury.[7] The first of these was an agreement on transport security, covering travel documents, containers, ports and aviation security. It envisaged joint G8 action in international bodies such as the International Civil Aviation Organisation (ICAO) and International Maritime Organisation (IMO). The summit provided useful pressure to complete this agreement, but the heads themselves did not have to intervene.

The second instrument embodied 'The G8 Global Partnership against the Spread of Weapons and Materials of Mass Destruction'. Its aim was to prevent nuclear, chemical or biological weapons falling into the hands of terrorists. The most important provision was a commitment by the G8 to raise up to $20 billion over 10 years to finance the destruction or clean-up of nuclear and chemical weapons and other material, initially in Russia but also in the other countries of the former Soviet Union.

After the Africa Action Plan, this agreement was the most important achievement of Kananaskis. The initiative had been driven by the United States, which launched a national programme in the 1990s to make safe plutonium and other fissile material in the former Soviet Union. (The heads had discussed this at Okinawa in 2000.) The US had already committed $10 billion to this activity and it became a major aspect of US/Russian relations since Bush began his meetings with Putin. The increased concern with terrorism since 11 September 2001 helped to persuade the rest of the G7 to commit a matching $10 billion.[8] But in return they insisted that the Russians give proper local support to their assistance projects in Russia. Funds that they had earmarked earlier could not be spent because of Russian reluctance to provide adequate access or legal and insurance cover.

The negotiation of the agreement at Kananaskis took up a great deal of time, between expert officials, political directors, sherpas and the heads themselves. Under pressure, the Russians reverted to Cold War reflexes and resisted giving the necessary assurances until the last moment. Exchanges among the heads themselves were needed to ensure that the Russians were fully committed to facilitating this programme on the ground and the matter was only resolved at a bilateral between Putin and Bush.[9]

Middle East

One day before the summit opened, Bush made a major speech outlining a new basis for a democratically based Palestinian state and its relations with Israel.[10] This speech had been delayed by the spate of suicide bombings and it looked as if it might distract attention from the main summit agenda. But in fact the Middle East peace process was discussed with other items over dinner, as planned. The most striking aspect of the speech was a refusal by Bush to deal with Arafat as Palestinian leader (though he did not name him) because he was tainted with terrorism. The other G8 heads welcomed the US proposals on how Palestine should become a viable state, which reflected in part European ideas. They took the position that the Palestinians had the democratic right to choose their own leaders, though Blair, Berlusconi and Chrétien, in different ways, showed some sympathy with Bush's frustration with Arafat. There was thus no open disagreement at the summit, but no great advance either.[11]

Other Regional Issues

The heads discussed Afghanistan (including the destruction of the opium crop), India/Pakistan and North Korea over dinner.[12] All the regional issues selected by the heads had strong links with terrorism or weapons of mass destruction. It was widely expected that Bush would raise Iraq, but there was no evidence that he did so.

Africa

In 2001 the G8 heads had launched the 'Genoa Plan for Africa', as an immediate and spontaneous initial response to the 'New African Initiative' presented to them there by Mbeki, Obasanjo and Wade. The heads set up a Group of Africa Personal Representatives to prepare their definitive response, to be agreed at Kananaskis.

Over the next year the New African Initiative mutated into the New Partnership for Africa's Development (NEPAD).[13] The key concepts underlying the NEPAD were:

- African countries must take responsibility for their own development. They must not blame their problems on others or rely on programmes imposed from outside.
- African countries must set and attain better standards of political governance and economic management. They should hold each other accountable for meeting these standards and set up a system of peer review for this purpose.
- Regional and sub-regional economic integration in Africa should be encouraged and the flight of African capital should be reversed.
- Better domestic performance on these lines should encourage Western countries to offer aid and market access and make Africa more attractive to private foreign investment. This would enable Africa to end its marginalisation in the international economic system.

The G8 Africa Action Plan adopted at Kananaskis welcomed NEPAD and sought to respond to it while leaving its ownership clearly with the Africans. The key concepts of the Action Plan were:

- G8 countries would set up 'enhanced partnerships' with African countries that were seeking to meet the NEPAD standards.
- The NEPAD peer review would influence the G8 in their choice of 'enhanced partners', though each G8 country would make its own assessment.

- The G8 countries had already promised at Monterrey in March 2002 to increase their total aid spending by $12 billion per year over five years.[14] The Africa Action Plan stated that half or more of this new aid money 'could be directed to African nations that govern justly, invest in their own people and promote economic freedom'.

This awkward phrasing on aid for Africa, which attracted criticism from development NGOs, reflected a difference within the G8. The Europeans, with Canada, were eager to commit 50% to deserving African countries. The United States was reluctant. Bush did not want to provide grounds for Congress to attach conditions to the Millennium Challenge Account, the channel for the new aid announced at Monterrey.[15] This issue was discussed up to the last moment and had to be settled at head of government level.

The Africa Action Plan brought together G8 commitments in two political areas (peace and security and strengthening governance) and six economic ones (trade and investment, debt relief, expanding knowledge, improving health, agriculture and water resources). In the mass of detail, it was difficult to distinguish ongoing commitments and new ones. Several areas, such as trade, health and education, overlapped with the 'economic growth' item on the summit agenda and are treated further below. Other salient features were:

- The peace and security chapter was distinct from the others. It dealt mainly with countries that would not meet NEPAD standards; it set deadlines (rare in the rest of the Action Plan) for enabling Africa to deal with its own conflict prevention; and it promised action on named trouble-spots like the Congo and Sudan.
- The other chapters broadly corresponded to the detailed provisions of the NEPAD, but the match was not perfect. The Action Plan noted the Africans' interest in infrastructure, but did not endorse it, nor did it react to NEPAD ideas on debt relief. It was weaker than NEPAD on trade access and environmental issues, but gave more attention to women and civil society.

The African leaders at Kananaskis reacted positively to the Action Plan. Obasanjo said it was not perfect, but it was a good beginning. The G8's support for NEPAD provided enough impetus for it to be adopted by the leaders of all African countries at the meeting chaired by Mbeki on 9 July 2002 that converted the old Organisation for African Unity (OAU) into the African Union.[16]

Yet it was clear at Kananaskis that both sides had a great deal more to do. On the African side, one major weakness of NEPAD was that, although it called for more participatory democracy, it had been handled so far entirely at head of state level. This had provoked widespread criticism from NGOs that it was being imposed from on top without consulting those who would be most affected by it. It was not clear how the actions envisaged by NEPAD could be put into effect at the grassroots. Another uncertainty was whether the peer review process (which was voluntary) would succeed in overcoming the traditional African reluctance to criticise one another or in changing the behaviour of non-cooperative states like Zimbabwe.

On the G8 side, the promise of $6 billion of additional aid per year was attacked by NGOs as imprecise and inadequate.[17] In fact, this would amount to a very large supplement to existing aid levels. Aid spending was constrained by the absorptive capacity of African countries and their institutions. If these countries really improved their standards of governance, additional aid and private finance should be forthcoming. A more serious weakness was the absence of any systematic approach in the follow-up to the Action Plan. Several G8 countries, including the US, UK and Canada, took advantage of the summit to announce additional aid for Africa. But each announcement was uncoordinated and they were difficult to compare with each other. The implication of the Action Plan was that G8 members would each act on their own to set up 'enhanced partnerships', without this being a joint activity. Though there would be follow-up in the G8 context, there was no coordination of the Action Plan elsewhere.

Economic Issues

There was a brief but lively discussion among the G8 heads of developments in their own economies. Like the G7 finance ministers, they expressed confidence in the economic recovery, though there was some anxiety about accounting standards in the light of the recent corporate scandals in the United States. The heads expressed support for Latin American countries, naming Brazil though not Argentina.[18] But most of their economic discussion concerned developing countries, especially poor ones, and therefore overlapped with the Africa Plan. The results were mixed.

Debt Relief and the HIPC

Debt relief was the main topic for the G7 meeting. The heads agreed to fund the shortfall emerging in the World Bank Trust Fund to finance debt relief under the HIPC, up to $1 billion. While the finance ministers had discussed this issue at Halifax, they had not been able to agree a figure, because of US hesitation. Under persuasion from Blair and others, Bush agreed to the $1 billion total.[19] US readiness to accept a precise figure here helped to induce the rest of the G7 to make the commitments sought by the Americans in cleaning up Russian nuclear and chemical weapons and installations. This was an example of the cross-issue deals that were possible at summits but seldom in fact happened.

Trade and the WTO

The G8 heads committed themselves to resist protectionist pressures and to complete the Doha round on time by the end of 2004. In the Africa Plan they amplified this by reaffirming the negotiating mandate on agriculture and promising more capacity-building and market access for poor countries. Canada announced national measures to admit the products of least-developed countries duty-free (except for eggs, poultry and dairy produce), thus matching the EU measures announced in 2001. But otherwise these G8 commitments were no advance on the status quo; they did not correct the unfavourable impact of recent US trade measures nor promise action to accelerate the negotiations in Geneva. This was a disappointment to the Africans.[20] They had hoped for precise G8 commitments to improve access for their agricultural exports, but France was reluctant to go beyond what had been agreed at Doha when launching the new negotiations in the WTO.

Education

The G8 education task-force produced a clear report, stressing the importance of not only getting children into school but keeping them there and of doing more for girls. The report accepted the argument of the World Bank that countries that organised themselves effectively to make good use of aid should receive the aid they needed. The G8 heads endorsed the report and 'agreed to increase significantly our bilateral assistance' for primary education. A similar commitment was contained in the Africa Action Plan and both the US and Canada announced more aid for education. But it was clear that this response would consist of piecemeal national contributions rather than a joint effort. The G8 did not commit themselves to help the 18 countries identified by the World Bank as deserving 'fast-track treatment', 11 of which were in Africa; nor to increase their aid to education on the scale that the World Bank had recommended, so as to meet the Millennium Development Goal in this area.[21]

Health, Including AIDS

The G8 promised in the Africa Action Plan enough resources to eradicate polio. But the leaders ignored the funding pressures on the Global Fund to fight AIDS, tuberculosis and malaria, which they had launched only the year before. The Fund had got under way very fast in committing funds for projects, though it had already received far more bids than it could meet. In April 2002 it had committed $616 million to be spent over the next two years on 58 projects, more than half in Africa. However, if these projects were extended over five years, that would exhaust almost all the Fund's resources, which stood at $2 billion.[22] Thus the Fund already needed replenishment, but the G8 made no move in response to this. Though the US committed another $500 million to fight AIDS, this was outside the Global Fund.[23] When the G8 were reluctant to sustain this instrument that they had launched only a year before, it cast doubt on the reliability of their other pledges.

Sustainable Development

The G8 heads accepted Annan's concept that the meetings at Doha in November 2001 (for trade), Monterrey in March 2002 (for finance) and Johannesburg in August 2002 (the World Summit on Sustainable Development - WSSD) formed an ascending sequence. They incorporated that concept in the Africa Action Plan.

But after the failed preparatory meeting in Bali the preparations for the WSSD were in trouble, partly because of differences between the G8 members.[24] Despite the presence of Mbeki and Annan, the G8 leaders showed no sign of intervening to make the Johannesburg meeting a success, for example by making a joint commitment to take part themselves. Chirac spoke at great length about sustainable development and said publicly that he had urged all his G8 colleagues to attend. But he and Blair were the only heads to indicate they would be there. In the event, the other Europeans and Chrétien also went to Johannesburg, but Bush did not.[25]

Assessment of the Kananaskis Summit

The organisation of the Kananaskis summit was handled skilfully by the Canadians. They worked to ensure good continuity in the summit process, so that issues launched at Genoa were properly followed up. They focused on their chosen agenda, delegating other issues to subsidiary ministerial groups. They simplified the process at the summit itself, so that the heads could concentrate on the key issues and strike deals where needed. Chirac said that he intended to follow the Canadian model in 2003.

Kananaskis did what G8 summits were intended to do. The heads acted to resolve issues that had not been settled at lower levels, in addition to giving their authority to work prepared by their officials. The direct intervention of the heads could be seen in:

- The decision on Russia hosting a summit in 2006 and on the summit sequence;
- The negotiation of the programme to clean up nuclear and chemical material in the former USSR;
- The figure of $1 billion to replenish the HIPC Trust Fund;
- The financial commitment to underpin the Africa Action Plan.

The attacks of 11 September 2001 inevitably brought terrorism onto the summit agenda, so that the political content of Kananaskis was much greater than Okinawa or Genoa. Kananaskis produced two agreements in this area, the one on weapons of mass destruction being of great importance and demonstrating the benefits of having the Russians in this forum. But terrorism was accommodated without undermining the economic objectives of the summit and these were not even upset by the last-minute attention to the Middle East.

Kananaskis completed an entire summit sequence, starting in Lyon 1996, in which the G8 had constantly returned to problems of development. Little attention was given in 2002 to other economic issues, such as the financial system. But there was a growing risk that the G8 summit could lose its capacity to intervene in these subjects or could neglect danger signals, as happened at Denver in 1997 before the outbreak of the Asian financial crisis.

However, despite the new attention to terrorism, the summits were still concerned with managing the advance of globalisation. The most intractable problem here was that poor countries could miss all the potential benefits of globalisation and thus fall further behind. Precisely because it was so intractable, this problem of enabling poor countries to benefit from globalisation had become lodged with the G8. Despite a series of initiatives in debt relief, IT and infectious diseases, the G8 found this a Sisyphean task. Much of the economic agenda at Kananaskis, apart from Africa, covered areas where G8 initiatives, after initial progress, showed signs of running out of steam, either because of inadequate resources (like education and health) or because they met domestic resistance (like trade access).

The combination of the Africa Action Plan with the NEPAD was the latest initiative in this field. Having launched the process at Genoa on their own personal decision, without advance preparation, the G8 heads now had to make good their promises. The work on Africa revealed some of the strengths of the G8 process: its ability to launch innovative initiatives, to embrace a wide range of different issues and to combine political and economic actions. But both in Africa and the G8 the process only came together at the summit, not at lower levels. There was no clear mechanism for coordination of G8 action that would be robust enough to survive the inevitable setbacks on the African side. The G8 and NEPAD combination achieved lift-off at Kananaskis, but it was not securely in orbit.

It was therefore welcome that Chirac, as the next summit host, said that Africa would still have the top priority at Evian in June 2003. The G8 Africa Group was retained in being and was intended to serve as a tracking mechanism in following up the Action Plan. Continued G8 summit attention to Africa could help to provide impetus to NEPAD and its peer review mechanism. But the coming year could also be used to improve the coordination of G8 and wider Western policy towards Africa at levels below the summit.

From the outset the summits were intended to promote a system of collective management involving North America, Europe and Japan, with shared responsibilities. Kananaskis could be seen as a test of how far Bush was prepared to participate in multilateral arrangements and how far he was driven by a unilateralist agenda determined by domestic political interests. In the international economic field the message up till then had been mixed. On the credit side the US showed enough flexibility to ensure the Doha round was started and launched a surprising new commitment on increasing aid at Monterrey. But domestic pressures prompted unhelpful unilateral actions on the Kyoto Protocol, steel tariffs and the new farm bill.

In the event, the summit provided some useful guidance on how Bush operated. Though others took the first initiative on Africa, Bush clearly endorsed the high priority given to Africa and did not try to sidetrack it. He was committed to the general approach of the Action Plan and NEPAD and ready to allocate new funds to African programmes. But his Africa policy was his own, looking forward to his visit there in 2003, and he was reluctant to coordinate with others.[26] In the discussion of other economic issues, Bush showed no sign of flexibility on trade or sustainable development, but it was not clear that he was put under pressure. Over weapons of mass destruction, an issue that was now driven by the terrorism agenda, he was looking to his G8 colleagues to support something that the US was doing already and he formed an alliance with Putin for the purpose. So the conclusion was that Bush would promote collective action, not only as part of the terrorism agenda but also in other areas. But within that collective action he would decide what the United States did without much reference to what others were doing.

Conclusion

In terms of the criteria, the Kananaskis summit showed *leadership,* in that it reached agreements that were not attainable at lower levels, and was innovative in several aspects of summit format. It was *effective* in reconciling domestic and international pressures over Africa, debt relief and the Global Partnership, though not in other economic subjects. Good *solidarity* was achieved on most issues, except perhaps the Middle East. The results on Africa were *durable,* despite the difficulties, though many NGOs did not find them *acceptable*. Finally there was broad *consistency* between political and economic issues, though there were some signs of inconsistency within the Africa programme.

Kananaskis would be remembered as a one of the most successful G8 summits. It was well-prepared and well-organised, so that the heads could make their mark. It escaped the tensions of Genoa the year before. The heads exerted themselves to conclude two far-reaching agreements associated with substantial spending commitments over many years ahead. The G8 Africa Plan, in its link with NEPAD, could be the instrument of historic change - but only, as Annan said, if both the G8 and the Africans did all that they had promised to do.[27] Finally, Kananaskis marked a new direction in summit activity in its focus on those political and economic issues, often treated in combination, that advanced the anti-terrorist agenda. Thus the summit series that began at Birmingham and focused on globalisation was now over. A new series, focused on terrorism and the roots of terrorism, began at Kananaskis and would persist at least till Gleneagles in 2005.

Notes

1 Quoted in Q. Peel, 'Keeping the Posse Together', *Financial Times,* 29 October 2001. Zoellick also made a link between trade liberalisation and fighting terrorism - see E. Alden and M. Mann, 'Washington Signals Push on Free Trade', *Financial Times,* 25 September 2001.

2 This account is closely based on Bayne 2003a.

3 For an evaluation of the security operation, see several articles in *Calgary Herald,* 28 June 2002. The Herald's estimate of the cost is in Canadian dollars, C$300-400 million.

4 See contrasting articles from before and after the terrorist attacks by J. Harding, 'Globalisation's Children Strike Back' and 'Clamour Against Globalisation Stilled', *Financial Times,* 11 September and 10 October 2001.

5 P. Wells, 'Anti-G8 Group Shouts Intolerance', *Calgary Herald,* 26 June 2002. The idea of civil society representing 6 billion – i.e. the rest of the world - started at Genoa. See della Porta and Reiter 2002, p. 121.

6 The idea that IDA should give more grants had been launched by Bush just before the Genoa summit - see Chapter 7 above. The initial reaction from other G7 members was sceptical, but a year's intense negotiation had produced a reasonable compromise. See A. Beattie, 'US and Europe Set to Agree Aid Compromise' and 'G7 Ties Up Some Cash for Indebted Nations', *Financial Times,* 10 and 17 June 2002.

7 The heads did not actively discuss action against terrorist finance, though this was running into problems. See J. Burns, 'Concern over Terror Fund Tracking', *Financial Times,* 10 June 2002, reporting the anxiety of the FATF.

8 See 'The G8 and Proliferation - Getting What You Pay For' *The Economist,* 29 June 2002.

9 Further background on this issue is available on the website of the Strengthening the Global Partnership Project - www.sgpproject.org. On follow-up action, see A. Jack, 'Russian Nuclear Rubbish Tip Challenges Clean-up Experts', *Financial Times,* 19 November 2002.

10 See 'George Bush's Plan for Peace', *The Economist,* 29 June 2002. This eventually led on to the preparation of the 'Road Map', see 'Floundering without a Map', *The Economist,* 21 December 2002.

11 R. Wolffe and others, 'Europeans to Seek Bush Change of Heart', *Financial Times,* 27 June 2002.

12 The increase in the Afghan opium harvest after the removal of the Taliban was causing great concern. See J. Burns, 'Flood of Heroin Expected as Eradication Falters', *Financial Times,* 7 May 2002.

13 For a pre-summit view on NEPAD, see 'Africa's Economies - an African Cure', *The Economist,* 22 June 2002. Good scholarly analyses of NEPAD and its genesis are in De Waal 2002 and Van der Westhuizen 2003.

14 In fact this total included extra money from all EU member states, while Japan's aid was contracting. See Chapter 8 above, with notes 33 and 34.

15 In fact, it soon appeared that African countries would be major beneficiaries of the Millennium Challenge Account. See J. Lamont, 'Africa Set to Benefit in $5bn US Plan to Reward Good Governance', *Financial Times,* 11 December 2002.

16 C. Hoyos and N. Degli Innocenti, 'Africa Launches a Union to Fight War and Poverty', *Financial Times,* 10 July 2002.

17 An Oxfam spokesman described it as "peanuts", which was widely reported - see C. Adams and others, 'G8's Africa Rescue Plan "Peanuts", Say Aid Agencies', *Financial Times,* 27 June 2002. This was partly due to confusion with the figure of $64 billion quoted as the total financing needs of NEPAD. Michel Camdessus, the French APR, had made clear earlier that a massive new fund was not on offer - J. Lamont and A. Beattie, 'G8 Cannot Provide Immediate Backing for New African Fund', *Financial Times,* 16 February 2002.

18 Brazil had drawn $10 billion from the IMF on 14 June and needed a new $30 billion rescue in August, R. Lapper and R. Colitt, 'Brazil to Use IMF's $10bn Credit Line to Defend Currency' and C. Giles, 'Markets Rise as $30bn Rescue Package for Brazil is Unveiled', *Financial Times,* 14 June and 9 August 2002. Argentina had defaulted on its $155 billion debt at the end of 2001, see Chapter 7, note 12.

19 C. Adams, 'UK Leads Way on $1bn Debt Relief', *Financial Times,* 27 June 2002.

20 The South African finance minister attacked US Treasury Secretary Paul O'Neill over trade policy during his visit to Africa before Kananaskis. See A. Beattie, and J. Lamont, 'US Farm Bill Arouses African Fury', *Financial Times,* 24 May 2002.
21 See Chapter 8 above, with notes 50-52.
22 See Chapter 8 above, with notes 43-45 and reports on the Global Fund's website, www.theglobalfund.org.
23 A. Beattie, 'US Plans to Boost AIDS Campaign', *Financial Times,* 20 June 2002.
24 C. Hoyos and V. Houlder, 'Plans for UN Meeting Face Agenda Crisis', *Financial Times,* 10 June 2002.
25 N. Dunne, 'Bush Absence Dashes Greens' Hopes', *Financial Times,* 19 August 2002.
26 Bush's visit, originally planned for January 2003, was delayed by the Iraq crisis. It finally took place in July, after the Evian G8 summit.
27 Annan is quoted in R. Cornwell, 'Western Powers pledge £4bn for Africa', *Independent,* 28 June 2002.

Chapter 10

Reconciliation: Evian 2003

The political environment for the G8 summit deteriorated sharply over the year following Kananaskis. The war in Iraq split the G8 members right down the middle. Britain, Italy and Japan supported the American strategy; France, Germany, Russia and Canada opposed it. This divided not only the G8 but also its European members, raising anxieties about the future of the transatlantic relationship and the political cohesion of the European Union. Over several months in early 2003, Bush had no direct contacts with Chirac or Schroeder.[1]

The Evian Summit was successful in producing a truce among the heads, restoring personal contact between them and demonstrating revived unity. Fortunately, the fighting in Iraq was over well before the summit. Agreement had been reached in the UN Security Council on Resolution 1483, which allowed attention to shift to less controversial issues concerned with rebuilding the country.[2] But the heads themselves struck few solid agreements to give depth to this reconciliation. This was in spite the mass of summit documents, prepared in advance, which departed from the simpler format in force since the Birmingham summit of 1998. However, Evian was innovative in extending the outreach of the summit, as the heads had two sessions with non-G8 leaders.

Preparations for Evian

Evian was Chirac's second chance to preside over a summit, since he had hosted the 1996 summit in Lyon, which had first identified development as a G7 priority. He gave a lot of personal attention to the summit and his aims were ambitious. In many respects, the summit organisation worked well. The French maintained the Canadians' procedural innovations from 2002 and adapted them as follows:

- The summit was held in the Hotel Royal and the Ermitage Hotel in Evian, which were within the same landscaped grounds. G8 delegations could move freely between the two. The media centre was at Publier, 3 miles (5 km) from Evian and the press were accommodated in ski resorts, about 30 miles (50 km) away. Non-G8 leaders were lodged at Lausanne across Lake Geneva.
- The Evian region was protected by elaborate security, involving up to 15,000 police and troops. The French prevented any demonstrations in the area, so that the main protest activity of this kind took place in Switzerland. A march on 1 June, attracting up to 100,000 people, was peaceful. But there was destructive rioting over several days in Geneva and Lausanne. The Swiss police found this hard to control and German reinforcements had to be used. Chirac indicated that France would pay compensation for damage done.[3]

- The French provided facilities for an 'alternative summit' of civil society organisations at Annemasse - 20 miles (30km) away from the action at Evian. The meeting produced a range of recommendations, all critical of the G8 (and NEPAD). Chirac commended this activity in public, but offered no reaction of substance.

Chirac's ambitious approach was less successful in the policy preparations. In contrast to Genoa and Kananaskis, Chirac chose a very broad agenda for Evian. This was grouped under four themes - solidarity, responsibility, security and democracy - that could embrace almost anything. Just before the summit, weaker prospects for growth, together with the fall of the dollar against the euro, led Chirac to declare that the summit should focus on restoring confidence in the world economy.[4] The G8 Africa Group continued work chaired by Michel Camdessus (former Managing Director of the IMF), who insisted on keeping it distinct from the main sherpa process. The preparations thus threw up a very wide range of topics. In consequence, the documentation issued from Evian was copious. In addition to the chair's summary, 16 G8 declarations, action plans and reports were issued. This added up to 68 pages of documents, more than any other previous summit.

In the run-up to the summit, there were meetings of G8 environment ministers, development ministers (following a precedent set by Canada in September 2002) and ministers of interior and justice (chiefly on terrorism issues). These meetings mainly pursued their own agenda, independent of the summit. The G8 finance ministers (including Russia for the first time) met in Deauville on 17 May. The conclusions on growth and exchange rates were insubstantial. There was no advance on the debt relief programme for heavily indebted poor countries (HIPCs). The ministers issued instead a document on procedures for handling middle-income debtors through the Paris Club. A second document focused on improving aid quality, giving prominence to issues of governance stressed by the United States. G8 foreign ministers met in Paris on 22-23 May and covered conflict prevention and regional issues. The UN Security Council had just adopted Resolution 1483 and this provided the basis for consensus on Iraq, with G8 ministers themselves adding little.

The Evian Summit, 1-3 June 2003

Exceptionally, the same group of G8 leaders gathered at Evian on 1 June as had met at Genoa in 2001 and Kananaskis in 2002 (except for Konstantine Simitis for the Greek EU presidency). After the discord on Iraq, everyone was concerned to put the past behind them for the duration of the summit and looked forward to future co-operation. They had all met informally the day before at the tercentenary celebrations in St Petersburg. The process of personal reconciliation had begun there, at a meeting between Bush and Putin where they declared their friendship was strengthened by recent troubles.[5] At a bilateral Bush-Chirac meeting in Evian, the body language looked good and Chirac publicly refused to take offence because Bush left the summit early for meetings in the Middle East. Chirac also took opportunities to stress his common ideas with Blair, for example on Africa. Schroeder (who arrived late), Koizumi, Berlusconi and Chrétien (at his last G8 summit) were less prominent. But supporters and opponents of the war in Iraq all seemed to mingle and no one appeared discontented or left out.[6]

Programme and Outreach

There was no G7 meeting at Evian. For the first time, Putin was admitted from the start. The first day (1 June) was occupied with two major outreach events: a working lunch and meeting with a large non-G8 group, followed by a working dinner with Africans only. The G8 proper began on 2 June with a morning session on economic issues. Lunch was devoted to security issues, especially terrorism, and regional problems. The afternoon session (after Bush had left) covered sustainable development. There was a free debate over dinner, with no agenda. On 3 June there was a brief session to agree on the chair's summary.

The first outreach event was a major innovation. The G8 heads met a group of leaders from 11 developing countries: China, India, Brazil, Mexico, Malaysia and Saudi Arabia as major players in the international system; Nigeria, South Africa, Algeria, Senegal and Egypt, as the NEPAD Steering Committee. Switzerland was present, as a reward for its close cooperation in summit organisation; Morocco was invited but did not attend. The heads of the UN, IMF, World Bank and WTO were also there.

By prior agreement, no statement was issued from this meeting; Chirac's comments to the press focused on the informal style rather than the content. Those invited were clearly pleased to be there. Some, especially Hu Jintao of China, took the opportunity for bilateral contacts; others, like Luiz Inácio Lula da Silva of Brazil, spoke at length to the assembled media. But the main interest was in whether such an outreach meeting should become a regular feature of G8 summits. Chirac clearly believed that it should and claimed Blair (summit host in 2005) shared his view. But he was careful not to commit Bush, the host in 2004.

Africa

A more substantive meeting followed between the G8 and the Africans (less Hosni Mubarak of Egypt, who had left to prepare to receive Bush on 4 June). This was in fact the fourth time the G8 had met these African leaders, going back to Okinawa. The meeting considered a solid, 20-page report from the G8 Africa Group on the implementation of the Africa Action Plan agreed to in 2002. Individual G8 members, including the EU, had also published their own reports of measures they had taken.

The four Africans - Obasanjo, Mbeki, Wade and Bouteflika - jointly briefed the press after the meeting. The main points to emerge were:

- The Africans insisted on their ownership of the New Partnership for Africa's Development (NEPAD) and on their own responsibilities. They sharply rejected criticism that they had not consulted civil society. They drew attention to agreement on the African Peer Review Mechanism - 15 African countries had undertaken to accept its disciplines.[7]
- They were encouraged by the actions taken by the G8 to increase help for Africa, singling out the American programme on AIDS and the British proposal for an International Financing Facility. They also drew comfort from the points made earlier by other non-G8 leaders, such as Lula of Brazil. Obasanjo said: 'On the whole we are satisfied with the progress made, but we should continue to build on this'.
- The G8 Implementation Report confirmed a strong increase in aid commitments for Africa over the last year by most of the G8.[8] But the record was of piecemeal actions, with little coordination, making comparisons difficult.
- A major advance was the G8/Africa Peace Support Plan. This built on the Africa Action Plan and laid out a programme for creating African capacity to intervene by 2010, with G8 support. Much of the rest of the Implementation Report described sample projects, without making clear which were new and which ongoing.

The Africans were clearly discontented by the lack of progress on debt relief, for both low- and middle-income countries, and on removing agricultural subsidies and other trade barriers. The main discussion on AIDS took place with the Africans also. These three issues are discussed further below.

The conclusion that emerged at Evian was that NEPAD was moving forward, although slowly. A nucleus of serious participants was coming together, who could provide an example to others. The G8 effort still seemed poorly co-ordinated, but there were signs of a more coherent approach based on support for good governance and transparency, which were themes that motivated the Americans. For the future, it was decided that the G8 would extend cooperation beyond the Africa Personal Representatives (APRs) to other OECD countries and the IMF and World Bank. There would be a further report to the G8 heads by 2005 at the latest. The Africans clearly hoped the G8 would continue to give their continent high priority. Blair and Schroeder indicated that they were ready to invite African leaders to the summits they expected to host in 2005 and 2007 respectively. The Americans made no commitment for 2004, even though Bush carried out his postponed African visit in July, shortly after Evian.[9]

Economic Issues

In the first session of the G8 proper, the leaders had a lively exchange on growth prospects, with sharing of experience on structural reforms. This exchange was reflected in optimistic language in the chair's summary about the revival of growth in 2003. But while Chirac called this a message of confidence, in fact the G8 leaders did nothing themselves to affect growth. Exchange rates were not mentioned in the chair's summary; Chirac answered questions in public with the gnomic comment that 'each of us considers exchange rate stability is important to support growth'.[10] After this session, the G8 issued three declarations discussed below: Co-operative G8 Action on Trade; Fostering Growth and Promoting a Responsible Market Economy; and Fighting Corruption and Improving Transparency.

Trade

The trade document was a disappointment. It contained general commitments to promote a productive WTO ministerial meeting at Cancun in September and to conclude the negotiations on the Doha Development Agenda successfully and on time. There was useful emphasis on capacity-building. But there was no advance on the main contested items:

- Agricultural trade did not attract special treatment, either here or in the African documents, despite the strong concern expressed by the Africans themselves. Earlier in 2003, Chirac had floated ideas on suspending all forms of support for agricultural exports.[11] But nothing survived of these proposals, except some awkward language on trade preferences. Chirac explained publicly that they had met resistance from the Americans, who were prepared to see action on EU measures, but not on their own.
- The problem of access to medicines was recognised, but not resolved. Both the trade document and the health paper issued later (see below) simply urged that the matter be settled before Cancun.

Blair and Chirac told the press that everyone realised that hard decisions would be needed before Cancun. But these decisions were not taken at Evian.[12]

Responsible Market Economy, Corruption and Transparency

The other two economic documents were linked and were a fusion of French, American and British ideas. These reflected the G8's aim to restore confidence and improve economic performance worldwide. They sought to encourage:

- Better corporate governance and sound regulation, in response to financial and other business scandals;
- Voluntary moves by firms in social responsibility;
- Stronger implementation of the OECD's Bribery Convention;
- Action in the UN and the Financial Action Task Force (FATF) against corruption, money-laundering and other financial abuses;
- Transparency in financial management in developing countries;
- A first move towards greater transparency in the management of extractive industries (hydrocarbons and mining).

These proposals depended on voluntary co-operation and largely relied on existing institutions. The advance was not in the ideas themselves (only the last was really new) but in having agreed G8 positions on them.[13]

Political Issues

Terrorism and Non-Proliferation

The lunch-time discussion focused on terrorism and on non-proliferation of weapons of mass destruction (WMD), with much attention to North Korea and Iran.[14] The main political document was the Declaration on Non-proliferation of WMD. This confirmed G8 commitments to use the main treaties and international instruments, as well as 'if necessary other measures in accordance with international law'. The declaration conveyed a stern message to North Korea on dismantling any nuclear weapons programme and a more nuanced request to Iran to comply with International Atomic Energy Agency (IAEA) rules. Putin undertook not to help Iran build up nuclear weapons capacity.[15]

Six more specific documents were issued, comprising:

- *Action Plan on Building Capacity to Combat Terrorism* This promised co-ordinated assistance from the G8 to countries needing help in denying support for terrorists, in bringing terrorists to justice and in improving anti-terrorist defences. It created a Counter-Terrorism Action Group (CTAG) to work closely with the UN. However, it did not indicate the levels of aid that might be available.
- *Action Plan on Transport Security* This expanded on the measures adopted in 2002, with special attention to the illegal use of hand-held missile systems (MANPADS).
- *Statement and Supporting Action Plan on Securing Radioactive Sources* These documents focused on the psychological impact of a terrorist attack using radioactive material stolen, from example, from hospitals. They advocated a range of actions in support of current IAEA programmes.
- *Action Plan on the Global Partnership and Associated Officials' Report* This set out at length the progress since the agreement reached at Kananaskis in 2002 to clean up nuclear and chemical weapons and other materials in Russia. While the promised funds were being committed, more needed to be done to facilitate projects on the ground.[16]

Some parts of this extensive documentation were more valuable than others. The commitment to capacity-building was a new initiative, which merited summit attention. But the documents on transport security and the Global Partnership were 'work in progress', following up last year's agreements. The plan on radioactive sources mainly backed up measures already adopted in the IAEA. All this activity stemmed from US initiatives. The Americans were using the G8 process to drive their non-proliferation agenda across various fronts, intended to guard against any possible terrorist threats on the model of 11 September 2001. In general, the rest of the G8 was content to follow the US lead.

On his way to Evian, Bush had made a speech in Cracow on 30 May, proposing that states should take powers to search ships and aircraft suspected of carrying WMD. This appeared to lie behind the phrase 'if necessary other measures in accordance with international law' in the main political declaration. No agreement was reached on this at Evian. But discussion between the G8 and others continued afterwards, leading to agreement on the Proliferation Security Initiative (PSI).[17]

Regional Issues

These were covered concisely in the chair's summary. Iraq itself was barely discussed, since no one wanted to disturb the delicate balance of UN Security Council Resolution 1483. On the Middle East, the rest of the G8 welcomed Bush's move to become personally involved in the peace process, based on the 'Road Map'.[18] The G8 also discussed economic support for the peace process and policy towards Syria. There was renewed concern over drug trafficking from Afghanistan, a promise of help to Algeria after its earthquake, and a strong message to Zimbabwe on human rights.[19]

Sustainable Development

The afternoon session on 2 June went over some issues already discussed with non-G8 countries, as well as opening up some new ones. Not many clues emerged on how the discussion went among the heads themselves. But five more action plans were issued, covering health, water, famine, science and technology for sustainable development, and marine environment and tanker safety. Debt and aid were covered in the chair's summary.

Health

As part of his 2003 State of the Union address, Bush had announced an Emergency Plan for AIDS, increasing American AIDS-related assistance by two-thirds to $15 billion over five years.[20] At Evian Bush challenged the rest of the G8 to match his pledge of $1 billion for the Global Fund to fight AIDS, Tuberculosis and Malaria (since the US contribution could not exceed one third of the total). The Europeans indicated readiness to see the EU put up another $1 billion, subject to confirmation at the next European Council. This would leave a third $1 billion to find from other sources. The chair's summary and the action plan contained no specific pledges, but confirmed support for the Global Fund and the pledging conference due in Paris in July. These moves were widely applauded. But it later emerged that Bush's $1 billion for the Global Fund was spread over five years. Despite urging from Chirac and Blair, the EU declined to commit another $1 billion.[21]

The passage on access to medicines repeated the declaration on trade in directing G8 ministers and officials urgently to establish a multilateral solution before the WTO Cancun meeting. There was rather weak language on research into diseases affecting developing countries, which contrasted with a reference to the additional G8 pledges of US$500 million to eradicate polio made since Kananaskis. The passage on Severe Acute Respiratory Syndrome (SARS) stressed the merits of international cooperation in checking the disease.

Water

This topic was given high priority by Chirac in his summit objectives and he had sent a personal message to the meeting of the third World Water Forum in Kyoto.[22] But the action plan adopted at Evian seemed rather insubstantial. The G8 committed themselves to 'assisting as a priority' countries that paid attention to clean water policy and to 'give high priority in official development aid allocation to sound water and sanitation projects'. But no figures were given, nor even a promise to increase aid levels. Unlike the American AIDS commitments, the European Commission's proposed 1 billion euro Water Fund was not used to lever more commitments of finance from others.[23]

Famine

This subject was a priority objective for the United States, but here again the action plan lacked bite. Most of it covered familiar issues of emergency relief; long-term food security was given briefer treatment. The plan noted past spending (over $3 billion in 2002 for emergency aid and long-term assistance alike). But the most substantial commitment for the future (which was also made in the Africa Plan Implementation document) was a pledge to reverse the decline in official aid for agriculture.

Financing for Development

The chair's summary instructed the finance ministers to do more work on increased resources, including the new International Finance Facility proposed by the UK.[24]

Debt Relief

The passages on debt in the Africa Plan Implementation Report and in the chair's summary contained little comfort for the Africans concerned about both low-income and middle-income debt. For the latter, the leaders confirmed the decisions taken by their finance ministers on the Paris Club. On HIPC debt, a long paragraph in the summary confirmed that the G8 members had met their Kananaskis pledge to replenish the World Bank Trust Fund but offered nothing more. The Africa document only noted where G8 members had carried out the promises of 100% debt relief they had made back in 2000.

Science and Technology for Sustainable Development

The action plan promised co-operation in global observation, in energy technologies (including renewable energy) and in agriculture and biodiversity. The proposed activities mainly relied on existing programmes and institutions and sought to involve developing countries. But this document managed to produce a common G8 position on environment and climate change issues despite the US withdrawal from the Kyoto Protocol. The aim was to establish the use of new technologies as the solution to the challenge of climate change over the long term.

Marine Environment and Tanker Safety

The first part of this action plan promoted a range of measures to preserve and manage fisheries and to protect the oceans, mainly following up commitments made at the WSSD in August 2002. The second part advocated actions stimulated by the sinking of the *Prestige* off the coast of Spain earlier in the year: faster phasing out of single hulled tankers, measures to prevent them transporting heavy-grade oil and guidelines on ports of refuge. Much of the follow-up on both points would take place in the Food and Agriculture Organization (FAO), the United Nations Environment Programme (UNEP) and the International Maritime Organization (IMO).

These two action plans represented the first time the G8 had succeeded in reaching agreement on any environmental topics for several years. As such, it was a welcome advance, on which more could be built in future. But this result was only achieved by avoiding controversial issues, such as European resistance to GMOs and the US absence from the Kyoto Protocol on climate change and the Biodiversity Convention. (The chair's summary noted, however, that those G8 members that had ratified Kyoto wanted to see it enter into force - which was meant to put pressure on Russia.)

Assessment of the Evian Summit

Canadian Prime Minister Chrétien, when asked to name the single best thing that came out of Evian, said: 'It was a good meeting - it could have been a disaster!' Evian was timely as an occasion for reconciliation among the leaders and successfully served this purpose. From Evian onwards, all the G8 heads were talking to each other again. But Evian was a truce, rather than a lasting peace, and there were plenty of fundamental differences, especially between Chirac and Bush, which could cause tension over the months ahead. At his final press conference, after Bush had left, Chirac repeated in public points he had made in the meetings about the illegality of the war in Iraq, adding that 'it is easy to make war alone; it is less easy to make peace alone'.[25]

Once the Iraq factor was discounted, Evian showed the same pattern of subject-matter that had emerged in the summits of the 2000s. In short:

- The capacity of the G8 heads to influence mainstream economic issues was dwindling. The heads could have a worthwhile discussion among themselves, as they did at Evian. But they did not really make a difference - power rested with the finance ministers. Evian also made a weak contribution in trade, like all the G8 summits except Genoa.
- The economic agenda was now dominated by development issues, which read across into the dialogue with the Africans. Evian, like previous summits, made some innovations here. But once again G8 decisions were attacked by articulate and experienced NGOs, such as Oxfam and Médecins Sans Frontières, as being inadequate responses to the problems and not living up to earlier pledges.
- The political agenda of items stimulated by the terrorist attacks of 11 September 2001 continued to grow. In fact, it made good sense to use the G8 to co-ordinate the fight against terrorism on its widest definition. This would often involve issues that combined political and economic elements, such as Africa and anti-terrorist capacity-building, which the heads of government were best able to handle.

Part of the purpose of G8 summits was to facilitate direct exchange among the leaders. But another part was reaching agreements among them that could not be reached elsewhere, to show that they had used their meeting well. Despite the record volume of documentation, there were very few agreements at Evian that required the intervention or attention of the heads. The only decisions that met this criterion were:

- The replenishment of the Global Fund, with $1 billion from the EU to match the $1 billion from the US - but this was undermined when it emerged that the American pledge was spread over five years;
- The continued commitment to Africa, to ensure the G8/NEPAD momentum was maintained;
- The joint language on non-proliferation, especially that aimed at North Korea and Iran;
- The commitment to help countries build up anti-terrorist capacity.

In other areas the leaders endorsed conclusions prepared by their officials, but they added nothing of their own and their authority, although useful, was not essential to further movement. Some topics, like water and famine, were new to the summit, but the results were insubstantial. Others produced results that were worth having, but did not merit the attention of the heads. In short, Evian was not a summit that scored very high in advancing co-operation that would not otherwise have taken place.

The immediate impact of Evian was also muffled by the mass of documentation, where it was always difficult to distinguish new commitments from ongoing ones. The broad agenda and voluminous paperwork were departures from the practice, in force since 1998, of limiting the topics and shortening the papers, so that the heads themselves could concentrate on the key issues. The experience of Evian suggested that the Americans would be well advised to return to the Birmingham model in 2004.

Another procedural aspect of Evian was more constructive - the involvement of leading non-G8 countries, including China, India, Brazil and Mexico for the first time. The advance of globalisation was making it impossible for the G8 to maintain their closed circle, for all its advantages of efficiency and informality. They needed to engage other leading players in the international system. This element of the Evian model could work well in future years, with the G8 inviting the four major countries given above, plus a shifting choice of others, to an unscripted meeting either before or after the main G8. This would prevent the G8 being trapped in a standard list of non-G8 guests, who might not all be suitable every year. The continued link with Africa was still justified. Africa was the most deprived continent; its problems combined politics and economics; and NEPAD offered the best hope of revival for years, firmly rooted in African initiative. But the G8/NEPAD link needed better co-ordination of effort at the level below heads of government.

Conclusion

In terms of the criteria, Evian showed *leadership* in promoting some valuable procedural advances. But the substantive results, though copious in quantity, were weak in quality and often did not deserve the attention of the heads. There were some *durable* moves in non-proliferation, but the decision on the Global Fund soon unravelled. The attention given to Africa was maintained, which was welcome to the African leaders, but Evian was no more *acceptable* to outside opinion than its predecessors. There was also a lack of *consistency* between the summit's ambitious aims and the actual results achieved, while inconsistencies persisted within the Africa programme.

Yet the Evian summit served its essential purpose of reconciliation among the G8 leaders. In that context it proved *effective* and restored *solidarity*. Domestic opinion in many G8 countries was very hostile to the war in Iraq - and this included the countries allied to the US, as well as those that opposed American policy. Nevertheless, all the heads recognised the international imperative of the G8 working together better. There would still be many occasions in future when they would disagree over policy towards Iraq, for example over reconstruction or debt relief. But after Evian it was clear that the G8 members were back on course in pursuing their goal of collective management of the international system, in selected economic and political issues.

Notes

1 When Chirac spoke by telephone to Bush on 16 April, after the fall of Baghdad, it was their first direct contact since 7 February. During March it was suggested that when

Bush came to the Evian summit, he would stay in Geneva, not on French soil. But Chirac promised the summit would not be a shouting match. See R. Graham, 'French Leader Adopts an Olympian Tone' and P. Spiegel and R. Graham, 'Chirac Talks to Bush but Chilly Relations Remain', *Financial Times,* 19 March and 16 April 2003.

2 The resolution was adopted on 22 May, a week ahead of the summit. M. Turner and others, 'Iraq Sanctions End as UN Accepts Coalition Control', *Financial Times,* 23 May 2003, gives the main elements.

3 F. Williams, 'Geneva Clears Up After Protests as France Pressed to Foot Bill', *Financial Times,* 3 June 2003.

4 A. Gowers and R. Graham, 'Giscard Calls on Summit to Forget Iraq War Split', reporting Giscard's interview with *Financial Times*, 26 May 2003.

5 J. Harding and A. Jack, 'Leaders' Differences Fail to Stem Flood of Affection', *Financial Times*, 2 June 2003.

6 However, press reports noted that Bush and Schroeder never seemed to speak to each other. See R. Graham and J. Harding, 'US and French Presidents Try to Heal Split over Iraq War' (the Bush/Chirac bilateral) and J. Harding, 'Body Language Exposed Tensions Behind the Words', *Financial Times*, 2 and 4 June 2003.

7 The 15 countries that had signed up by 31 May 2003 were: Algeria, Burkina Faso, Cameroon, Congo (Republic of), Ethiopia, Gabon, Ghana, Kenya, Mali, Mozambique, Nigeria, Rwanda, Senegal, South Africa, Uganda.

8 Despite these efforts, there was continuing evidence of economic hardship in Africa, see 'Cursed, Twice Over' (hunger and AIDS), *The Economist*, 15 February 2003 and B. Stocking (Oxfam director), 'Africa's Suffering Endangers Everyone Else', *Financial Times*, 18 February 2003.

9 See 'America and Africa' and 'George Bush Visits Africa', *The Economist,* 5 and 12 July 2003. Before his visit, the UNDP issued a report showing how African countries were missing the Millennium Development Goals, M. Turner, 'African Nations "Off-Track" in Reducing Poverty', *Financial Times,* 9 July 2003.

10 Chirac is quoted in R. Graham, 'G8 Vague on Timing of Recovery', *Financial Times,* 4 June 2003.

11 Chirac launched his idea, without advance warning, at a Franco-African summit. It was later commended by Lamy. See J. Johnson and others, 'Surprise at Chirac's Farm Trade About-Turn' and G. de Jonquières and T. Buck, 'Chirac Plan on Farm Subsidies Hailed by Lamy', *Financial Times,* 22 and 26 February 2003.

12 The EU reached agreement on CAP reform by the end of June, while the US accepted a deal on access to medicines shortly before Cancun; see T. Buck, 'EU Farm Deal Lifts Trade Talks Hopes' and F. Williams, 'WTO Deal on Cheap Drugs Ends Months of Wrangling', *Financial Times,* 27 June and 28 August 2003. But both decisions were long overdue and their lateness hindered the preparations for Cancun.

13 The last idea, the Extractive Industries Transparency Initiative, was beginning to gather support in Africa. See 'Oil and Development', *The Economist,* 25 May and C. Hoyos, 'Africans to disclose Details of Oil Deals', *Financial Times,* 19 June 2003.

14 Concerns about North Korea's and Iran's nuclear programmes are analysed in 'Iran's Nuclear Plans' and 'Diplomacy Needs Backing' (North Korea), *The Economist,* 1 March and 12 April 2003.

15 J. Blitz, 'Summit Leaders Draw Together Over WMD', *Financial Times,* 3 June 2003.

16 See 'Taking Nunn-Lugar Global', *The Economist,* 25 January 2003.

17 See J. Harding and others, 'Allied Move to Curb WMD Poses New Test', *Financial Times,* 2 June and 'George Bush's Travels', *The Economist,* 7 June 2003. By September the PSI had 11 active members, including France and Germany, and the Americans were

pressing Russia and China - see 'Counter-Proliferation', *The Economist,* 20 September 2003.

18 Bush went direct to the Middle East from Evian, to promote the 'Road Map'. See J. Harding, 'Bush Steps up Involvement in Search for Peace', *Financial Times,* 29 May and 'A Good Beginning', *The Economist,* 7 June 2003.

19 On drugs in Afghanistan, see J. Burns, 'Warning on Resurgence of Afghan Drugs Trade', *Financial Times,* 17 April 2003.

20 A. Beattie and G. Dyer, 'US Triples HIV-AIDS Budget for Poor Nations', *Financial Times,* 30 January and 'AIDS - the Other War', *The Economist,* 1 February 2003.

21 For initial approval, see 'AIDS, Africa and the G8 - the Right Direction', *The Economist,* 7 June 2003. For the unravelling, see J. Blitz, 'Blair, Chirac Urge EU Cash for AIDS Fund', J. Dempsey and A. Beattie, 'EU Leaders Back Away from AIDS Pledge' and J. Sachs, 'A Miserly Response to a Global Emergency', *Financial Times,* 18 and 21 June and 17 July 2003.

22 Camdessus, the French APR, was also the chair of the World Panel on Financing Water Infrastructure, which called for a doubling of aid for water projects. But the meeting of the World Water Forum was not very productive. See J. Mason and V. Houlder, 'Ways Set Out to Increase Access to Clean Water' and B. Rahman, 'No Plans, No Money from Kyoto Meeting', *Financial Times,* 6 and 24 March 2003.

23 The idea, first floated at the WSSD, later ran into trouble with the EU member states. See R. Minder, 'WHO Chief Attacks EU Water Aid Delay', *Financial Times,* 9 October 2003.

24 This was meeting resistance - A. Beattie, 'Brown Plan to Reform Global Financial System Meets Opposition', *Financial Times,* 14 April 2003.

25 I heard Chrétien (in his last G8 appearance) and Chirac make these comments at their post-summit press conferences.

Chapter 11

The Shadow of Iraq: Sea Island 2004

As at Evian the year before, Iraq provided the essential context for the G8 summit of 2004. For many months, Iraq had produced only bad news for the US and the other members of the coalition. But a week before the summit the tide turned when an interim government was formed in Iraq and began to gain acceptance. As the heads were arriving at Sea Island, a UN Security Council Resolution was adopted unanimously, giving solid international backing for the transfer of power and the continued presence of coalition troops.[1] These events created a good foundation for G8 agreement on the broader Middle East initiative, the key innovation of this summit. There were useful political decisions on non-proliferation and peace support in Africa. In contrast, the economic agenda took second place.[2]

Summit Preparations and Outreach

The organisation of the summit largely followed the model established at Kananaskis and Evian:

- The heads of government met in the exclusive resort of Sea Island, off the coast of Georgia. G8 delegations were lodged nearby on St. Simon's Island and in Brunswick. The international media centre was in Savannah, 80 miles (130 km) away; Bush, Chirac and Koizumi visited it.
- Security both at Sea Island and in Savannah was very tight, with the historic waterfront of Savannah barricaded off. The cost of these precautions was given as $25 million. They were not needed against demonstrators, however, since very few turned up and they were outnumbered by media and police.
- Unlike previous years, the American hosts made no attempt to engage civil society organizations. There were no facilities provided for them at Savannah or elsewhere, while NGOs such as Oxfam and Greenpeace were not allowed to circulate papers in the media centre.
- The documentation, as at Evian, was prolific and often confusing. Some key documents, like the 'chair's summary', only appeared very late. Apart from the chair's summary, a total of 15 G8 statements and action plans were issued, only one less than Evian. Some of these were very short, but others were supported by detailed annexes explaining what the G8 were already doing. Few of the action plans were actually discussed by the heads themselves. The comprehensive media briefings given by the Americans often announced their content before the G8 met to consider the relevant topic.

The Americans had originally intended to have no meetings with non-G8 countries. As the summit approached, however, they sought to involve regional leaders in the launch of their Middle East reform initiative. But many countries, such as Egypt and Saudi Arabia, declined to accept an invitation to the summit, so that a supplementary meeting was laid on with African leaders.[3] In the end, the G8 met with a mixed Middle Eastern group on the first day - Afghanistan, Algeria, Bahrain, Jordan, Turkey and Yemen, plus the new Iraqi President - and a strong African contingent on the second - Algeria, Ghana, Nigeria, Senegal, South Africa and Uganda.

Meanwhile the idea of outreach to major non-G8 powers such as China, India and Brazil clearly remained active and several G8 heads gave their views in public. Chirac continued to advocate a regular meeting on the lines of the one he had held at Evian. The new Prime Minister of Canada, Paul Martin, favoured a meeting at heads' level of the countries in the G20 finance ministers, of which he had been the first chair. Berlusconi envisaged enlarging the G8 to admit China and India. Blair, when asked, was cautious on enlargement but expected outreach to continue in 2005, when he would host the summit at Gleneagles in Scotland.

The Americans also resisted having many meetings of G8 specialist ministers in the run-up to Sea Island. Only G8 ministers of interior and justice met on terrorism issues, on 11 May. The G8 foreign ministers, who met in Washington on 14 May, had a brief session with Bush, but issued no agreed statement. Their debates were dominated by Iraq and Israel/Palestine. France and Germany, though negotiating actively for a new UN Security Council resolution, made clear that they would still not send troops to Iraq, so that the US and UK had ceased to press for this by the summit.[4] The G7 finance ministers met in New York on 23 May and issued a statement giving an optimistic forecast for the world economy, in spite of worries about oil prices. Brief comments on remittance flows, entrepreneurship in development, and debt relief for poor countries foreshadowed decisions to be announced at the Sea Island summit.

The Sea Island Summit, 8-10 June 2004

Martin of Canada was the only newcomer, apart from Bertie Ahern of Ireland for the rotating EU Presidency. Otherwise, the same group met around the G8 table as at Genoa, Kananaskis and Evian. But several of them were facing elections or loss of office. Martin would go to the polls on 28 June, when the Liberals lost their majority but remained the largest party. Bush was seeking re-election in November - and was successful. Prodi's term as European Commission president would expire within the year. Blair was expected to hold elections in 2005, through he was confident he would still be there to chair the next summit. Others, such as Chirac, Schroeder, Berlusconi and Koizumi, though themselves under no electoral threat, were meeting a loss of political support at home.[5] Only Putin, recently re-elected, was really secure. These domestic political factors were a greater constraint on the heads than they had been in earlier years.

The leaders' performance at the summit could only by judged on the basis of their press conferences. Bush himself came over as energetic and determined, with a visceral commitment to see things through in Iraq. He made his points by the force, not the subtlety, of his arguments. Chirac was individualistic as always, going out of his way to distance himself from the United States and to provide the grit in the G8 oyster.[6] Schroeder, in contrast, was much more conciliatory to Bush and was engaged on the Middle East and on debt relief. Blair was less visible than in previous years, perhaps holding his fire for Gleneagles in 2005. Koizumi pressed the points of direct concern to Japan, especially on North Korea, while backing Bush on Iraq. Martin drew on his experience as the only former finance minister in the group. Berlusconi, Putin, Prodi and Ahern made no clear mark on the proceedings.

All the G8 heads except Koizumi had met on 6 June at the 60th anniversary of the D-Day landings in Normandy. They were welcomed by Bush at Sea Island during 8 June in time for a social dinner, with spouses and other guests. Bilateral meetings had already begun that day, and the whole programme provided ample time for these. The morning sessions on 9 June covered the world economy, international trade and entrepreneurship for development. After a working lunch with regional leaders, the G8 issued their Middle East reform plan and spent the afternoon on transport security and non-proliferation. Their working dinner covered regional issues. On 10 June, the G8 turned to development issues, leading up to their working lunch with the Africans. Martin and Prodi left before the end, but some others met Bush again at Reagan's state funeral in Washington on 11 June.

Economic Issues

World Economy and Trade

The initial exchange on economic prospects for the world and for each G8 member reflected the buoyancy of growth almost everywhere. US briefing singled out the Eurozone as lagging behind the rest of the G8 as well as major emerging markets. But Chirac contested this and expressed concern at the size of the US budget and external deficits, which could unsettle exchange rates and interest rates.

The G8 issued a statement on trade urging the resumption of negotiations in the WTO's Doha Development Agenda by the end of July. This reflected recent exchanges on the framework for negotiations, but contained no commitment on what would happen after July. It stressed the gains that developing countries could make by removing their own trade barriers, but recognized that the pace of this would vary between countries. It did not refer to the latest European Commission proposal to eliminate agricultural export subsidies, since this was resisted by France.[7] Although trade was actively discussed by the G8 and was pressed again by the Africans on 10 June (see below), none of the briefings suggested the leaders themselves gave it high priority. So this was only a low-power, short-term commitment.[8]

Broader Middle East

The Americans had always intended the centre-piece of the Sea Island Summit to be the launch of a far-reaching initiative to encourage political and economic reform in the countries of the Middle East and North Africa, from Morocco to Afghanistan. (Pakistan was originally included, but it was later regarded as belonging to South Asia, not the Middle East.) This idea was acceptable to the rest of the G8, as it closely matched the EU's Mediterranean programme in force since 1995, called the Barcelona process. But when the Americans began soundings of regional countries early in 2004, a draft of their proposals leaked out and led to very adverse reactions. Egypt and Saudi Arabia in particular said they could not accept a process of reform that was dictated from outside.[9]

Despite this reaction, knowledge of the US initiative encouraged indigenous moves toward political and economic reform within countries of the region. This was driven by the private sector (business and civil society), but was also taken up by some governments and found rather hesitant expression at the Arab League Summit in May.[10] Meanwhile, G8 summit preparations worked intensively on the US ideas to convert them into a form that could be more acceptable in the region. In particular, the rest of the G8 saw no chance that the US broader proposals could gain support unless they were linked to progress both in Iraq and in the Israel/Palestine dispute.[11]

The unanimous adoption of the UN Security Council resolution on Iraq thus met one essential condition for agreement on the broader Middle East initiative and greatly lightened the atmosphere as the summit opened. Blair also pressed Bush over breakfast on 9 June to revive the Israel/Palestine peace process, based on the Road Map and the work of the 'Quartet' (US, EU, Russia and the UN). At the G8 lunch with Middle Eastern leaders, all the guests insisted that they were pursuing home-grown reform plans out of conviction, because their peoples demanded it. Each country was distinct, but there was no 'clash of civilizations' and democracy was compatible with Islam. This was evident from Turkey, as the Turkish Prime Minister later pointed out to the press.

The G8 then issued two documents. The first was a political declaration establishing the 'Partnership for Progress and a Common Future in the Region of the Broader Middle East and North Africa'. This pledged G8 support for reform in the region, based on universal values, such as freedom, democracy and the rule of law. The declaration established some specific principles: reform could not be imposed from outside; each country was unique; government, business and civil society would be involved as full partners; and reform was a long-term effort, which required 'a generational commitment'.[12]

The second document, the 'G8 Plan of Support for Reform', embodied eight new initiatives, together with an account of existing G8 activities in the region that contributed to reform. Two initiatives were political and institutional: the establishment of a 'Forum for the Future' among G8 and regional countries, and a 'Democracy Assistance Dialogue'. The other six were economic and social, focused on micro-finance, education and literacy, training for employment, private sector development, financing and the investment climate. The Forum for the Future would involve not only governments (foreign and economic ministers) but also business and civil society. Participation in these programmes would be voluntary. But it was clear that the G8 hoped that all countries from Morocco to Afghanistan would be ready to take part, including those major regional powers absent from the summit, such as Egypt and Saudi Arabia. The Americans were prepared to admit Libya, Syria and Iran to everything if they renounced support for terrorism and possibly to some of the activities even without this.

The Partnership document incorporated substantive commitments on Iraq and on Israel/Palestine, as described below. There was also a separate statement on the Gaza withdrawal and Middle East peace, issued after the G8 had discussed this further over dinner on 9 June.

Iraq

The Iraq passage set out a strong collective G8 commitment to helping 'the fully sovereign Iraqi interim government' to rebuild Iraq and make it peaceful, democratic and prosperous. Some differences persisted, however. While the principle of debt reduction for Iraq was accepted, American ideas for near-complete debt forgiveness were opposed vocally by France and more quietly by Germany, Russia and Japan, on the grounds that this was far more than was on offer to very poor countries without oil resources. In fact the matter was not discussed by the heads and it was remitted to the Paris Club.[13] The media made much of the way Chirac disagreed with Bush (and Blair) over whether NATO could be involved in Iraq. This was later resolved at the NATO summit on 28-29 June, after the new Iraqi government had made a formal request for technical assistance and training, though France continued to make difficulties.[14] Despite these differences, the documents reflected much closer G8 agreement on Iraq than before. France, Germany and Russia, while still critical of the US invasion, rallied behind the new Iraqi government and were satisfied by the safeguards in the UN resolution. This rapprochement was confirmed at the EU/US summit later in June.

Israel/Palestine

When Ariel Sharon visited Washington in April 2004, Bush not only welcomed his plan for Israeli withdrawal from Gaza but also made suggestions about the shape of a final settlement that abandoned established principles deemed essential by the Palestinians.[15] This had been very badly received in the Arab world. The G8 summit essentially brought the peace process back on track again and sought to stimulate forward movement. The Partnership document invoked the basic UN resolutions and endorsed the objective of 'two states living side by side in peace'. It confirmed the central position of the Quartet in advancing the Road Map. This language was intended to appeal to Arab countries and dispose them to look positively on the broader reform initiative. The separate statement on Gaza commended the Israeli withdrawal plan and called for immediate action by the Quartet to take forward the Road Map, while both sides should end all acts of violence.[16]

Terrorism and Non-Proliferation

The afternoon discussions on 9 June resulted in the issue of a substantial Action Plan on Non-Proliferation, bringing together a range of issues mainly derived from US initiatives. The key elements were as follows:

- *Nuclear Non-Proliferation* The document agreed on a number of measures to strengthen the capacity of the International Atomic Energy Agency (IAEA). There was no consensus, however, on the radical US proposal to ban the transfer of nuclear enrichment technology to any state that did not already have it.[17] The G8 only undertook to apply a one-year moratorium to such transfers, in the hope of agreement on a definitive regime by the 2005 summit.
- *Proliferation Security Initiative (PSI)* This measure, launched by Bush in 2003 just before the Evian Summit, was intended to inhibit the trafficking of weapons of mass destruction and delivery systems. By the time of the 2004 summit, all G8 countries including Russia had become full participants and the PSI had already proved its worth by the interception, in October 2003, of a ship carrying nuclear equipment to Libya.[18]
- *Global Partnership* This initiative had been a major achievement of the 2002 Kananaskis summit, which committed $10 billion (from the US) plus $10 billion (from other G7 countries) over 10 years to make safe or dismantle nuclear and chemical weapons and installations in Russia and to retrain Russian nuclear scientists. The Sea Island summit welcomed other contributors to the programme and envisaged spreading it to other countries of the former Soviet Union and to Libya and Iraq. But against this progress, implementation remained very slow, because of persistent problems with access to sensitive areas and with legal and insurance protection in Russia.[19]
- *Non-Proliferation Challenges* The G8 gave a stern warning to North Korea to dismantle all its nuclear programmes and a strong exhortation to Iran to meet all its obligations to the IAEA. Libya was commended for ending its WMD programs. Koizumi endorsed the decision on North Korea, though he stressed his conviction that Kim Jong-Il now wanted to get rid of nuclear weapons.[20]

The G8 also returned to the issue of transport security, first raised at Kananaskis in 2002. The summit adopted the 'Secure and Facilitated International Travel Initiative' (SAFTI), focused on improved practices to deter terrorist attacks on air transport, working with the International Civil Air Organization (ICAO).

Regional Political Issues

Over dinner on 9 June, the leaders returned to Israel/Palestine, as noted above. They also discussed Afghanistan (especially drugs), Haiti and Sudan, on which they issued a short declaration.[21]

Development Issues

The heads had a first discussion of the private sector's role in development on 9 June and issued an Action Plan on Entrepreneurship and the Eradication of Poverty. They returned to development issues for the main morning session on 10 June. They issued six more declarations and action plans: on health issues (separate plans for HIV/AIDS and polio); on ending famine; on transparency and combating corruption; on debt relief; and on science and technology for sustainable development.

These documents clearly emerged from detailed preparatory work. Most of them were adopted on the nod, without debate by the G8 leaders. The heads did, however, have a serious exchange on finance for development. Chirac, who had been reticent on trade (especially agriculture), spoke out in favour of the British initiative for an International Finance Facility (IFF). This, however, was resisted by the US, Germany and Japan, though Schroeder gave hints of future flexibility both on the IFF and debt relief. But in general the G8 were hesitant over increased aid commitments, because of budgetary pressures in continental Europe and Japan and fears of Congressional resistance in the United States.[22]

Entrepreneurship and Development

The G8 action plan on this topic drew on a report prepared for the UNDP by Martin and Mexican ex-president Ernesto Zedillo. Martin introduced the discussion among the heads and was pleased by the outcome. Earlier summits, such as Lyon 1996 and Denver 1997, had focused on foreign private investment as a force for development. But this was the first time the G8 sought to mobilize foreign remittances (estimated at $100 to $150 billion a year) or to assist private sector operations within developing countries, through improving the business climate, developing local finance for housing and water supplies, and promoting micro-finance. Most of the action plan encouraged work already under way in bodies such as the UNDP and the World Bank, but the G8's endorsement was intended to give a worthwhile boost to this activity.[23]

Health

On HIV/AIDS, the G8 agreed action to develop and disseminate a HIV vaccine. This built on a US national programme and aimed to strengthen international cooperation in creating, testing and manufacturing such a vaccine, with a report to the 2005 summit.[24] The Americans had earlier intended to seek increased contributions to the Global Fund to fight AIDS, Tuberculosis and Malaria. But they decided not to press for this, when others argued for building up the operational capacity of the Global Fund before committing more finance.[25]

On polio, the G8 undertook to meet any funding gap in the WHO's Polio Eradication Initiative, with the aim of ending polio in the six countries where it was still active - India, Pakistan, Egypt, Afghanistan, Niger and Nigeria.

Famine

The document on famine and food security built on the Evian Famine Action Plan. It sought to work with the agricultural development programme launched by the African Union with help from the FAO, and focused specially on ending famine in Ethiopia.

Transparency and Fighting Corruption

The G8 document reported progress on commitments made at Evian under this heading. A particular innovation was the encouragement of national 'transparency compacts', where countries would get help in introducing greater openness and efficiency into government operations. Georgia, Nicaragua, Nigeria and Peru were the first countries to enter into such compacts.

Debt Relief

In a short statement on debt relief, the G8 undertook to extend the life of the HIPC programme until the end of 2006 and to top up the financing if necessary. This was a small advance on what the G7 finance ministers had said and could lead to a commitment of up to $1 billion, though no figures were given. However, there was no agreement on improving the terms of debt relief, where the UK and the US were arguing for up to 100% relief on institutional as well as G8 bilateral debt, when this was needed to ensure 'debt sustainability'.[26] The finance ministers were simply asked to report by the end of 2004.

Science and Technology for Sustainable Development

The G8 document, which only became public four days after the summit, gave backing to the Japanese 'Reduce, Reuse and Recycle' initiative. It also provided a review of actions taken since the action plan on this topic issued at Evian. It was clear that some leaders - such as Chirac - would have liked a fuller discussion of the global environment.

Africa, including Peace Support

The G8 commitments on health and famine were directly relevant to Africa. In addition, the Sea Island summit, like Evian, built on the commitment in the 2002 G8 Africa Action Plan to make the Africans capable of resolving violent conflicts among themselves by 2010. The new African Union was committed to providing troops for peace support operations on the continent and was already intervening in Sudan. But often the African troops were poorly trained and equipped and could not be moved to where they were needed.[27] The G8 therefore issued an Action Plan on Expanding Global Capability for Peace Support Operations, aimed at training 75,000 troops for peace-keeping operations by 2010, initially in Africa but also in other countries. There would also be measures to train 'heavy police' (like French gendarmes and Italian carabinieri). In addition, the G8 undertook to develop transport and logistics support arrangements by the time of the 2005 summit. The Americans were asking Congress for $660 million to finance their share of this programme.[28]

The summit ended with a working lunch attended by six African presidents. Four were regular participants at G8 summits - Bouteflika, Mbeki, Obasanjo and Wade. John Kufuor (Ghana) and Yoweri Museveni (Uganda) were newcomers and Museveni made a long and impressive intervention about the importance of better trade access.[29] Speaking at a joint press conference afterward, Obasanjo welcomed the continued involvement of the G8 with NEPAD. He expressed appreciation for the decisions on peace support, HIV/AIDS and famine, while stressing the contribution the Africans themselves were making to policy in these areas. But he noted that the G8 members were still debating internally about agricultural subsidies and more generous debt relief, implying that the G8 response was less than the Africans had hoped. There was also a sense of some disappointment among the Africans that this year's summit was not better integrated into the ongoing G8/NEPAD process. As Obasanjo said, they did not come all the way from Africa just to have lunch.

Assessment of the Sea Island Summit

The Middle East reform initiative was the outstanding innovation from this summit. It responded to the problems of a chronically troubled region. These problems included:

- Widespread political dissatisfaction with autocratic regimes;
- Economic sluggishness, despite massive oil wealth, and persistent high unemployment;
- Low standards of education and restricted opportunities for women;
- Many entrenched territorial disputes, especially Israel/Palestine.

Furthermore, the broader Middle East was the major source of international terrorism, threatening not only the West but also the stability of the region itself.

Only the G8 summit had the capacity to develop a response to such a wide range of problems, because of the supreme authority of the leaders and their ability to combine political and economic responsibilities. Such a combined response was necessary, as political unrest and economic under-performance were feeding on each other. The broader Middle East initiative was thus an example of the good use of the summit's potential, with intensive preparatory work being given high-level collective impetus by the heads of government.

The successful launch of the initiative faced three immediate threats, which could strain the fragile consensus reached at Sea Island and lead to recriminations among the G8:

- The situation in Iraq could deteriorate in the months ahead, as insurgent groups sought to destabilize the interim government;
- The efforts to revive the Road Map in Israel/Palestine could prove abortive, with violence persisting there too;
- Leading countries of the region, such as Egypt and Saudi Arabia, might continue to remain aloof.

In practice, the initiative survived these threats in the five months following Sea Island. Iraq's interim government took over power in late June, but a high level of insecurity persisted, with suicide bombs and hostage-taking. After some hesitant moves between Israel and the Palestinians, the familiar stalemate returned, with violence from both sides. Even so, foreign and finance ministers from all the regional powers (except Iran and Syria) took part in meetings with the G8 on the margins of the UN General Assembly and the Annual Meeting of the IMF and World Bank. These meetings were to prepare for the first session of the 'Forum for the Future', to be held in Morocco later in 2004.

There were also more fundamental obstacles to the reform programme. Unlike the G8's involvement in Africa, the initiative did not come from within the region. Many regional states remained suspicious of US intentions and resistant to any outside dictation. The G8 documents sought to dispel these fears, but the result could be that the desired reforms never achieved strong momentum, for two reasons:

- The more autocratic regimes paid lip service to the ideas of reform, but continued to stifle effective opposition;[30]
- The programs offered by the G8 were not sufficiently purposeful or well resourced to make any impact, economically or politically.

These dangers were well understood by the G8. This explained their stress on action over the long term, moving at a pace acceptable to regional countries and treating each one individually. Participation was bound to be incomplete at the outset, for example because of the strained US relations with Syria and Iran, though the hope was that they could join in due course. There was no decision on whether the initiative could embrace the Muslim countries from the former Soviet Union and the Russian attitude to this was not clear. But these countries too would benefit greatly from being involved.

In addition to the Middle East, the Sea Island Summit marked some advances on other political issues, reflecting the priority given to them since the terrorist attacks of 11 September 2001. The measures on transport safety were politically motivated and extended work begun at Kananaskis in 2002, though they hardly deserved summit attention. The peace support action plan was intended to meet another Kananaskis commitment from the Africa Action Plan. Summit attention should help to mobilize the substantial funds required. The non-proliferation action plan pulled together for the first time a number of distinct programmes, which were all initiated by the Americans but had gained participation from the rest of the G8. This gave added authority to these programmes, though the summit was not used to overcome remaining obstacles.

In contrast, the economic discussions were less productive. Despite the usual lively exchange on the world economy, the heads could not go beyond what their finance ministers had said. The trade document had a very limited shelf life and lacked longer-term commitment, while there were no advances on the trade access issues of great concern to the African leaders present.

In the development issues covered, there were some innovative features, especially the mobilization of remittances for development and the measures to improve transparency of government operations. These were directed, more than before, to domestic aspects of development, rather than the external contribution of aid, trade or foreign investment. Though valuable, they were also intrusive and would need careful handling to ensure developing countries had 'ownership' of the processes involved. Elsewhere, the economic documents either gave G8 support to existing US programmes (as on HIV/AIDS) or reported progress in implementing earlier commitments. The debt relief undertakings ensured that the HIPC programme remained operational, but did not improve it. The science and sustainability document kept alive the modest initiative begun at Evian in 2003. In general, the results achieved from Sea Island on these items seldom needed the intervention of heads of government.

Conclusion

The Middle East initiative from Sea Island scored well against all the criteria. There was innovative *leadership* in a contentious area and strong *solidarity* among the G8. The initiative *effectively* integrated politics and economics, while the parallel progress on Iraq and Israel/Palestine showed *consistency*. The G8 did their best to make it *acceptable* to the regional powers and to ensure *durability*. The other summit results were less impressive and many issues hardly deserved summit attention. There was *effective* and *durable* progress on peace-keeping in Africa, but no *consistent* movement on the economic issues of concern to the Africans, notably trade and debt. There was some *durable* movement on proliferation issues, though also some strains on *solidarity*.

The Americans left their distinctive mark on the organization of the summit and the conduct of both the preparations and the discussions among the heads. The documents to be issued by the summit were almost all worked out in advance in every detail, giving the heads little opportunity to make any personal impact on the outcome. American press briefings were full and highly informative, but said more about US proposals than collective G8 positions. In short, the Americans took great pains that their version of events should prevail.

This showed that, six years after the Birmingham summit, the reforms introduced there were at risk of serious erosion. The practice of only heads coming to the summit, with small delegations, was now well entrenched. But the aim of a short agenda with a limited set of specific items had been replaced by broad, all-embracing themes. Instead of a few concise documents, there was a confusing plethora of action plans and supporting documents. The summit had shifted away from any domestic issues, such as jobs and crime, to a total concentration on international problems. It had moved from a largely economic agenda, with politics only on the side, to a growing emphasis on politics, or at least politics and economics combined. Some current trends were driven by events, especially the response to terrorism. Others were welcome advances, such as the launch of integrated economic and political programmes and the growing interest in outreach to non-G8 countries. But the G8 heads risked losing the capacity to strike deals and launch initiatives through personal interaction, unless Blair could return to a more austere simplicity of format for the Gleneagles summit of 2005.

Notes

1 See J. Drummond and others, 'Wrangling Ends as Iraq Picks Leaders', *Financial Times,* 2 June, W. Hoge, 'Security Council Backs Resolution on Iraq Turnover', *New York Times,* 9 June and 'Iraq's New Government' and 'Iraq's UN Resolution', *The Economist,* 5 and 12 June 2004.

2 This chapter is based on my 'Impressions of the Sea Island Summit', accessible on www.g8.utoronto.ca.

3 The refusals by Arab leaders are noted in P. Webster and R. Watson, 'West Reaches out to Heal Rift with Muslims', *The Times,* 27 May and S. Weisman, 'Bush Plan for Group of 8 to Hail Democracy in the Middle East Strains Ties with Arab Allies', *New York Times,* 6 June 2004.

4 Michel Barnier, the French Foreign Minister, set out the French position in an interview with *Le Monde,* 14 May 2004.

5 The Upper House elections in Japan weakened Koizumi's standing; see D. Ibison, 'Koizumi Dealt Heavy Blow in Japanese Poll', *Financial Times,* 12 July 2004.

6 This image is taken from the leader 'Gallic Grit in the American Oyster', *Financial Times,* 12 June 2004. See also J. Harding and J. Chaffin, 'Banter Hides Depth of Bush-Chirac Rift', *Financial Times,* 11 June 2004.

7 T. Buck and others, 'EU Offers to Scrap Farm Export Subsidies' and 'EU's Farm Subsidy Offer Irks French', *Financial Times,* 10 and 11 May 2004.

8 However, the G8's comments on the pace of liberalisation were well received by developing countries and the Doha negotiations were successfully re-launched. See R. Colitt, 'Framework Sought for Farm Talks' and F. Williams and G. de Jonquières, 'Big Trade Nations Hail Key Deal on Subsidies', *Financial Times,* 15 June and 2 August 2004.

9 See G. Dinmore, 'US Plan for "Greater Mideast" Sees Key Role for G8 Summit', R. Khalaf and J. Dinmore, 'Reforming the Arab World - the US is Serious' and

J. Dempsey, 'EU Changes Tack to Foster Mideast Reforms', *Financial Times,* 27 February and 23 and 25 March 2004.

10 M. Bishara, 'Another Arab Summit Ends in Words But No Deeds', *International Herald Tribune,* 25 May 2004. The preparations for the summit had been difficult and it had had to be postponed once.

11 For a scholarly analysis, see Everts 2004.

12 For immediate comment, see 'The Transatlantic Alliance' and 'Democracy for Arabs', *The Economist,* 5 and 12 June 2004.

13 See A. Beattie, 'Bush to Press for Write-Off of Iraq's Debts', *Financial Times,* 9 June 2004. The matter was still not resolved when G7 finance ministers met in October - A. Balls and C. Giles, 'G7 Promises Progress on Debt Relief', *Financial Times,* 4 October 2004.

14 See R. Graham, 'French President Spells out Limits on Iraq Support' and G. Dinmore and others, 'NATO Plans Iraq Mission Despite Chirac', *Financial Times,* 11 June and 3 July 2004.

15 H. Morris and others, 'Bush Backs Israeli Plan to Keep Settlements', *Financial Times,* 15 April 2004.

16 For a scholarly analysis of the prospects for an Israel/Palestine settlement, see Hollis 2004.

17 This idea, among others, was launched by Bush in a speech in February, but resisted by the Europeans. See M. Huband and others, 'Bush's Safeguards Depend on Global Teamwork to Foil Black Market' and S. Fidler, 'Europe to Block Freeze on Spread of Nuclear Processing', *Financial Times,* 13 February and 22 May 2004.

18 For details of the interception, see S. Fidler and M. Huband, 'Turks and South Africans Helped Libya's Secret Nuclear Arms Project', *Financial Times,* 10 June 2004.

19 See 'Nuclear Nightmares', *The Economist,* 5 June 2004 and the reports accessible on www.sgpproject.org.

20 There was clear agreement on dealing with North Korea through the six-party talks, see 'North Korea's Diplomacy', *The Economist,* 24 January 2004. Koizumi's view is reported in D. Pilling, 'N Korea "Ready to Abandon Nuclear Arms" - Koizumi', *Financial Times,* 8 June 2004. But there was tension between the US and the Europeans over how best to handle Iran, see R. Khalaf, 'Nuclear Proliferation - Iran Feels Confident', *Financial Times,* 9 September 2004.

21 On the crisis in Darfur, Sudan, see 'Special Report - Sudan', *The Economist,* 15 May 2004 and note 27 below.

22 James Wolfensohn, President of the World Bank, was strongly critical of G8 countries aid performance. He is quoted in this sense in C. Swann and E. Crooks, 'Low Levels of Aid for Poor "Unacceptable"', *Financial Times,* 26 April, and again in A. Balls, '"Terrorism and Iraq have pushed Development off the World's Agenda"', *Financial Times,* 24 September 2004.

23 See 'The Importance of Remittances to Developing Economies', *The Economist,* 31 July 2004.

24 On the prospects for a vaccine, see F. Williams, 'AIDS Vaccine a Decade Away', *Financial Times,* 3 September 2004.

25 Despite the confusion after Evian, pledges to the Global Fund had risen to $5.5 billion - see Chapter 8 above.

26 See C. Swann and A. Fifield, 'G8 Pledges to Extend Debt Relief for Poorest States' (the finance ministers) and 'Blair and Brown to Push for Extended Debt Relief', *Financial Times,* 24 and 31 May 2004. As noted in Chapter 5, note 36, the British and American approaches were not really compatible.

27 See 'African Peacekeepers', *The Economist,* 13 March, D. White and A. England, 'Africa Ready for Peacekeeping Burden - If Someone Pays', and A. England, 'Darfur's Green Berets Take Pride in African Union Mission', *Financial Times,* 31 July and 26 September, 2004.

28 For immediate comment, see 'Peacekeeping in Africa', *The Economist,* 19 June 2004.

29 Kufuor had also spoken out on the importance of trade access for African countries, in D. White, 'Africa Needs Aid and Access to Markets', *Financial Times,* 27 April 2004.

30 See J. Atterman, 'Arab Liberals Need Careful Nurturing', *Financial Times,* 3 August 2004.

Chapter 12

Summit Performance III: Africa, Terrorism and Non-Proliferation

The G8 summits of the seventh series, from Kananaskis onwards, operated in the shadow of the terrorist attacks of 11 September 2001. Inevitably, the fight against terrorism became the top priority. But the earlier priority of managing globalisation did not disappear. The two were superimposed on each other and overlapped. In particular, the original American strategy of not only fighting the manifestations of terrorism but also attacking its roots gave a new impetus to measures to help poor and conflict-ridden states, especially in Africa, that could easily become the sources of terrorists. Thus the Genoa Plan for Africa, adopted by the G8 in July 2001, proved to be very timely.

But concern with terrorism also brought more political items to the summit's attention, at the expense of the traditional economic agenda. The G8 became concerned with measures to counter terrorism itself and with preventing the proliferation of weapons of mass destruction - nuclear, chemical and biological - that might fall into the hands of terrorists. Terrorism and non-proliferation had occasionally featured in G7 summits, going right back to the 1970s. They now became recurrent summit themes, which were pursued for political motives, though they often contained economic elements.

This chapter looks separately at Africa and at terrorism and non-proliferation, to assess the G8 summits' performance in these areas. As with Chapters 5 and 8, it will review briefly how earlier summits treated these issues and then offer a detailed analysis of G8 achievements from Kananaskis onwards. The familiar criteria will be applied - leadership, effectiveness, solidarity, durability, acceptability and consistency. The effectiveness criterion, however, has been expanded to cover the summit's ability to integrate politics and economics as well as to reconcile domestic and international pressures.

Africa at the G8 Summits

Africa was rarely discussed at early summits and was hardly ever the subject of G7 decisions.[1] It only became a leading topic at the last summit of the G7 cycle, Denver 1997. The results were disappointing and led to no specific follow-up at Birmingham or Cologne. The G7 made no attempt to involve African countries in the process.

But as the first G8 summits addressed the concerns generated by globalisation, the heads inevitably became aware that Africa was the continent most affected by crippling debt burdens, the digital divide and infectious diseases, like AIDS and malaria. The measures adopted on debt relief at Cologne, on IT at Okinawa and on health issues at Genoa were largely intended to benefit the poor countries of Sub-Saharan Africa. The G8 heads were therefore ready to respond to the New African Initiative put before them at Genoa 2001 and adopted their 'Genoa Plan for Africa' without delay, going beyond the advice of their officials. This decision launched the heads into what proved their most innovative campaign of the first G8 summit sequence, in the way they combined economic and political elements and entered into a systematic relationship with non-G8 countries.

The Emergence of NEPAD

By the end of the 1990s, Africa was in a tragic state. While a few African countries had achieved impressive growth performance, for most of them growth had either failed to keep up with their population or had been going backwards absolutely. African countries were chronically vulnerable to drought, flood, famine and disease. Many were also crippled by the new scourge of AIDS, which was cutting back production and life expectancy, overwhelming health and education programmes and threatening the whole fabric of society. Furthermore, numerous African states were devastated by civil war or undermined by decades of autocratic government and systematic corruption. Such countries, including 'failed states' like Somalia, could easily become the breeding grounds for terrorist movements.

In Africa, many years of external aid programmes had failed to produce results and there was widespread disillusion. There was no model of indigenous development based on intra-African cooperation. Most countries still looked to their former colonial powers, to the European Union or to the international financial institutions, holding them responsible when they failed to prosper. Africa was becoming marginalized in the international system and reaping few or none of the benefits of globalisation.

Late in 2000, Mbeki of South Africa joined with Obasanjo of Nigeria and Bouteflika of Algeria to introduce the Millennium Africa Plan (MAP), aimed at reversing this downward trend and launching a new African renaissance.[2] Over the next year they discussed their ideas widely with fellow African leaders, who made their own contributions. The MAP was combined with the Omega Plan drawn up by Wade of Senegal and with ideas originating with the UN Economic Commission for Africa (ECA) and its Ghanaian Secretary General, K. Y. Amoako. This combination of proposals mutated into the New African Initiative and reached its final form in October 2001, as the New Partnership for Africa's Development.[3]

The NEPAD proposals, which covered peace-keeping, political governance and economic development, differed from all previous African approaches to the revival of their continent. Up to then, Africans had tried to put the blame for their troubles onto others: on the legacy of colonialism, on the inequity of the international system or on the inadequacies of aid flows and development institutions. This time, Mbeki, Obasanjo, Wade and their colleagues accepted that Africans were themselves to blame for their problems and that they had to take responsibility for their own recovery. This meant correcting their own failures, not only in domestic economic policy but also in political governance, by strengthening democracy and respect for the law. They recognized that unless they did that, they could not expect richer countries or international institutions to provide the official aid, private investment, trade access, debt relief and other forms of external help that they needed.

The NEPAD enabled the Africans to take ownership of their own political and economic revival.[4] They were no longer seeking to excuse failure by attributing it to policies imposed from outside. They set standards for themselves, in both economic and political behaviour, and undertook to hold each other accountable for their programme's implementation. The NEPAD further provided for an African peer review mechanism, based on a concept developed by the Economic Commission for Africa.[5] A rigorous system of peer review would inevitably mean African countries comparing and criticising each other's economic and political performance. This was seen as a necessary part of attracting outside aid and investment. But it was a major innovation for the continent, because it departed from the traditional approach of the Organisation for African Union (OAU), which had resisted such differentiation and insisted that all African countries should be treated alike.

The sponsors of NEPAD gradually overcame resistance, so as to ensure that their approach had the full support of all 54 OAU members. The original NEPAD Steering Committee of South Africa, Nigeria, Senegal, Algeria and Egypt contained only one least-developed country and was not regionally balanced. So it was underpinned by a 15-state Implementing Committee, with three countries from each African sub-region, including many poor ones.[6] Meanwhile, the OAU was itself transformed into the new African Union, with Mbeki as its first president.[7] This was distinct from NEPAD, but provided the essential institutional backing for many of its actions, especially in peace-keeping and conflict prevention.

The G8 Africa Action Plan

Mbeki, Obasanjo and Bouteflika had met the G8 at the dinner before Okinawa and decided that this was the best method to approach potential Western backers at the highest level. They got themselves invited to the Genoa outreach dinner, with Wade, and their ideas impressed the G8 profoundly. In the Genoa Plan for Africa the G8 promised to help the Africans, provided they honoured their own undertakings and took responsibility for their own renewal. Genoa set up a special group of Africa Personal Representatives (APRs), to report direct to the G8 heads.[8] This group worked closely with African countries during the following year to produce the G8 Africa Action Plan, for adoption at the Kananaskis summit of 2002.[9] The four African presidents - Mbeki, Obasanjo, Wade and Bouteflika - were invited to the summit again, this time as participants rather than guests.[10]

As recorded in Chapter 9, the Africa Action Plan was a response to NEPAD, but insisted that NEPAD's ownership remained with the Africans. The G8 picked up from NEPAD the concept of 'enhanced partnerships', which G8 countries would set up with African countries that were seeking to meet the NEPAD standards and submit themselves to peer review.[11] The Action Plan brought together G8 commitments in two political areas (peace and security and strengthening governance) and six economic ones (trade and investment, debt relief, expanding knowledge, improving health, agriculture and water resources). The peace and security chapter set deadlines for enabling Africa to deal with its own conflict prevention and promised action on named trouble-spots like the Congo and Sudan. The other chapters of the Action Plan broadly corresponded to the detailed provisions of the NEPAD on governance and economic development.

The Africa Action Plan could be seen not only as a response to NEPAD but also as a weapon in the fight against terrorism launched since 11 September 2001. The G8, like the sponsors of NEPAD, recognised that Africa suffered from a lack of strong political institutions and the persistence of civil conflict, as well as declining economic standards. This influenced the construction of NEPAD and the Africa Action Plan, so that they combined economic development with elements dedicated to peace and security and to improved governance, which both sides considered necessary.

The Africa Action Plan had its shortcomings. The first problem concerned finance. Although the Africans had constructed NEPAD in a form that was calculated to attract outside support, the financing formula in the Africa Action Plan was complex. G8 countries had already promised at the UN meeting on financing for development, at Monterrey in March 2002, to increase their total aid spending by $12 billion per year over five years. Under the Action Plan, half or more of this new aid money could go to Africa, but there was no assurance of unified G8 funding.[12]

Second, the Africa Action Plan involved a group of donor countries, each with its own programmes and priorities. The Kananaskis summit was the occasion for announcements of increased aid and trade access for Africa (sometimes shared with other countries) by the United States, Britain and Canada. But these were all national initiatives, not coordinated and often difficult to compare one with another. There was no decision at Kananaskis to create coordination machinery, either among the G8 themselves or between the G8 and the Africans.[13]

Third, while the Africa Action Plan followed the economic parts of NEPAD fairly closely, there were some significant differences, where the Africans did not get all they hoped for. The Action Plan did not endorse the NEPAD proposals for infrastructure projects or for more generous debt relief. It was weaker than NEPAD on trade access and on environmental issues, while both documents seemed reluctant to face up to the challenge of AIDS.

While the Africans present at Kananaskis welcomed the Action Plan as whole, they were disappointed not to be offered improved trade access for their agricultural products. At the summit itself, the French insisted that, on agricultural trade, the G8 could go no further than what was agreed at the WTO meeting at Doha in November 2001. Canada announced new measures after the summit to liberalise access for the exports of least developed countries, comparable to measures already introduced by the EU.[14] But these still exempted certain food products. In this area the G8 countries still seemed too inclined to give way to domestic pressures, when these clashed with the objective of helping Africa.

Progress after Kananaskis

Kananaskis kept the G8 Africa Personal Representatives group in being, with a mandate to make recommendations to the 2003 summit, and Chirac promised Africa would still have high priority there. At Evian, the four African presidents met the G8 again and the APRs produced a solid report on the implementation of the Action Plan. Individual G8 members also issued their own reports. It was clear that all the G8 members had been much more active in Africa than they would have without the stimulus of NEPAD, though there was no coordination of effort and it was hard to distinguish new commitments from the recycling of old ones. The main collective achievement was the G8/Africa Peace Support Plan, to advance peace-keeping. The Africans also announced agreement on the African Peer Review Mechanism. The Africans were pleased with progress, but still unhappy about trade access and debt relief.

Evian called for another report to the G8 heads in 2005. The Americans had not originally intended to feature Africa at the Sea Island summit of 2004. They only invited the African leaders as an afterthought and follow-up to the Action Plan was not integrated into the summit discussions. But there was another major advance in peace-keeping. The G8 made a major commitment towards training and logistic support, for which the US alone was seeking $660 million from Congress. The Africans present recognised the benefit they would receive from G8 cooperation over finding and testing an HIV/AIDS vaccine and from help promised to fight famine. But they sought to make clear the extent of their own efforts in health and agriculture and they repeated their anxieties over trade access and debt. Blair made it known that Africa would be a major theme for the Gleneagles summit of July 2005, when the African leaders could expect to take part again. He had already announced, in February 2004, the formation of a Commission for Africa, with members drawn from the G8 and Africa, from government and private sector, to generate stronger public support for measures to help Africa and report before Gleneagles in 2005.[15]

Prospects for NEPAD and the G8's Support for Africa

During several years of NEPAD and the G8 Africa Action Plan running in tandem, the process had moved from the innovative planning stage into the tougher and more demanding implementation stage. This made it possible to see how both the Africans and the G8 were responding to the problems that arose and draw some conclusions about the longer-term prospects.

Peace-keeping

The chapter of the Africa Action Plan on peace and security contained the clearest commitments and targets. It was here that the earliest progress was made, in the form of the G8/Africa Peace Support Plan. By the beginning of 2004, there were signs that conflict was receding in Africa.[16] The African Union (AU) began to develop its capacity for peace-keeping, sending forces and observers to Burundi and to Darfur in Sudan.[17] These efforts earned strong backing from the G8, who undertook to provide the training and logistic support that the Africans lacked.[18]

Governance

NEPAD had begun very much as an enterprise driven at head of state level. Because of this 'top-down' approach, NEPAD was criticised by Western NGOs as being out of touch with the grass-roots.[19] But the African leaders rejected this criticism vigorously and NEPAD started to attract more positive scholarly interest.[20] The African Parliament linked to the AU held its first meeting.[21] NEPAD required African countries to be ready to criticise each other, which had never happened under the OAU. This was now beginning under the AU, which was refusing to recognise governments that came to power by coup d'etat. But the old tradition still protected those in power, as was shown by the continued reluctance to attack President Robert Mugabe's regime in Zimbabwe.[22]

The governance elements of the NEPAD process continued to advance, driven by a nucleus of committed countries. The African Peer Review Mechanism, with 17 participants, started work in February 2004. Ghana, Kenya, Mauritius and Rwanda were the first to have their standards of governance evaluated.[23] The hope was that others would want to join in once they saw that NEPAD discipline was paying off. However, this progress was not sufficiently recognised by the G8. Although they had welcomed NEPAD because the Africans would set standards of governance and be accountable, G8 members were still insisting on their own standards, which held up aid disbursement. The Americans were slow in bringing the new Millennium Challenge Account into operation and their choice of African beneficiaries took little account of the NEPAD peer review mechanism.[24]

Economic Development

There were some promising economic signs here also.[25] The OECD recorded that most African economies performed well in 2003, with average growth at 3.6%, while the prospects for 2004 and 2005 were even better.[26] This recovery was due mainly to more stable political conditions, stronger industrial commodity prices and increased aid flows. But the evidence continued to show that Sub-Saharan Africa was off-track for meeting most of the Millennium Development Goals. Much of the support promised by the G8 was slow to take effect and sometimes denied altogether, in aid, debt relief and market access.

Official Aid Flows More aid was being committed to African countries than before, following the pledges made at Monterrey and Kananaskis to increase total aid to Africa by $6 billion per year. But it was unclear whether donors would meet their Monterrey pledges and in any case this increase was held to be insufficient to meet the Millennium Development Goals.[27] The World Bank calculated that a doubling of aid was necessary worldwide, from $50 billion to $100 billion; this led to the British proposal for an International Finance Facility, so far only backed by

France among the rest of the G8. The UN Millennium Project argued for even larger increases.[28] Support for primary education (goal no. 2) offered a specific example of aid falling short. The World Bank reported inadequate funding to support the countries, many of them in Africa, selected for 'fast-track' funding under the 'Education for All' programme.[29]

Debt Relief There was growing recognition by the IMF and World Bank that the debt relief offered by the HIPC programme was inadequate. Pressure for more generous relief came from the Africans, from NGOs and eventually from two G8 members - the UK and the US.[30] But the summit could not do more than extend the life of the programme and ensure the World Bank Trust Fund was replenished. The G7 finance ministers did not resolve the issue in October 2004, in part because the US and UK disagreed among themselves. The United States favoured converting all loans to HIPC countries to grants, but without providing extra money for the Fund and Bank. The United Kingdom was convinced that this would require additional funds and offered to contribute ten percent of the total.[31]

Trade Access African countries increasingly pressed the G8 for better trade access and criticised protective measures like US cotton subsidies and the Farm Bill adopted in 2002.[32] At first, the Africans were inclined to welcome the failure at Cancun, but Amaoko, the Secretary General of the ECA, realised how much the collapse of the Doha Development Agenda could hurt Africa.[33] African countries became active members of the G90 in the WTO, often working with NGOs. They drove a hard bargain in the 2004 resumption of the Doha negotiations, so as to ensure the EU and the US made firm commitments on agriculture.[34] But so far the G8 countries have not done more than promise that African concerns will be met in the context of the Doha Development Agenda.

Many of these shortcomings on aid, trade and debt relief were due to unresolved differences among the G8 partners. The Africa Action Plan contained no mechanism to coordinate the actions being taken to help Africa, so as to produce a collective impact and to go wider than just the G8. In an effort to correct this, the G8 Africa Group was supplemented, from November 2003, by the African Partners Group, which brought together G8 and non-G8 aid donors, African countries and international institutions. But this has not solved the problem of coordination among the G8 themselves, which only really takes place under the pressure of the summit once a year.

Performance under the Criteria

The G8 summit performance on Africa scores quite well under the criteria, but there are some weaknesses:

- The G8 heads showed clear *leadership* in devoting so much attention to Africa and adopted an innovative approach. They responded to the personal approach of the African leaders and developed a systematic link with them.

They gave their authority to a wide-ranging programme of action, which deserved the attention of heads of government.

- The G8 were *effective* in combining the political and economic elements of the African programme in a way the summits had rarely done before. However, they were much less effective in overcoming domestic resistance to measures of benefit to Africa, especially in trade access.
- *Solidarity* was strong for the Africa programme as a whole. The UK, France and Canada were the most enthusiastic, but the United States took a full part. The US was even prepared to join in a collective financial commitment, but insisted on maintaining its own standards for aid programmes.
- Africa's problems would need attention long past 2015, the target year for the Millennium Development Goals, so that it was too soon to say if the programme would prove *durable*. But early signs were promising, in that G8 involvement, first aroused at Genoa in 2001, was still fully engaged in the approach to Gleneagles in 2005.
- The G8 members insisted from the start on African ownership of NEPAD, to ensure *acceptability* of their Action Plan. They later developed the new Africa Partners Group to associate non-G8 countries and international institutions. There was resistance at first from civil society, because the whole process was driven from the top, but this was slowly being overcome.
- The G8 Africa strategy was broadly *consistent* with the G8's position in other economic and political areas. But this was a weakness as well as a strength. G8 shortcomings in trade access, debt relief and primary education weakened the impact of what they could offer for Africa and were the cause of NGO criticism. In general, the peace-keeping and governance elements made more progress, while the economic commitments lagged behind.

Terrorism and Non-Proliferation: Early Summit Treatment

These issues were among the earliest political topics to be treated by the G7 summits, alongside their main economic agenda. Hijacking and hostage-taking, both aspects of terrorism, preoccupied the summits from Bonn I 1978 to Venice I 1980 and were the subject of political declarations, the first of their kind. Interest in state sponsorship of terrorism, especially by Libya, revived from London II in 1984 and this became the principal subject of discussion among the heads at Tokyo II in 1986. A G7 group of counter-terrorism experts was formed at this time.

The Tokyo II summit was successful in producing G7 agreement on this subject, after the American bombing raid on Libya had threatened to divide the Americans from the rest. Thereafter the threat receded, to revive again at Lyon in 1996, when US servicemen were attacked in Saudi Arabia, just days before the summit. This was an early example of the summit reacting to a terrorist operation motivated by Islamic extremism, of the same kind as the 11 September attacks.

Nuclear issues, including proliferation, went back as far as 1977, when the US tried to prevent Germany and France from selling reprocessing technology to Brazil and Pakistan. The Chernobyl disaster of 1986, just before the Tokyo II summit, gave the G7 heads (especially Kohl) an abiding interest in nuclear safety, especially in Central and Eastern Europe. After the end of the Cold War in Europe, this was combined with concern about nuclear smuggling, as the break-up of the USSR weakened the security of nuclear weapons and installations and put many nuclear scientists out of a job. A G8 expert group on non-proliferation, including nuclear smuggling, was founded in 1993 on a Japanese proposal. When the special Nuclear Safety and Security Summit met in Moscow in April 1996, nuclear smuggling and the protection of nuclear material were major items on its agenda.[35]

The G8 Summits and Terrorism

At the first four G8 summits, terrorism was discussed by the foreign ministers, but hardly attracted the attention of the heads. The terrorist attacks on the US embassies in Kenya and Tanzania in 1998, now attributed to Al-Qaeda, happened some weeks after the Birmingham summit.

Immediately after 11 September 2001, the direction of the G8's work on terrorism changed. State sponsorship of terrorism took second place, once the Taliban regime had been driven from Afghanistan in November. The first priority was defence against trans-national terrorist networks, especially Al-Qaeda and its affiliates. The G8 did not address the whole range of counter-terrorist activities, but concentrated on obstructing the financing of terrorism, preventing terrorist attacks on means of transport and helping countries build counter-terrorist capacity. G8 work on non-proliferation, considered separately below, focused on keeping weapons of mass destruction out of the hands of terrorists.

Financing of Terrorism

The G8 rapidly concluded that trade and transport sanctions, used in the past against states sponsoring terrorism, would have no effect on trans-national networks like Al-Qaeda. But there was scope to inhibit the financing of terrorism and the G8 (strictly the G7) had an instrument ready to hand for this.[36]

Back in 1989, the Paris summit had launched the Financial Action Task Force (FATF), to penalise the laundering of the proceeds of drug trafficking and organised crime. The FATF spent the 1990s helping its 28 members, mainly from OECD, to develop effective counter-measures against money-laundering. In 2000, the FATF decided to identify publicly countries whose financial systems gave too many opportunities to criminals and published a list of 15 such 'non-cooperative jurisdictions'. The G7 leaders at Okinawa endorsed a report from their finance ministers, which commended the FATF's action and added that countries that did not mend their ways would be vulnerable to counter-measures, even though Russia was on the list. This led to progress between Okinawa and Genoa, which enabled five jurisdictions to be taken off the list in 2001, including Russia, though six new countries were added.[37]

Early statements by G7 finance ministers in response to the terrorist attacks, on 25 September and 6 October 2001, established an Action Plan to penalise terrorist financing and mobilised the FATF for this purpose. G7 and other FATF countries overhauled and redirected their money-laundering legislation to target the financing of terrorism - often revealing shortcomings in their earlier measures. The FATF was given a new mandate to attack terrorist finances and lost no time in drawing up detailed guidance.[38] This formed the basis for wider campaigns against terrorist finance, especially through the IMF, which gained remarkable worldwide support. By February 2002, when the G7 finance ministers met again, nearly 150 countries had issued orders to freeze terrorist assets and over $100 million had already been frozen.[39] These actions were endorsed and commended by the G8 heads at Kananaskis, though without discussion. After this initial spurt, however, progress slowed down and it proved very hard to track down terrorist funds through the banking system, because of the use of clandestine unregulated channels. But despite frequent warnings that new efforts were needed, terrorist finance never became a topic for discussion among the heads.[40]

Protecting Means of Transport

The attacks of 11 September were made by hijacking civil aircraft and using them as destructive weapons. They were followed by other attempts to blow up aircraft, either by bombs on board or missile attacks from the ground. So better protection of aircraft and other means of transport were a natural focus for G8 action, with the initiative coming from the United States.

Kananaskis adopted a wide-ranging agreement on transport security, covering both air and sea transport of passengers and goods. Evian followed this with a specific agreement on protecting aircraft from attack from the ground, by hand-held rocket systems (MANPADS). Sea Island endorsed another broad agreement called the Secure and Facilitated International Travel Initiative (SAFTI), focusing on procedures to deter terrorist attacks on aircraft and their passengers.

All these agreements were driven by security considerations, which tended to override economic factors. They required detailed discussions among officials and often led to tense exchanges, especially when the US appeared to insist on more stringent rules for international travel than it applied domestically. Most of the follow-up to the G8 agreements was pursued through international institutions, especially the ICAO and the IMO. While having these agreements on the summit agenda helped to stimulate agreement among the G8, it was never necessary for the heads to discuss them explicitly or to resolve differences at their level.

Capacity-Building

The Americans and the rest of the G8 soon realised that many poorer countries needed help to build up their defences against terrorism. The Evian summit adopted an Action Plan on Building Capacity to Combat Terrorism, which was one of the few decisions taken there which justified the involvement of heads of government. The Action Plan offered assistance to governments in keeping out terrorists, in tracking them down and bringing them to justice. Such assistance would be coordinated through a new Counter-Terrorism Action Group (CTAG), working with the UN. But no financial amounts were specified and by Sea Island the heads seemed to have forgotten about their initiative.

Summary on Terrorism

Given the importance attached by the United States to the fight against terrorism, the amount of collective action by the G8 heads seems rather meagre. The deep disagreements over Iraq can explain why it was omitted from the agenda at Kananaskis and Evian. But Afghanistan, where they did agree, was hardly discussed either. The heads did not consider the measures needed to restore Afghanistan as a viable state. The only topic regularly covered was the revival of opium growing, as a source of heroin, but without the G8 having a visible impact on the problem. Terrorist finance was delegated to the finance ministers; transport measures never needed more than summit endorsement on the nod; and capacity-building soon went off the heads' agenda. The conclusion must be that the US preferred to keep major areas of anti-terrorist action in its own hands. Collective management was only used in areas where international channels were well-established, such as finance, transport and non-proliferation.

The G8 Summits and Non-Proliferation

The attacks of 11 September 2001 also changed the priorities for action in the field of non-proliferation. The main fear now was that weapons of mass destruction - nuclear, chemical or biological - would fall into the hands of terrorists. Governments mainly became a target if they were likely to be the channel whereby WMD reached terrorists, though the nuclear ambitions of both North Korea and Iran remained serious concerns. As with terrorism, the initiative always came from the Americans, whose objectives were set out in a series of speeches by Bush.[41] But there was rather more visible input by other G8 members.

The Global Partnership against the Spread of WMD

The Global Partnership, a major initiative from Kananaskis, built on work endorsed by earlier G7 and G8 summits (especially Okinawa) to counter nuclear smuggling, especially of plutonium, out of the former Soviet Union. The Americans had already developed programmes - the Nunn-Lugar initiative - to destroy nuclear, chemical and biological weapons, to make safe nuclear installations in Russia and to retrain Russian scientists. They had committed substantial sums for this purpose, though most of this was spent in the United States. Other G7 members, such as the UK, had developed programmes to be carried out inside Russia, but found these frustrated by bureaucratic obstruction. The promise of better cooperation, extracted with difficulty from Putin at Kananaskis, encouraged the rest of the G7 to match the $10 billion already committed by the US. Over the next two years the scale of the problem in Russia was clearly defined, other countries were added to the subscribers and the financing targets were almost met. But the disbursement of funds was extremely slow. Putin proved unable to unblock the problems at lower levels and projects still faced problems of access, legal protection and insurance cover.[42]

The Proliferation Security Initiative (PSI)

Just before the Evian summit, Bush made a speech in Cracow on 30 May 2003. There he advocated measures to prevent the international movement of WMD and their delivery systems, whether by sea, air or land. This would be achieved by intercepting ships, aircraft or other means of transport that were known or suspected to be carrying WMD. The idea was discussed at Evian, but no immediate G8 agreement was reached, as the US at first sought measures that would enable any ship under suspicion to be stopped and searched on the high seas. In later discussion this provision was watered down, so that the Proliferation Security Initiative, as agreed, only allowed for searches in port or coastal waters with the permission of the territorial state, or on the high seas with the permission of the country under whose flag the ship was sailing. Comparable provisions were agreed for aircraft. Since many countries were prepared to concede such permissions in advance, the PSI could still prove effective.[43]

By the Sea Island summit the PSI was well established and all G8 countries had signed up to it, including Russia. In October 2003 a suspected German ship sailing from Dubai to Tripoli was stopped and searched and proved to be carrying equipment for Libya that could only be used in developing nuclear weapons.[44] This was decisive in persuading the Libyan government to abandon its WMD programme and to reveal the extent of its arsenal and its international sources - see further below.

Exporting Reprocessing Technology

On 15 September 2003 and 11 February 2004 Bush made two more major speeches advocating further non-proliferation measures. The actions proposed in the first speech, made to the UN General Assembly, were later endorsed in the comprehensive Security Council Resolution 1540.[45] The second speech advocated the strengthening of the disciplines applied by the IAEA to countries with nuclear power programmes, to prevent these being used in the construction of WMD. Both the UN Security Council resolution and the bulk of the measures relating to the IAEA were welcomed by the G8 at Sea Island. The rest of the G8 were happy to see the US working through multilateral institutions in this sensitive field.

On one US proposal, however, agreement could not be reached. The Americans suggested there should be no more transfers of nuclear enrichment technology to countries that did not already possess it. The rest of the G8 resisted this as discriminating against poor countries and depriving them of the option to develop nuclear power as an energy source. The G8, however, agreed on a one-year moratorium on such exports, in the hope of reaching a consensus by Gleneagles 2005.[46]

Hard Cases: North Korea, Iran, Libya and Iraq

In his State of the Union address on 29 January 2002, Bush identified North Korea, Iran and Iraq as 'an axis of evil', because they were the most likely source of WMD for terrorists.[47] In addition to these three, Cuba, Libya, Sudan and Syria were regarded with deep suspicion by the Americans.[48] The countries of the 'axis', together with Libya, were all the subject of exchanges among the G8, though in very different ways.

North Korea The nuclear ambitions of North Korea, together with the prospects for North/South reconciliation, had been a recurrent concern of the summits of the 1990s. At Okinawa the prospects for reconciliation had seemed good. But these hopes received a sharp reversal in October 2002, when North Korea revealed that it had an active nuclear arms programme and withdrew from the Nuclear Non-Proliferation Treaty (NPT).[49] Not only the United States, but also Japan and Russia among the G8 members were directly concerned. Although the North Koreans tried to deal with the US and its Asian neighbours separately, the Americans wisely insisted on working through a six-nation group, composed of North and South Korea, China, Russia, Japan and the US, which began meeting in August 2003.[50] The United States sought and obtained backing from the whole G8 at Evian and Sea Island that the objective should be the complete and irreversible ending of North Korea's nuclear weapons programme.

Iran The problems with Iran were different. From 2002 onwards the Americans tried to convince their G8 partners that the Iranians were using their nuclear power programme (for which they were getting help from Russia) as cover for nuclear weapons development.[51] The US wanted early punitive action taken against Iran in the IAEA and the UN Security Council. But the Iranians denied any wrongdoing and remained members of the NPT. The Europeans wanted to try persuasion as well as pressure, so that the appeal to Iran from Evian contrasted with the warning to North Korea. Russia, however, said it would suspend its assistance programme.

In November 2003 the foreign ministers of France, Germany and the UK, with general EU backing, struck a deal in Tehran whereby the EU would provide help to Iran in return for it allowing IAEA inspectors to confirm the peaceful nature of its nuclear programme.[52] But the inspectors found evidence of Iranian deception, so that the IAEA adopted a highly critical resolution, provoking Iran to declare it would withdraw from the deal. The G8's message to Iran from the Sea Island summit was tougher than the year before. But the Europeans still tried to keep their diplomatic approach alive, despite some tension with the US.[53]

Libya Though Libya had been ostracised for twenty years because of its sponsorship of terrorism, the Libyan government eventually accepted responsibility for the Lockerbie bombing of 1986. The US and UK launched discreet talks (begun under Clinton and pursued under Bush) on normalising relations in return for Libya abandoning its WMD programme. The interception of the ship carrying nuclear equipment in October 2003 made the Libyans realise that their intentions were known and two months later Gadaffi decided abruptly to make a complete disclosure of Libya's plans and to start dismantling its stocks of WMD.[54] This move was strongly welcomed by the G8 at Sea Island, where the heads also recommended that Libya should benefit from the Global Partnership.

Iraq In contrast to the others, the threat from Iraq's WMD was never discussed by the G8. Neither Bush nor any of the other heads raised Iraq at Kananaskis - with hindsight, a discussion there might have saved much pain. At Evian the reconciliation among the G8 was so recent that no one wanted to discuss such a sensitive subject. By Sea Island it was becoming clear that Iraq's WMD programme, which the UK and US had made a reason for invading, no longer existed.

Summary on Non-Proliferation

The G8 achievements on non-proliferation were more substantial than on terrorism as such. The United States clearly concluded that this subject could best be pursued by using multilateral institutions, like the UN and the IAEA, or plurilateral instruments like the Global Partnership, the PSI and the Korean six-party conference. While most of the initiatives came from the US, there were active interventions from the Europeans (over Iran) and Japan and Russia (over North Korea), which tempered the American strategy. All were engaged in the Global Partnership, which depended on Russian involvement, and in the PSI, where Germany had facilitated the interception of the ship carrying nuclear material to Libya. The only exception to this pattern was Iraq.

Performance under the Criteria

The G8 summit's performance gets a broadly positive assessment in this area:

- The summits showed clear *leadership* in proliferation issues, moving the treatment of issues forward cumulatively and introducing innovative measures. They were less active themselves in other terrorism subjects, though their interest in transport security and terrorist finance helped to ensure agreement was reached at lower levels. But the G8 did not show leadership over Afghanistan and then Iraq. If they had, they could have avoided a lot of trouble.
- On these subjects, the summits were *effective* in reconciling political and economic pressures, though usually at the expense of economics. But they were not effective in overcoming the domestic obstacles in Russia to the Global Partnership.
- *Solidarity* was maintained quite successfully on most subjects. Although the initiative almost always came from the United States, the other G8 members were prepared to give support and suggest modifications. So collective

management was achieved, not always on American terms, though tension persisted over some issues, such as Iran.

- It is too soon to judge whether the measures adopted would be *durable*, but in both the non-proliferation agenda and in transport security there was successful practice of iteration, whereby subjects came back to the summit to be improved and expanded.
- Most of the decisions adopted were pursued in broader multilateral or plurilateral contexts, which helped to ensure their *acceptability*. Measures like the Global Partnership and the PSI were successful in attracting support from non-G8 governments. NGOs and epistemic communities began to take a positive interest in the non-proliferation programmes.
- The requirements of *consistency* were only moderately well satisfied. Aspects of terrorism were neglected, while US policy on Iraq did not fit in with the rest of the agenda. There was some concern that the requirements of transport security and blocking terrorist finance would be economically damaging to poor countries and the promised capacity-building assistance was slow to appear.

Lessons from the Summit Record

The lessons that can be drawn from the G8 summit achievements on Africa, terrorism and non-proliferation reveal how the summit changed after 11 September 2001.

Leadership

The most striking example of leadership was the G8's joint programme with the group of African presidents sponsoring NEPAD. This was highly innovative in establishing the first systematic link between the G8 and another group of countries. The G8 heads insisted that the Africans should retain responsibility and 'ownership' of the strategy to revive their continent. They gave priority to Africa as a key element of their fight against the root causes of terrorism. There was also good leadership in the G8's cumulative non-proliferation programme. However, terrorist finance, which was left to finance ministers, in fact seemed more deserving of summit attention than transport security, while the Americans kept other important terrorism subjects off the G8 agenda.

Effectiveness

The Africa programme was highly effective in combining political and economic elements, in a way never attempted by the G7 summit. A similar model was used in the broader Middle East initiative adopted at Sea Island, though without the same impetus from the region. The summit was thus developing a new capacity to integrate politics and economics. In contrast, the G8 summits were not very effective in reconciling international and domestic pressures where these applied to these subjects. Resistance to the Global Partnership persisted within Russia, while the G8 were least forthcoming to Africa in areas like trade access that required changes in domestic policy. This lack of economic generosity contrasted with the readiness of the G8 to put up large sums for political purposes, like the Global Partnership and peace support in Africa.

Solidarity

Overall, there was good solidarity among the G8 members, though with a marked difference between Africa and the other items. The African programme was essentially driven by the UK, Canada and France. But the US, though not an originator, was still a very active participant, taking the lead in specific areas like AIDS and famine relief. On all the terrorism and proliferation items, the United States took the initiative and the others were ready to follow. They were only too pleased when Bush decided to use international channels to pursue its counter-terrorism agenda, but still intervened to modify or restrain American approaches, for example on Iran, the PSI and transfers of reprocessing technology. While terrorism items might follow the pattern of the early G7 summits, where nothing much happened without US initiative, Africa was a clear example of genuine collective management.[55]

Durability

It was hard to tell, so soon after the measures were taken, whether they would prove durable. A true African renaissance would take many decades, so the G8/NEPAD link would require the same 'generational commitment' as the broader Middle East initiative adopted at Sea Island. Similarly, the effects of the non-proliferation and other counter-terrorism measures could only be felt over the long term. But the G8 so far showed commendable stamina on Africa, meeting African leaders every year and keeping up the momentum on both economic and political fronts. Non-proliferation was also treated iteratively, with new measures being added at successive summits.

Acceptability

The Africa programme had early problems of acceptability, because it seemed to be limited to exclusive groups of G8 and African leaders, who imposed decisions from the top. Once the G8 Action Plan and NEPAD were established, it became easier to involve other countries, the private sector and international institutions, who were represented in the Africa Partners Group and the Commission for Africa created by Blair. But the process would continue to attract criticism as long as Mugabe was in power in Zimbabwe. The measures on non-proliferation, terrorist finance and transport security were all fed into wider institutions, which made them more acceptable, though controversy over Iraq meant that anything started by the United States was likely to attract resistance.

Consistency

There were signs of inconsistency over Africa. In contrast to the progress made in peace-keeping and standards of governance, the G8 adopted too slowly, or not at all, the measures needed - in aid volume, primary education, debt relief and trade access, etc - to help Africa to meet the Millennium Development Goals embodied in NEPAD. Most of the terrorism and non-proliferation measures were consistent with each other and fitted into broader international frameworks, though this consistency was upset by US policy on Iraq. But there was a wider concern whether the advance of the political agenda was consistent with the G8's original vocation as an economic summit.

Conclusion

This chapter of performance assessment has concentrated on those issues to which the G8 heads gave the most attention during the seventh summit series to date. This attention was sustained over several summits and led to clear results on Africa, terrorism and non-proliferation. These results could be added to the progress made in financial architecture, debt relief, trade and development, as recorded in Chapters 5 and 8. But there were other issues, which the G8 either treated only inconclusively or on which they persistently failed to agree. Environmental issues like climate change and food safety were raised at every G8 summit, but the underlying transatlantic differences were not resolved. (Despite this, Blair has stated his attention of making climate change a priority subject for Gleneagles 2005.) The heads compared notes on economic prospects every year, but without taking operational decisions. A similar process was seen in areas such as employment, education and conflict prevention, which were treated briefly at summit level, but then dropped off the agenda again. All these other topics, however, will be included in the final chapter of conclusions, Chapter 14, which will consider how far the summits of the first G8 sequence met their objectives.

Notes

1 It featured, for example, at Bonn II 1985, see Putnam and Bayne 1987, p. 202.

2 See V. Mallet and R. Lambert, 'Mbeki Reveals Africa Development Plan', *Financial Times*, 27 November 2000.

3 The full text of the NEPAD document is accessible through the website www.nepad.org. For a fuller account of its origins, see De Waal 2002 and Van der Westhuizen 2003.

4 This concept of 'ownership' is an important parallel with the post-war Marshall Plan. The comparison between the Marshall Plan and the G8/NEPAD link is explored in Bayne 2003, on which the African part of this chapter is based.

5 The ideas for peer review were spelt out in the ECA's 'Compact for African Recovery' of April 2001. The ECA established contact with the OECD, the institution with the most extensive experience of peer review in policy coordination, so that the OECD could advise the Africans on the demands of peer review. See De Waal 2002 and

www.uneca.org. The OECD has since begun producing, with the African Development Bank, the *African Economic Outlook*, see www.oecd.org and note 26 below.

6 The original membership of the NEPAD Implementing Committee comprised the presidents of: Southern Africa - Botswana, Mozambique, South Africa; West Africa - Mali, Nigeria, Senegal; Northern Africa - Algeria, Egypt, Tunisia; East Africa - Ethiopia, Mauritius, Rwanda; Central Africa - Cameroon, Congo (Brazzaville), Gabon. From July 2002 Libya replaced Tunisia.

7 The African Union was formally created on 9 July 2002 and set up a number of pan-African institutions modelled on the European Union. See C. Hoyos and N. Degli Innocenti, 'Africa Launches a Union to Fight War and Poverty', *Financial Times,* 10 July 2002. The African Union incorporated a number of ideas promoted by Gadaffi of Libya. It looked as if acceptance of these ideas, plus a seat on the Implementing Committee, was the price of getting Gadaffi's acceptance of NEPAD. See De Waal 2002, pp. 467-469.

8 The first chair of the group was Bob Fowler, lately Canadian ambassador to the UN and concurrently sherpa for the Kananaskis summit; he remains Canadian APR. The French APR, who took over the chair before Evian, was Michel Camdessus, former Managing Director of the IMF. The British APR was of ministerial rank, first Baroness Amos and then Hilary Benn, Secretary of State for International Development.

9 The G8's 'Africa Action Plan', as well as the earlier 'Genoa Plan for Africa', is accessible on www.g8.utoronto.ca.

10 Mubarak of Egypt was also invited to Kananaskis, but could not attend. He was present at Evian for the large outreach meeting, but did not stay for the Africa session. He declined an invitation to Sea Island because of reservations about the broader Middle East initiative.

11 The concept of 'enhanced partnership' was also derived from the ECA's 'Compact for African Recovery' - see note 5 above.

12 This was a major difference between the G8's relations with Africa and the Marshall Plan - see note 4 above.

13 The need for such machinery, and suggestions for it, are the theme of Maxwell and Christiansen 2002.

14 The European Union undertook in March 2001 to admit all products from least developed countries free of duties and quotas, though with transitional arrangements for bananas, rice and sugar. The Canadian measures matched those of the EU, except that eggs, poultry and dairy produce were not covered. For the United States, access was provided under the Africa Growth and Opportunity Act of 2000. See Chapter 8 above, with notes 20 and 21.

15 See P. Vallely, 'Blair Backs New Drive to Transform Africa's Dire Outlook', *Independent,* 27 February 2004. The Commission has since met in London in May and in Addis Ababa in October 2004; its report is due in March 2005.

16 D. White, 'More Signs of Peace But Progress is Slow', *Financial Times* Davos Survey, 21 January 2004.

17 A. England, 'Darfur's Green Berets Take Pride in African Union Mission', *Financial Times,* 26 September, 2004.

18 See G. Dinmore and C. Adams, 'US Backs Extended African Union Mission in Darfur', and C. Adams, 'Blair Pledges EU Force to Aid Africa', *Financial Times,* 6 and 8 October, 2004.

19 See the critique in Chabal 2002.

20 See for example, the recent study by the US Council for Foreign Relations, Atwood, Browne and Lyman 2004. This is summarised in Atwood and Lyman 2004.

21 J. Reed, 'Pan-African Parliament Holds its First Session', *Financial Times,* 17 September 2004.

22 Mbeki was especially loath to attack Mugabe. Obasanjo was ready to be more critical, as he showed at the Abuja Commonwealth Heads of Government Meeting in November 2003.

23 A total of 17 countries were ready to submit to peer review: Algeria, Angola, Burkina Faso, Cameroon, Ethiopia, Gabon, Ghana, Kenya, Mali, Mauritius, Mozambique, Nigeria, Republic of Congo, Rwanda, Senegal, South Africa and Uganda. Angola and Mauritius had joined the list in Chapter 10, note 8. See 'African Leaders Invite Criticism', *The Economist,* 21 February 2004.

24 The first MCA beneficiaries were announced in June 2004. Of the eight Africans, half had accepted NEPAD peer review (Ghana, Mali, Mozambique, Senegal) but half had not (Benin, Cape Verde, Lesotho, Madagascar). See G. Dinmore, 'US Scheme Rewards Good Governance With Aid', *Financial Times,* 3 June 2004.

25 See 'Survey - Sub-Saharan Africa', *The Economist,* 17 January 2004.

26 See *African Economic Outlook,* 2003-2004 (OECD 2004), accessible on www.oecd.org.

27 The OECD was doubtful about Monterrey commitments - see A. Beattie, 'Capacity of Rich Nations to Fulfil Pledges on Aid Questioned', *Financial Times,* 29 January 2004.

28 On the World Bank and the IFF, see Chapter 8 above with note 31. Jeffrey Sachs and the Millennium Project argued for an increase of $75 billion per year till 2015; see Sachs 2004 and 'How to Save the World', *The Economist,* 30 October 2004.

29 A. Beattie, 'Rich Nations Tackled Over Education Initiative Fund' and A. Balls, 'Donors Fail on Education Funding', *Financial Times,* 25 March 2003 and 29 March 2004 - see Chapter 8 above, with notes 50-52.

30 For early African pressure on the World Bank, see J. Lamont, 'African Censure for World Bank over Drive to Reduce Poverty', *Financial Times,* 22 October 2002. For later arguments, see C. Swann, 'Poor Countries Debt Relief "Failing"' and K. Watkins, 'Africa's Burden of Debt is Far Too Heavy', *Financial Times,* 13 and 22 September 2004. Kevin Watkins is Research Director of Oxfam.

31 See A. Balls and A. Beattie, 'Differences between US and UK to Stall Debt Relief Deal' and A. Balls and C. Giles, 'G7 Promises Progress on Debt Relief', *Financial Times,* 30 September and 4 October 2004. A good review of the issues is in 'Debt Relief - Clean Slate', *The Economist,* 2 October 2004.

32 See F. Williams and G. de Jonquières, 'US Fights Plea by Africans Over Cotton', *Financial Times,* 11 September 2003 and A. Beattie, and J. Lamont, 'US Farm Bill Arouses African Fury', *Financial Times,* 24 May 2002.

33 D. White, 'Failure of World Trade Talks May Harm Smaller African Nations', *Financial Times,* 25 September 2003.

34 See F. Williams, 'G90 Talks Threaten to Derail Outline Trade Pact' and G. de Jonquières and F. Williams, 'Poorer Nations to Soften Trade Stance', *Financial Times,* 9 and 14 July 2004. The needs of poor countries in the WTO are discussed in G. de Jonquières, 'Call for Trade Rule Overhaul to Favour Poor Nations' (on report for the Commonwealth Secretariat of a group chaired by Joseph Stiglitz) and S. Page, 'Making Doha a Better Deal for Poor Countries' *Financial Times,* 21 June and 27 July 2004.

35 See Hajnal 1999, p. 13 and Kurosawa 2002, pp. 118-119.

36 Wechsler 2001, written before 11 September, had already drawn attention to Osama bin Laden's use of clandestine financial networks.

37 Russia was still on the 'non-cooperative' list at the time of the Genoa summit, but came off it later in 2001; see Bayne 2002, pp. 35-36.
38 See 'Terrorist Finances', *The Economist,* 29 September 2001 and H. Williamson, 'Global Financial Taskforce Needs Overhaul to Fight Terrorism', *Financial Times,* 3 October 2001.
39 E. Alden, 'Complex Finances Defy Global Policing', *Financial Times,* 21 February 2002.
40 See 'Terrorist Finance - Follow the Money', *The Economist,* 1 June 2002, C. Norgren (President of the FATF) and J. Caruana, 'Wipe out the Treasuries of Terror' and S. Fidler, 'Al-Qaeda Outsmarts Sanctions, Says UN', *Financial Times,* 7 April and 28 August 2004.
41 A good review of US aims is in the article by John Bolton, Under-Secretary of State for Arms Control and International Security, 'An All-Out War on Proliferation', *Financial Times,* 7 September 2004.
42 See the latest reports of the Strengthening the Global Partnership Project, accessible on www.sgpproject.org. The participants in this project have regularly warned about the problems of implementation, see M. Turner, 'Plans to Secure WMD "Fall Far Short"', *Financial Times,* 19 November 2003.
43 For a full analysis of progress under the PSI, see *The Monitor* 2004.
44 For details of the interception, see S. Fidler and M. Huband, 'Turks and South Africans Helped Libya's Secret Nuclear Arms Project', *Financial Times,* 10 June 2004. See also note 54 below.
45 See the Bolton article recorded in note 34 above.
46 See Chapter 11, note 17.
47 'American Leadership: the Axis of Evil' and 'Weapons Proliferation: Know Thine Enemy', *The Economist,* 2 February 2002, pp. 13-14 and 24-26.
48 'State-Sponsored Terrorism: the Seven Deadly Sinners', *The Economist,* 25 May 2002.
49 A scholarly analysis of the onset of the Korean nuclear crisis is in Bleiker 2003.
50 See 'Dealing with North Korea', *The Economist,* 23 August 2003. These talks have continued in being, though with many ups and downs - see A. Fifield, 'Fresh Push to Revive North Korea Talks', *Financial Times,* 18 October 2004.
51 For a scholarly analysis of Iran's nuclear ambitions, see Bowen and Kidd 2004. See also 'Iran's Nuclear Plans', *The Economist,* 1 March 2003.
52 R. Khalaf, 'Iran Still Urged to Give Arms Assurance', *Financial Times,* 22 October and 'Give Diplomacy a Chance' *The Economist,* 22 November 2003.
53 G. Smyth and J. Johnson, 'Europe Trio Seeks Guarantee on Iran Nuclear Policy' and G. Dinmore, 'G8 Bid to Heal Rift on Iran', *Financial Times,* 30 July and 18 October 2004.
54 'Libya's Weapons of Mass Destruction', *The Economist,* 3 January 2004. In September the US lifted the sanctions it maintained on trade and investment with Libya - E Alden, 'US Lifts Trade Embargo Against Libya', *Financial Times,* 21 September 2004.
55 On American leadership and the G7 summits, see Putnam and Bayne 1987, pp. 272-273.

CONCLUSIONS

Chapter 13

Concentrating the Mind: Summit Process

Dr Johnson said: 'When a man knows he is to be hanged in a fortnight, it concentrates his mind wonderfully'.[1] Though less extreme than execution, summit meetings like the G8, where heads of government meet informally in a small group, are also a device to 'concentrate minds' on cooperative decision-making, so as to respond to intractable problems where international and domestic pressures interact. This chapter examines how this decision-making process works, at the G8 summit and in the G8 system as a whole, and how it has changed as a result of new demands in the early 21st century.[2]

For the twenty-odd years of the G7 summits, decision-making took place on two closely knit levels. One level comprised the heads of government themselves and the foreign and finance ministers who always accompanied them to the summit. The second was composed of a small team of bureaucrats led by the head's personal representative or 'sherpa'. Follow-up to summit decisions was entrusted to wider international institutions. This hermetic system served the G7 summit well in its earlier years. But it did not offer an adequate response to the pressures of advancing globalisation, which brought many new subjects onto the summit agenda and many new actors, both state and non-state, onto the international stage.

During the first sequence of G8 summits, as summarised in Chapter 1, the shape of the decision-making process changed radically. The heads of government detached their flanking ministers and began meeting by themselves. The supporting apparatus, at both official and ministerial level, became much more complex and developed a life of its own. Many more outside players became involved both in the preparation of the summits and in their follow-up.

This chapter looks back over the summit narratives to draw out the key questions in G8 decision-making since the Birmingham summit of 1998. How far did the G8 heads of government (listed in Tables 13.1 and 13.2) regain personal control of the summit process? Or did they still rely on the preparatory work of the G8 apparatus? What was the impact of wider outreach to non-G8 countries and the private sector? What were the pressures on the size and membership of the summit? The analysis seeks to distinguish three levels of input to the process:

- The contribution of the heads of government themselves;
- The contribution of the supporting apparatus;
- The contribution of other actors, both state and non-state.

The question of membership has an impact on all three levels.

Table 13.1 G8 Heads of Government, Sixth Summit Series, 1998-2001

Summit	*Birmingham May 1998*	*Cologne June 1999*	*Okinawa July 2000*	*Genoa July 2001*
Country				
United Kingdom	**Blair**	Blair	Blair	Blair
Germany	Kohl	**Schroeder**	Schroeder	Schroeder
Japan	Hashimoto	Obuchi	**Mori** (Obuchi)	Koizumi
Italy	Prodi	D'Alema	Amato	**Berlusconi** (Amato)
Canada	Chrétien	Chrétien	Chrétien	Chrétien
France	Chirac	Chirac	Chirac	Chirac
United States	Clinton	Clinton	Clinton	Bush
Russia	Yeltsin	Yeltsin	Putin	Putin
EU Commission	Santer	Santer	Prodi	Prodi
EU Presidency	Blair (UK)	Schroeder (Germany)	Chirac (France)	Verhofstadt (Belgium)

Note

Names in bold indicate the summit host and chair. In 2000-2001 Obuchi and Amato prepared the summit, but were no longer in office when it was held.

Table 13.2 G8 Heads of Government, Seventh Summit Series, 2002-2005

Summit	*Kananaskis June 2002*	*Evian June 2003*	*Sea Island June 2004*	*Gleneagles July 2005*
Country				
United Kingdom	Blair	Blair	Blair	***Blair***
Germany	Schroeder	Schroeder	Schroeder	*Schroeder*
Japan	Koizumi	Koizumi	Koizumi	*Koizumi*
Italy	Berlusconi	Berlusconi	Berlusconi	*Berlusconi*
Canada	**Chrétien**	Chrétien	Martin	*Martin*
France	Chirac	**Chirac**	Chirac	*Chirac*
United States	Bush	Bush	**Bush**	*Bush*
Russia	Putin	Putin	Putin	*Putin*
EU Commission	Prodi	Prodi	Prodi	*Barroso*
EU Presidency	Aznar (Spain)	Simitis (Greece)	Ahern (Ireland)	*Blair* (UK)

Note
The heads given under Gleneagles offer the best estimate of those likely to be present. But Blair expects to hold elections before July 2005 and Berlusconi may be forced to, while Martin leads a minority government.

Under each heading, there will be separate consideration of the contribution to organisation and preparation, to the summit itself and to follow-up. The findings are summarised under each heading as the chapter proceeds, while the conclusions assess the interaction of the three levels with each other.

The Contribution of the Heads

The G7 summit was conceived as a personal encounter of the leaders of the world's most powerful economies. The founders believed that bringing the heads of government together would lead them to understand better both the domestic problems of their peers and the international responsibilities that they all shared. This would enable them to solve, through personal interaction and original ideas, problems that had baffled their bureaucrats. The bureaucrats themselves ought to be kept out of the process entirely.[3]

This vision soon proved to be out of reach. But the prospect of informal and spontaneous contacts, at which they could develop their own ideas, continued to exercise a powerful attraction on the heads. During the 1990s, the heads increasingly complained that the agenda and the documents were too long, giving them no scope to make their own input. But the reforms introduced at Birmingham revived hope among the heads that they could at last take direct control of the summit process. This section considers how and where the heads were able to act in their personal capacity in the G8 summit process, without relying on their officials and the rest of the apparatus.

The Heads and Summit Organisation

The G7 heads had always put a high premium on informal exchanges in a small, select group. As British Prime Minister Callaghan said in 1976:

> The numbers attending are small and compact. Discussions are businesslike and to the point. We do not make speeches at one another. We talk frankly but also as briefly as we can, and a lot of ground is covered.[4]

The G8 heads likewise professed to want summit procedures kept simple, although some of their own practices frustrated this. This desire for simplicity shaped their approach to the numbers involved and to summit membership.

Numbers Involved Ever since 1975, the heads had been flanked at the summits by their foreign and finance ministers, which involved quite a crowd around the table. Several attempts to meet without the ministers were frustrated, usually by Germany, Japan or the US.[5] By the mid-1990s, however, the agenda had grown so dense that the heads and their ministers were meeting at the summit in separate groups, with only rare plenaries. In 1998 Blair was able to separate the flanking ministers in time as well as space, so that from Birmingham onwards only the heads came to the summit, with ministers meeting separately beforehand.

'Heads-only summits' were clearly welcome to the leaders themselves. Meeting alone gave the heads greater freedom to develop their own ideas and to strike deals among themselves, as Chapter 14 explores. There were now only nine or ten seats at the table, depending on whether an extra seat was needed for the EU Presidency. When all the heads were reasonably fluent in English, as happened after Putin and Koizumi arrived, they could have a genuine debate. This helped to build up a sense of personal closeness and confidence, which was helped by unusual continuity among the G8 heads. As Tables 13.1 and 13.2 show, the group of leaders has remained unchanged from Genoa to Sea Island, except for the rotating EU Presidency and Martin's arrival in the last year.[6] Even where there was tension, as between Bush and Chirac, it was at least predictable.

For the first two G7 summits, at Rambouillet and San Juan, Puerto Rico, the heads had been lodged under one roof, but this practice lapsed thereafter. Since each G7 member had its own accommodation, there was no limit in the size of the supporting delegations, even though they never got into the meeting room. The United States and Japan tended to bring huge delegations, so that in Genoa the Italian hosts had to lodge them in cruise liners in the harbour. After 2001, security considerations obliged the summit to be held in secluded sites that could be easily isolated. This meant that once again the heads were all lodged in the same hotel or resort, with limited space for supporting delegations. This too was welcome to the heads, as it increased the scope for spontaneous meetings on the margin of the summit, as when Bush and Blair met at 6.30am in the gym at Kananaskis.

Summit Membership The G7 heads had also insisted on keeping the number of participating countries to a minimum. Giscard only accepted reluctantly the inclusion of Italy, Canada and the European Community. Once the size of the summit had been settled in 1977, at seven powers plus the EC, the heads resisted any move to add new members for twenty years.

The Birmingham reforms went against this trend by adding Russia as a formal member and making G7 into G8. This was easier for the G7 heads to accept now that supporting ministers no longer came to the summit. Despite the political advantages of this enlargement, it had drawbacks for decision-making. Yeltsin was not used to the informal mode and would make speeches at his colleagues. He was more interested in increasing Russia's prestige than in collective decisions. His successor Putin proved more flexible and participatory after he arrived at Okinawa. But this has made the G8 heads wary of extending invitations to other powers. The Russian experience showed that once a country had been invited, it could not be 'un-invited' without giving offence.

The evidence from the Kananaskis summit suggests that the heads themselves wish to preserve the intimacy of their exclusive grouping. There is no agreement among the heads at present to admit other countries to summit membership. When they decided at Kananaskis to allow Russia to host a summit for the first time, they also laid down a cycle of G8 presidencies for the rest of the decade, in a form that showed no sign of wanting to expand the participants further. It was their own decision, which took the sherpas by surprise. This view is likely to persist, as nearly all the G8 heads present at Kananaskis should meet again at Gleneagles in 2005 (see Table 13.2)[7]

The only conceivable change would be a decision to admit China, making G8 into G9.[8] Since the G8 heads had their conversation in Kananaskis, the case for admitting China has become much stronger. The Chinese economy has grown so big that it alone can have an impact on the world trading and monetary system. China is now active in the WTO, while on the margins of the IMF the G7 finance ministers have begun inviting China to their meetings.[9] Politically, China is increasingly influential both in Asia, where it cooperates with G8 members, for example over North Korea, and in the world at large, especially as a permanent member of the UN Security Council. On economic and foreign political grounds, therefore, China has a strong case, which it puts it well ahead of other aspirants such as India or Brazil.[10]

The problem is that China does not meet the standards of democracy that are an implicit criterion for summit membership, even for Russia. The G8 will hesitate to admit China until this problem has been resolved by political change within the country itself. The idea has been floated of inviting China to attend on condition that it launches moves to become more democratic.[11] But conditional membership of this kind is like the long apprenticeship served by Russia and China is unlikely to find such conditions acceptable.

The Heads and Summit Preparation

Agenda-Setting The host head of government has the responsibility for setting the agenda. Though many topics are carried over from previous summits, agenda-setting is the point at which the host has most influence over the proceedings. Most heads take the opportunity to intervene personally, by writing to, telephoning or visiting their peers.

The intention, following Birmingham, was that the agenda should be kept short and precise. But when their turn comes, every head of government wants to take advantage of the summit's capacity to innovate. They want to put a stamp of originality on 'their' summit. In consequence, each summit has tended to add one or more new subjects to the agenda. For example, Schroeder introduced conflict prevention at Cologne, Obuchi added IT and infectious diseases at Okinawa, Chrétien gave priority to terrorism at Kananaskis and Bush focused on Middle East reform for Sea Island.

The importance of these issues often merited summit attention, which led to valuable innovation. But none of them had been on the original G7 agenda; they had either been occasional topics at earlier summits or were wholly new. But once they were on the agenda, they could not easily be taken off again. This trend showed how different leaders, in search of innovation at the summit, were themselves increasing the agenda overload about which they complained. By the end of the first G8 sequence, the summit agenda and documentation had become as prolific as it had been before Birmingham.

The Heads at the Summit

The new format introduced at Birmingham gave the heads greater freedom to act on their own at the summit itself. But the initiatives they took personally, without relying on their officials, proved to be limited in scope.

Policy Initiatives Ideas for brand new policies seldom prevailed, if they had not been filtered through the preparatory process. There were several examples of this during the first G8 sequence, usually started by Chirac or Bush. Chirac's ideas for a new food safety organisation, proposed before Cologne, and for suspending agricultural export subsidies, launched before Evian, came to nothing. Bush's suggestions for more grants by the World Bank and for a new approach to the Israel/Palestine dispute were not endorsed at the Genoa and Kananaskis summits and needed more negotiation at lower levels.

Procedural Initiatives The most striking personal initiative by the G8 heads was at the Genoa summit, when, after the working dinner with African presidents, they agreed on their own 'Genoa Plan for Africa'. This was done without any advance preparation, mainly on the instigation of Blair, Chirac and Chrétien. But this 'Genoa Plan' was essentially a procedural decision. It laid down some principles and set an agenda for future work, but did not contain any new policy commitments. These had to wait until a year later, when they were embodied in the Africa Action Plan prepared by the G8 Africa Group. Another procedural initiative that came from the heads themselves was the agreement at Kananaskis to let Russia host the summit in 2006. This appeared to be a spontaneous proposal by Schroeder, naturally encouraged by Putin.[12]

Political Reflexes On occasion the political instincts of the heads led them to pick out certain issues and go against what their officials have prepared. At Genoa the political sense of Blair and his colleagues told them that the conclusions prepared on Africa, before the working dinner, would not be adequate, so that they acted to expand them. Putin showed himself just as alert to this as his G7 colleagues, when he decided not to press for debt reduction at Okinawa or to raise disarmament at Genoa, though his advisers had urged him to do so.

Domestic Motivation The G8 heads also made personal use of the summit to respond to domestic pressures or to advance their domestic agenda. Blair in 1998 and Schroeder in 1999 were newly elected left-of-centre leaders, who used the summit to advance their own domestic objectives in employment and social protection. Successive Italian prime ministers promoted conflict prevention because of the domestic disruption caused by the turmoil in the Balkans across the Adriatic, especially by flows of refugees. These political objectives and pressures, of course, did not always have positive effects. In 2003 and 2004 Chirac held up G8 decisions relating to agriculture in the WTO, because of his concern about popular reactions in France.

The Heads and Summit Follow-up

Once the summit was over, the leaders rarely intervened to ensure its conclusions are carried out. In October 1998, Blair sounded his colleagues on whether the worsening monetary crisis called for an extraordinary summit - but they were content just to issue a statement encouraging their finance ministers. Likewise, Berlusconi suggested a special summit after the terrorist attacks of 11 September 2001, but this found no support. These personal interventions by the summit chairs in policy follow-up were exceptional and were not backed up by the rest of the G8.[13]

The position was quite different as regards communicating the summit outcome to the media. All the heads took pains to convey their own views to their national press corps, who had followed them to the summit site. The leaders wanted to make a good impression back home, which often led them to stress their personal victories, rather than the agreed results achieved at the summit. Comparing national accounts often revealed inconsistencies, which could focus public attention on points of difference rather than agreement.

Summary of the Contribution of the Heads

The main personal contribution of the heads of government to decision-making at the G8 summit, independent of their officials, can be summarised as follows:

- The heads were attached to simplicity of process and had a strong preference for small numbers, in membership and people round the table;
- Personal initiative mainly appeared in agenda-setting (by the summit host) and procedural decisions at the summit, prompted by political reflexes and reflecting domestic pressures;
- The heads were rarely involved in implementation, but paid close attention to media treatment of the summit.

The prospect of meeting their peers at the top table thus concentrated the minds of the leaders, especially where this international encounter could also advance their domestic agenda.[14] At first sight, this record of the heads' personal contribution suggests rather a meagre harvest. But in fact the heads were more likely to take independent initiatives at the summit if they were dissatisfied with the way the summit process was working, as they had been in the mid-1990s. The heads had themselves re-directed summit work on UN reform at Halifax in 1995, terrorism at Lyon in 1996 and crime at Denver in 1997. After the Birmingham reforms the heads had less reason to intervene against the grain of the preparations. The new format allowed them more scope to innovate and strike deals based on the preparatory work, as emerges from the next section and from Chapter 14 below.

The Contribution of the Supporting Apparatus

Even before the first summit of all, at Rambouillet in 1975, it was clear that the subject-matter of international economics was too complex for the heads to reach decisions without some preparation. The heads reconciled themselves to playing roles at the summit which had been written for them by others, especially their personal representatives or 'sherpas'. This was the first stage in institutionalising the summits.[15]

The preparation of the summit is largely in the hands of the supporting G8 apparatus. Even what happens at the summit itself usually owes more to the preparatory process than to the personal intervention of the heads. This section therefore looks at what supporting G8 bureaucrats and ministers do, both on their own and in combination with the heads of government.

Participants in the G8 Apparatus

The Sherpas Traditionally, summit preparations have been in the hands of the personal representatives or sherpas, who are chosen either for their closeness to the head or their seniority in their parent department. There were some changes in national practice during the G8 sequence. Under Republican Presidents Reagan and George Bush senior, the US sherpa had been a senior State Department figure. Clinton, like his Democrat predecessor Carter, chose his sherpa from his White House staff - and his Republican successor George W. Bush continued the practice. Chancellors Schmidt and Kohl had always made the state secretary at the finance ministry the German sherpa, but Schroeder has moved the post to his Chancellery. The sherpas remained in charge of the process during the first G8 sequence, but their authority was being threatened by the growing complexity of the decision-making.

Sous-Sherpas and Political Directors The sherpas are supported by two 'sous-sherpas', one each from the finance and foreign ministries, to work on the main summit agenda, and by the 'political directors' from foreign ministries, to prepare foreign policy subjects. Up until the early 1990s the entire group would meet together. But by the time of the G8 summits the sherpas, each set of sous-sherpas, and the political directors were meeting separately, to cover the growing agenda. Plenary meetings of the full team became rare. In addition, groups of specialist officials have grown up to deal with recurrent summit themes, such as crime, terrorism or non-proliferation, and they would produce reports for the sherpa team.

Africa Personal Representatives (APRs) The Genoa Plan for Africa created the G8 Africa Group, composed of Africa personal representatives who were charged with the joint preparation of the Africa Action Plan and its subsequent follow-up. The APRs were to report direct to the heads, without being under the authority of the sherpas. This was not a problem before Kananaskis, as Bob Fowler, who first chaired the G8 Africa Group, was concurrently Canadian APR and sherpa. But when the chair passed to Michel Camdessus, the French APR, he insisted on keeping the Africa process separate from the sherpas. The APRs later developed the African Partners Group, with wider participation. But they still have a direct link to the heads of government and are required to produce a report for the 2005 summit.

Ministerial Groups At the outset G7 foreign and finance ministers attended the summit as supporting the heads. But each group steadily asserted its independence. During the 1980s the secretive G5 was absorbed into the public G7 finance ministers, while G7 foreign ministers began meeting on their own on the margin of the UN General Assembly. After Birmingham 1998, both groups would meet just before the summit, but also at other times through the year. G7 finance ministers would always meet on the margins of IMF meetings. G8 foreign ministers would meet as issues required it, as when they held a special meeting on conflict prevention in December 1999, to carry out a remit from the Cologne summit.

Other ministers became associated with the summit in the 1990s, largely thanks to personal initiatives by the heads themselves. This led to regular or periodic meetings of environment ministers (promoted by Kohl) and employment ministers (backed in turn by Clinton, Chirac and Blair). These have been supplemented during the G8 sequence by energy ministers (started by Yeltsin), education ministers (thanks to Schroeder) and development ministers (begun by Chrétien). Interior and justice ministers, who first met in 1995 and 1996, have had annual meetings since 2001 and are now focused on terrorism issues.[16]

Originally, these specialist ministers met to prepare for summits and carry out instructions from the heads. But as the G8 sequence advanced, they have detached themselves from the summit and pursued their own independent agenda. In contrast, the G7 finance ministers, though no longer at the summit, at first felt obliged to control what the heads were doing on financial issues. Up to Kananaskis, they supplied the heads with reports for them to endorse and issue at the summit. But this practice has lapsed, as the heads' attention has moved away from finance.

All these ministerial groups include the Russians, except the finance ministers who now meet as G8 just before the summit and as G7 for the rest of the year. Each has its own apparatus of supporting officials. Once the summit began meeting as heads only, these separate ministerial groups have no longer felt bound to preserve the strict G8 format. The foreign ministers have invited selected other countries to join them for meetings focused on specific problems - for example, on Balkan stability in June 1999, in response to the Kosovo crisis. Both foreign and finance ministers met their counterparts from Middle Eastern countries in September/October 2004 to prepare for the first meeting of the 'Forum for the Future' launched at Sea Island.

The finance ministers' meetings have been especially original in the formation of G7-based groupings as part of the new financial architecture agreed in 1999. The Financial Stability Forum includes monetary authorities from non-G7 countries as well as international associations of regulators.[17] The G20 is a permanent grouping, intended to contribute to reform of the international financial system, which includes the G8, the EU and eleven more 'systemically significant' countries. Martin, now Canadian Prime Minister, was the first G20 chair.[18] In addition, the G7 finance ministers have begun meeting their Chinese counterparts, as noted above. These developments have encouraged outside ideas for reforming the institutions. One idea is that the G7 should be collapsed into a 'G4', composed of the US, Japan, China and the Eurozone.[19] Another is that the G20 could usefully meet also at head of government level - see below.

The persistence of these ministerial groups is a consequence of the heads meeting alone at the summit. The heads, having decided to exercise their own freedom, have essentially allowed these other groups to operate independently too, rather than trying to keep control over an ever-expanding pyramid of activity. In practice only the foreign and finance ministers really prepare for the summit. Their ability to involve non-G8 countries in their meetings makes it easier for the heads to resist pressure to expand the summit itself.

The G8 Apparatus and Summit Preparations

Timetable Summit preparations are concentrated in several meetings each spring of the sherpa teams, to select the agenda and start drafting the necessary documents. In many ways the dynamics of summit meetings are reproduced at sherpa level. At these small gatherings, discussion is frank, with plenty of personal interaction.[20] The sherpas get to know each other well, they understand each others' domestic background and they develop a sense of solidarity and shared responsibility. The sherpas become adept both at seeing what arguments would prove convincing, against their colleagues' domestic backgrounds, and at picking up ideas from the others which they can use to good effect back home.[21]

Agenda-Setting This is the task for the first sherpa meeting of the year. The host head of government, as shown earlier, focuses on new ideas to make that year's summit distinctive. The sherpas, on the other hand, have to wrestle with the on-going summit agenda of items started but not completed in earlier years.[22] The difficult issues that come up to the heads often need recurrent summit treatment, like Africa or debt relief for poor countries. While most items can be handed on to other established organisations for follow-up (see below), sometimes the institutions are inadequate, so that the G8 remains responsible for them.

The agenda is thus always under pressure. The innovative ideas of earlier years can become recurrent items later. Although the Birmingham reforms were meant to check this inflation of the agenda, later summits have kept on adding new items without taking old ones off. Choosing an open-ended agenda, as the French and Americans did in 2003 and 2004, encourages this process. In general, the hardest part of agenda-setting for the sherpas is deciding what to leave out.

Impact of the Apparatus on the Summit Itself

The work of the sherpa team prepares agenda items for treatment by the heads at the summit itself in three different ways: endorsement of work in progress; promoting agreement at lower levels; and promoting agreement at the summit itself.

Summit Endorsement - Work in Progress Endorsement makes up the largest and the easiest part of the summit agenda and documentation. It consists of the heads putting their authority behind work that is going on elsewhere. Often this will be activity that has been generated by earlier summits, so that the heads give their blessing to work in progress. In other cases G8 governments find it useful to have the endorsement of their peers for policies they have decided to adopt already, since this can be useful in overcoming domestic opposition.

This part of the summit agenda, however, is most subject to inflation. There is a strong incentive for G8 governments to seek summit endorsement for as many of their policies as they can. Once the heads have lent their authority to a particular subject, they are often reluctant to abandon it, for fear that others should conclude that they have ceased to care about it. But the wider this endorsement is given, the more its value becomes diluted.[23]

The move to heads-only summits was intended to reduce the issues coming to the heads for endorsement and to allow more issues to be pushed down to other ministers. The process worked well in the early G8 summits and shortened the summit documentation considerably. The Canadians made further progress in 2002 by abandoning the usual communiqué and insisting that only issues actually discussed by the heads should appear in the 'chair's summary' that replaced it. But this progress was reversed at Evian and Sea Island, when the summit documentation was full of accounts of what the G8 had already done elsewhere.

Stimulating Agreement at Lower Levels A more demanding technique is where summit discussion, or even the prospect of it, is used to resolve differences between G8 members which persist at lower levels and may prevent agreement in wider international contexts. A good example was seen in the international financial architecture agreed after the Asian crisis. The essential work on this was done by the G7 finance ministers and their deputies. On some issues there were deep divisions between them, but the approach of the summits at Birmingham in 1998 and Cologne in 1999 gave them an incentive to resolve these differences. The heads gave their authority to what their finance ministers had agreed, without adding anything of their own.

The work done since 1999 in conflict prevention also illustrates this well. After the initial impulse from the heads at Cologne, the foreign ministers worked up a detailed programme at their meetings in Berlin in December 1999 and Miyazaki in July 2000. The imminence of the Okinawa summit, a week after the Miyazaki meeting, concentrated their minds, so that heads only needed to endorse what the foreign ministers had done, without having to discuss it themselves. At Genoa the heads left the generic subject wholly to their foreign ministers, but identified conflict prevention as a specific element of their African initiative. Accordingly, the chapter on peace and security contained some of the most precise commitments in the Africa Action Plan agreed at Kananaskis.

The G8 summits' main achievement in trade also falls into this category. Neglect of trade at the summits of the late 1990s meant that the G8 did not have an agreed view on launching a new round of trade negotiations. This contributed to the disastrous failure of the Seattle WTO meeting late in 1999. But in 2001 the approach of the Genoa summit was used to stimulate and confirm agreement between the trade negotiators of the EU, the US, Japan and Canada. This facilitated a much more successful outcome from the Doha WTO meeting later in the year.

Finally, the approach of the G8 summit encouraged UN negotiators to reach agreement on resolutions to be adopted by the Security Council. This happened over Kosovo in 1999 and over Iraq in 2003 and especially 2004, when the resolution was adopted unanimously hours before the start of the Sea Island summit. Over Iraq, the consensus reached by diplomats in the UN may well have spared the heads from what could have been a fractious discussion.

Stimulating Agreement at the Summit Itself The two techniques described so far cover most of the summit content and often they will produce the most important evidence of G8 cooperation. But the heads also play a more direct role. In some cases they have to engage their own authority to give the necessary impetus to a wide-ranging or innovative programme. The work on IT and the digital divide at Okinawa, the decision to launch the Global Fund at Genoa and the broader Middle East initiative agreed at Sea Island are all examples of this. In other cases agreement can only be reached through the intervention of the heads themselves. This applied to the peace arrangement for Kosovo in 1999. Detailed preparations had been made, but everything hinged on the position of Yeltsin, which did not become clear until he reached the Cologne summit in person. Most of the provisions of the Africa Action Plan had been agreed before the Kananaskis summit, but the direct intervention of the heads was needed to confirm the figure of $6 billion per year in extra aid for Africa.

In yet other cases the heads are able to reach agreements that are not attainable at lower levels. Debt relief for low-income countries provides an example of this. After a disappointing outcome from Birmingham, Schroeder's move to ease the German position enabled the heads at Cologne to advance agreement on this subject further than their finance ministers had taken it. In debt relief the summit became identified as the place where things happen, so that it attracted huge demonstrations to Birmingham and Cologne.

Again, at Kananaskis the heads were able to overcome US reluctance and fix a figure of $1 billion for replenishing the World Bank trust fund for debt relief, where their finance ministers had failed. Bush was prepared to accept this $1 billion figure, because the Europeans, Japan and Canada had agreed to match the US contribution of $10 billion over ten years to clean up Russian nuclear and chemical weapons and installations. The agreement on this could only have been reached among the heads, with the direct involvement of Putin, because at lower levels the Russians had refused the necessary guarantees of access and legal protection. The link between the two agreements illustrates the summit's potential to identify and conclude cross-issue deals - see Chapter 14 below.

Such agreements exploit the heads' wish for some achievements of their own. They are not happy when everything at the summit has been 'pre-cooked'. The sherpas therefore try to provide some scope for the heads to go beyond what has been prepared for them. Without this, the heads will be tempted to take their own unprepared initiatives. But this strategy does not always work - and once discord is registered at the summit it may be harder to find agreement elsewhere. This is shown by the summits' treatment of environmental issues throughout the G8 sequence. At Okinawa, for example, raising the issue to head of government level in advance of a climate change meeting at The Hague later in 2000 did not resolve the disagreements.

Domestic Motivation When the heads are ready to go a bit further at the summit than their officials or ministers, that usually reflects their judgement of the balance of domestic and international advantage in reaching agreement. Yeltsin knew that the Kosovo settlement was unpopular in Russia, but he did not want to alienate the support of the G7. Blair and Schroeder were aware of strong public interest in debt relief, mobilised by the Jubilee 2000 Campaign. Bush knew that Congress was so keen on the agreement to clean up installations in Russia that they would regard $1 billion for debt relief as an acceptable price. But these domestic political considerations can also work in the wrong direction. On climate change and biodiversity the strongest domestic pressures in Europe come from consumer groups and public opinion, while in North America they come from producers and business interests. So agreement on environmental issues may actually be harder to reach at the summit than lower down.

The G8 Apparatus and Summit Follow-Up

In contrast to agenda-setting and summit preparation, the sherpa network plays a smaller part in summit follow-up. The G8 ministerial groups, however, have a growing role in the implementation of summit conclusions. They have much greater flexibility than the summit itself, in the choice of when they meet and whether they involve other countries. But by far the largest responsibility for summit follow-up, however, still rests with wider international institutions. The contribution of these outside bodies is considered in the next section of this chapter.

Summary of the Contribution of the Supporting Apparatus

The contribution of the supporting apparatus to the summit, whether working on its own or together with the heads, can be summarised as follows:

- The sherpa network has grown more complex and been supplemented by semi-independent ministerial groups that have greater flexibility in timing and participation;
- In agenda-setting, the hardest task for the sherpas is to keep the agenda under control;
- Summit endorsement of existing policies is valuable, but becomes devalued if used too much;
- The prospect of summit discussion can stimulate agreement at lower levels, without a direct contribution from the heads being necessary;
- The sherpas try to take advantage of the heads' desire to achieve something of their own, so as to advance agreement at the summit beyond the preparations;
- Sherpas take little part in follow-up; supporting ministers do rather more, but most is done in wider institutions.

The imminence of the summit concentrates the minds of those involved in the preparations, whether these are the sherpa team or the groups of G8 (and G7) ministers, and often this is enough to produce agreement. Although the G8 system has become more dispersed, the heads-only summits since Birmingham can still have this concentrating effect and lead to productive results.

The Contribution of Other Actors

During the 1970s and 1980s, summit preparations were held tightly by the sherpas. The summit itself was likewise a closed event. Summit follow-up was entrusted to other institutions, without much direct involvement by the G7. During the 1990s, however, the self-contained character of summitry began to loosen up and this process accelerated rapidly in the first G8 sequence. This loosening was a response to the new demands introduced by advancing globalisation and was a direct consequence of the heads meeting on their own. Once the summits had detached themselves from their own ministerial apparatus, they gained greater scope to form links with outside actors, both other non-G8 governments and non-state groups. This also reflected the perception by the heads of government of their responsibility to explain policy decisions to their peoples and to reassure them about the impact of globalisation.

Other Actors in Summit Preparation

Throughout the G7 cycle, the summit participants kept preparations firmly in their own hands. Outside governments had little chance to influence the process directly, except for other member states of the European Community (later European Union), who were consulted to some degree by the Commission. The OECD also held its annual ministerial meeting a few weeks before the summit, so that the non-G7 members could make their views known. As for non-government influences, these hardly went beyond visits to the host head of government by business and trade union delegations under OECD auspices. But this hermetic character of the preparations was opened up during the first G8 sequence.

Non-G8 Governments and International Institutions The growing involvement of supporting ministers in the preparatory process has enabled other international institutions to be involved. G7 and G8 ministers often invite senior staff members from these institutions to join them. The supporting ministerial groups also allow other governments to become involved, because, as noted above, they are not limited to a strict G7 or G8 format. For example, G8 foreign ministers involved other states and institutions in developing the Stability Plan for the Balkans before Cologne, while finance ministers met their colleagues from selected Middle Eastern countries as part of their preparations for Sea Island.

Private Business and NGOs In 2000, the Japanese prepared the treatment of IT and the digital divide at the summit by involving a range of major multinational companies. They organised a special conference shortly before Okinawa and incorporated most of its findings in the summit's own report. Before Okinawa the Japanese sherpa team also involved international NGO groups in consultations on the agenda.[24] These consultations were repeated by the Italians in 2001 and have become a standard element of summit preparation.[25]

Other Actors at the Summit Itself

Non-G8 Governments Outreach from the summit itself also began at Okinawa and Genoa, when the G8 leaders met groups of heads of government from developing countries, mainly from Africa, over a working dinner. At Kananaskis four African leaders together with the UN Secretary-General joined the G8 heads for the launch of their Africa Action Plan, as participants rather than guests. The Africans likewise took part at Evian and Sea Island and will be invited to Gleneagles in 2005. A parallel group of Middle Eastern leaders came to Sea Island as well. These outreach meetings show the G8 heads engaged with leaders from specific regions where they have undertaken policy initiatives. The heads are concerned that these extra meetings could reduce the time available for discussion among themselves and will not want to be committed to meet the Africans or the Middle East group every year. There was in fact no requirement for an African meeting in 2004, as the G8 Africa Group were not due to report till 2005, while the Middle East leaders are not expected to be at Gleneagles.

At Evian the G8, for the first time, met a larger group of leaders from developing countries that included major powers like China, India, Brazil, Mexico and South Africa. With this outreach meeting the G8 members recognised that, as globalisation advanced, more countries have become influential players in the international system and need to be associated with their decision-making. But there is no clear consensus on how this broader outreach should be developed. Chirac has proposed that the large outreach meeting at Evian should become an annual event, without specifying who should attend. Martin has advocated meetings at head of government level of the G20 to consider specific major issues.[26] Bush decided against any large outreach meeting at Sea Island.

Blair expects to hold a large outreach meeting at Gleneagles of countries with an interest in the summit's agenda. As long as the G8 determines which non-G8 powers to invite each year, it retains the initiative over the development of outreach. But if the G8 heads should establish a recurrent link with a broader group of fixed membership, such as the G20, there would be cumulative pressure for the G8 itself to be absorbed into the wider grouping. Although this is widely advocated by outside commentators, it is not likely to appeal to the present members of the G8.[27] Whatever the merits of replacing the G8 by a larger representative group, this process would destroy the present advantages of direct contact and informality, to which the G8 heads are personally attached.

NGOs Private business firms have rarely been associated with the summit itself.[28] But the involvement of NGOs took off from Birmingham 1998, where the Jubilee 2000 Campaign organised a march of 50,000 people calling for debt cancellation. Since then, the host government has regularly met a delegation of NGOs present at the summit.[29] In 2000 the Japanese provided an NGO centre at the summit site, as did the Italians in 2001. But these procedures were disrupted by the violent riots in Genoa during the summit, where one demonstrator was killed. To avoid a recurrence of this and to provide greater security after the terrorist attacks of 11 September 2001, Canada held the 2002 summit in the remote mountain resort of Kananaskis, keeping NGOs (and the media) at a safe distance in Calgary. Likewise, France offered facilities for an 'alternative summit' at Annemasse, well away from Evian, but allowed no public demonstrations anywhere near the summit site. The United States did not offer any facilities for NGOs in 2004.

Other Actors and Summit Follow-Up

International Institutions In contrast to the preparations, summit follow-up has relied on other actors from the outset. The summits of the 1970s and 1980s largely delegated the responsibility for implementing their economic decisions to bodies like the OECD, the IMF and World Bank and the GATT. During this time the summit took a detached attitude to these institutions, handing down its decisions as *faits accomplis* and expecting them to be adopted without further debate.[30]

But this approach would no longer work in the 1990s, as more countries became active in the international system. While still relying on international economic institutions, the G8 heads have realised that they would have to use more tact and persuasion to get their ideas for reform accepted by the wider membership. Meanwhile, the expanding agenda has taken the summit deeper into unfamiliar policy areas. Its links have spread beyond economic bodies to various organs of the United Nations, as well as security institutions like the OSCE. In some subjects the summit has found the existing institutions to be inadequate, for example in crime and money-laundering. This has been a factor behind the creation of G8 ministerial groups, such as the interior and justice ministers.

Business and NGOs Both private business and NGOs had begun to be involved in summit follow-up during the 1990s. An initial involvement of private business came with the 'Global Information Society' conferences launched after the Naples summit of 1994. The renewed interest in IT at Okinawa led to the creation of the 'DOT-Force' to recommend ways to overcome the digital divide, with strong participation from business and also from NGOs. Business and NGOs were involved in two other programmes launched at Okinawa: the campaign against infectious diseases, leading at Genoa to the Global Fund to fight AIDS, tuberculosis and malaria; and the task-force on renewable energy. All these bodies adopted a 'multi-stakeholder' approach, as analysed in Chapter 8. The broader Middle East initiative also integrates private firms and civil society bodies in the reform process. The participation of the private sector has the merit of tapping additional sources of expertise and financial support, even though these new follow-up structures may be harder to integrate into the existing framework of international institutions. The active involvement of leading NGOs in these activities has been in striking contrast to the violent public demonstrations on the streets.

Summary of the Contribution of Other Actors

The contribution of other actors to summit decision-making can be summarised as follows:

- Summit preparations now give more access to other governments and international institutions, as well as to business and NGOs;
- Non-G8 governments have became active participants in parts of the summit itself, in a variety of combinations;
- International institutions have always been entrusted with summit follow-up, but the G8 now treats them more persuasively and systematically;
- Business firms and NGOs are increasingly used in follow-up, especially when existing institutions are inadequate.

In the early years, it was enough for the summits to make recommendations for these to concentrate the minds of others. But power is now much more widely spread, both among states and among other actors in the system, as a result of globalisation. The heads are developing techniques for associating non-G8 governments with their decision-making, while preserving the informal character of the G8 meetings. They are also reaching out to private firms and civil society, adopting a 'multi-stakeholder' approach. So other players are increasingly involved and contribute to the results, at the cost of more dispersed decision-making in the G8 system.

Conclusions

The main conclusions of the three preceding sections are:

- The heads of government have gained new freedom by meeting on their own. They contribute independently to decision-making by personal initiatives, especially in agenda-setting and procedural decisions, and by following their political reflexes. Meeting their international peers concentrates the minds of the heads most when this also advances their domestic agenda. But these personal interventions are a small part of the G8 summits' achievement, probably less than in previous years.
- Most cooperation at the summit still emerges from the work of the supporting apparatus, whether by the sherpa team or the growing network of G8 ministerial groups. The preparations enable the heads to add their authority to work in progress; to induce agreement at lower levels, without acting themselves; and at times to go further than is possible at lower levels. Holding the summit concentrates the minds of other ministers and bureaucrats, as well as the heads themselves. It has continued to do so, even though the summits have become more detached from their base.
- Other actors - non-G8 governments, international institutions, business and NGOs - are increasingly involved in summit preparation, in the summit itself and in follow-up. The institutions are treated more persuasively and systematically than before. This greater dispersion and transparency is necessary, if the summits are to concentrate the increasingly independent minds of other players in the system.

There are, however, tensions between the greater independence of the heads, the proliferation of the supporting apparatus and the growing involvement of other actors. For example:

- The heads have achieved their greater freedom at the expense of being less able to act directly on other centres of policy responsibility. For example, their regular exchange on macro-economic policy has become inconsequential, because it is not firmly linked with what their finance ministers are doing. Though Chirac wanted the Evian summit to give 'a message of hope' to the world economy, it was not really able to do so.
- Separating the supporting apparatus from the summit opens new opportunities for the ministerial groups, which have continued to grow during the first G8 sequence. These groups increasingly pursue their own agenda; the G8 format often enables them to agree common positions that they can pursue in wider international institutions. The heads have chosen to tolerate this independence and no longer try to keep control of the whole G8 system.
- Meeting alone also enables the heads to establish links with wider networks, such as non-G8 governments, private business and civil society. With the advance of globalisation, these have become essential contributors to decision-

making, especially in follow-up. Their involvement also helps to make the G8 process more transparent. But this dispersion of activity can make it harder to concentrate minds in the inter-governmental institutions, on which the summit still largely relies for implementation.

- The G8 heads have chosen to preserve the compact membership of the summit and show no enthusiasm for enlargement. But in response to the demands of globalisation the summit has developed closer contacts with non-G8 countries, both indirectly through ministerial meetings with wider membership and directly by inviting other leaders to join them at the summit.

The evolution of the summit process served to concentrate minds during the first G8 sequence. While there were some variations in achievement, the first five summits of the sequence successfully selected issues for treatment by the heads, leaving others to be dealt with at lower levels. They achieved some innovative results and struck deals among themselves. Non-G8 countries and the private sector were integrated into the process by means of the 'multi-stakeholder' approach pioneered at Okinawa. There was some loss of cohesion at Evian and Sea Island. Evian launched wider outreach and Sea Island was innovative on the Middle East. But the summits ceased to be selective and became swamped by too many subjects, not all of which deserved to be handled at the heads' level. The documentation became as voluminous as it had been before Birmingham. The G8 process thus had a clear impact on the summits' performance against their objectives, to be considered in the final chapter.

Notes

1 Boswell, *Life of Johnson*, vol. iii, p. 167 (19 September 1777).

2 This chapter is adapted from a paper originally delivered at a workshop of the European Consortium for Political Research (ECPR) in Grenoble in April 2001. Earlier versions have been published as Bayne 2004 and as my contribution to Reinalda and Verbeek 2004, a broader analysis of decision-making.

3 This view was held strongly by the founders Giscard and Schmidt; see Putnam and Bayne 1987, pp. 32-34.

4 Quoted in Putnam and Bayne 1987, p. 44.

5 Major's proposal in 1993 for a heads-only summit was declined by the newly elected Clinton, who did not want to cause tension with his Secretaries of State and Treasury. When Blair tried again in 1998, Clinton was more experienced in office.

6 Continuity is not a guarantee of higher performance, however. Evian and Sea Island were less productive than preceding G8 summits, as discussed in Chapter 14.

7 The only certain newcomers since 2002 would be Paul Martin for Canada and José Manuel Barroso for the European Commission. Martin is known to favour a summit of the G20, as a supplement to the G8 - see the discussion later in this chapter. His views on China's membership are less clear.

8 Japanese Prime Minister Obuchi tried to invite China, with other Asian powers, before Okinawa, but China declined. For an analysis of G8 relations with China, see Kirton 2001b.

9 China was first admitted to G7 deputies' meetings in 2003. In October 2004 it was invited to a G7 finance ministers' meeting for the first time, though only for part of the agenda. See A. Balls, 'G7 Invites China to Discuss Fixed Exchange Rate', *Financial Times,* 1 October 2004, and page 201 below.
10 Admitting China is one of the changes proposed in O'Neill and Hormats 2004 - and Bob Hormats is a former US sherpa. This paper also argues for consolidating the European G8 membership. While this is plausible at finance minister level - see note 19 below - it is highly unlikely at the summit, which deals with so many issues where the EU does not act collectively. While there are so many Europeans at the summit table, Canada is sure of its place to provide non-European balance.
11 See M. Goodman, 'The G8 Should Start Opening to China', *Financial Times,* 3 June 2004. Matthew Goodman has served in the Bush White House.
12 Schroeder had been so impressed by Putin at Okinawa that he argued there for dropping G7 meetings. The 2002 decision shows Germany delaying its turn to allow Russia into the sequence.
13 There are a few examples of regular follow-up at head of government level, such as the Sarajevo summit of July 1999 on Balkan reconstruction, which associated other countries.
14 This process is called 'reverberation' by Professor Bob Putnam in his model of 'two-level games', which he developed from his observation of the Bonn I summit of 1978. See Putnam 1988 and Putnam and Henning 1989.
15 For an account of the development of the sherpa process, see Putnam and Bayne 1987, pp. 48-61. A complete list of the summit participants, including the sherpas, from the beginning up to 2000 is in Sherifis and Astraldi 2001, pp. 217-253.
16 Peter Hajnal has provided the classic analysis of this development, see Hajnal 1999, especially pp. 35-44. I greatly welcome the prospect of a revised and updated edition of his work.
17 Kenen, Shafer, Wicks and Wyplosz 2004, pp. 71-74, explain the composition of the FSF. They show that G7 members still have a privileged position in the Forum, as having more representatives at the table.
18 See Kirton 2001a for an early account of the G20 and its role. His later analysis, in Kirton 2005, suggests that the performance of the G20 has dropped back since Martin ceased to chair it.
19 This proposal for a new key currency group is a principal recommendation of Kenen, Shafer, Wicks and Wyplosz 2004, see pp. 84-86. The report envisages the survival of the G8 summit - see p. 101.
20 As with the summit itself, the arrival of the Russians introduced rather more formality, with separate G7 and G8 sherpa meetings at first. But this has eased with the establishment of Andrei Illarionov as Putin's sherpa.
21 This again shows Putnam's 'two-level game' model at work, as in note 14 above.
22 The growth of 'iteration' at the summits is documented in Bayne 2000, pp. 200-208.
23 This is vividly described by Bob Fowler, as Canadian sherpa, in Fowler 2004.
24 For an analysis of the G8's relations with NGOs, see Hajnal 2002.
25 However, the US did not do this in 2004. NGOs also influence national preparations. Some of the environmental measures agreed at Okinawa, such as the task-force for renewable energy and the provisions on illegal logging, were British initiatives worked out in cooperation with NGOs - see Budd 2003.
26 Wider outreach has been a persistent French objective - see Chapter 2 above. Martin floated his idea in speeches on 29 April and 10 May 2004. The countries that met at Evian are not the same as the members of the G20. Both groups include the G8, with

the EU, and Brazil, China, India, Mexico, Saudi Arabia and South Africa. The Evian group, with a more political composition, adds Algeria, Egypt, Malaysia, Nigeria, and Senegal. The G20, of significant countries in the financial system, adds Argentina, Australia, South Korea and Turkey.

27 The idea that the G8 should be replaced by a wider more representative grouping has been advocated by outside commentators for several years, such as Jeffrey Sachs ('Global Capitalism - Making It Work', *The Economist,* 12 September 1998) and Michel Camdessus when at the IMF (see R. Chote, 'Camdessus Urges G8 to Embrace Other Countries' and T. Bardacke, 'Camdessus seeks Broader G8', *Financial Times,* 10 May 1998 and 14 February 2000). A more recent view is that the G20 should replace the G8, see Bradford and Linn 2004 and English, Thakur and Cooper 2005, though Kirton 2004 points out the obstacles.

28 However, both firms and NGOs took part in the presentation of the first DOT-Force report at Genoa in 2001.

29 This did not happen at Sea Island, but is likely to be reinstated at Gleneagles.

30 The G7 approach is assessed in Putnam and Bayne 1987, pp. 145-169.

Chapter 14

Staying Together: Summit Objectives

The G7 summit was originally founded with three objectives:

- To use the *political leadership* of heads of government to launch new ideas and overcome deadlock at lower levels;
- To *reconcile domestic and international pressures* that were generated by growing interdependence;
- To develop *collective management* among Europe, North America, and Japan, to replace original US hegemony.

Though the summit's agenda varied with the years, these objectives remained constant. But by the late 1990s the summit process no longer enabled the heads to achieve these objectives in conditions of advancing globalisation. Therefore the Birmingham summit of 1998 introduced fundamental reforms, converting G7 into G8 and ensuring that the heads could meet on their own. These reforms have now been in operation for a full sequence of seven summits, so that each G7 country has acted as host.[1]

This final chapter offers a judgement on whether these changes have enabled the G8 to meet their objectives more successfully and whether the objectives themselves have changed. The basis for this judgement is drawn from the earlier chapters of this book, including:

- The narratives of the seven summits from Birmingham 1998 to Sea Island 2004;
- The results achieved in the main issues treated by the summits - financial architecture, debt relief, international trade, development issues, Africa, terrorism and non-proliferation;
- Other issues attempted by the summits, including those pursued only superficially or where no agreement was reached.

The main argument of the chapter is that the first G8 sequence has revived and strengthened the summits' capacity for *political leadership*. The concept of *collective management* has been maintained and adapted, in spite of changes in the US attitude under Bush. In contrast, the summits' record in *reconciling domestic and international pressures* has not improved, but is rather getting worse. In addition, the summits have identified a fourth objective, which is *integrating international economics and politics*. These four elements are examined separately in the main body of the chapter.

On this judgement, the performance is mixed but on balance positive. The G8 heads therefore continue to value the summit as a policy instrument. The media, however, dwell on the negative aspects and remain sceptical. As well as overcoming the frustrations of the mid-1990s, the summit has survived two serious threats to its continued existence during this period. The first was an external threat, consisting of the violent riots that targeted the summit in Genoa, leading to the death of a demonstrator. The second threat was internal, being the bitter dispute over the invasion of Iraq, which divided the G8 down the middle before Evian. Having seen off both threats, the heads are not attracted by suggestions that the summit should enlarge itself to become more representative. They have preserved the G8 summit because they believe that staying together serves their interests best.[2]

Grading the G8 Summits

As noted in Chapter 1, earlier volumes on summitry - *Hanging Together* and *Hanging In There* - introduced a system of grading the summits in terms of their contribution to successful international cooperation. The grades for the G7 summits were given in Table 2.1 above. It is now time to suggest grades for the G8 summits. These are set out in Table 14.1 below.[3]

Table 14.1 G8 Summits and their Achievements, 1998-2004

Year	*Site*	*Grade*	*Achievements*
Sixth Summit Series - Globalisation and Development			
1998	Birmingham	B+	New format, crime
1999	Cologne	B+	Debt, Kosovo, finance
2000	Okinawa	B	Outreach, IT
2001	Genoa	B	Infectious diseases, Africa
Seventh Summit Series - Fighting Terrorism and its Causes			
2002	Kananaskis	B+	Africa, cleaning up WMD
2003	Evian	C+	Outreach, reconciliation
2004	Sea Island	C+	Middle East

The G8 summits from 1998 to 2001 - the sixth summit series - show the best run of grades since the summit cycle began. There are no A grades, but a consistent performance at B+ or B. This reflects the rejuvenation of the summit produced by the Birmingham reforms. There were innovative achievements in financial architecture, debt relief, IT and infectious diseases. The heads struck a deal over Kosovo, helped to launch the Doha Development Agenda and initiated the G8's involvement with Africa.

The summits from 2002 to 2004 - the seventh summit series - show a decline in performance from this high standard, as the effects of the reforms began to wear off. Kananaskis 2002 was another very successful summit. Though perhaps less innovative than its predecessors, it took substantial commitments on Africa and the heads were able to strike deals among themselves. Evian and Sea Island, however, suffered from having ill-defined agendas which generated too many documents of uneven quality.[4] While Evian made peace among the G8 heads after the divisions caused by Iraq, cooperative agreements were few and the main advance was in the outreach to major developing countries. The principal achievement at Sea Island was the broader Middle East initiative. Sea Island's grade is provisional, since it could be enhanced if Middle Eastern reform really takes off or reduced if the initiative runs into the sand.

As the G7/G8 summits have now been going for 30 years, all G7 countries have acted as host four times, while France and the US have hosted five summits. It is therefore possible to compare how different G7 countries have performed as host and chair. This is shown in Table 14.2 below; the G8 sequence begins with the UK in the fourth column.

Table 14.2 Comparison of Summit Grades by Host Country

Host	*1975-1981*	*1982-1988*	*1989-1995*	*1996-2000*	*2003-2004*
France	A-	C	B+	B	C+
United States	D	B	D	C-	C+
				G8 starts here	
United Kingdom	B-	C-	B-	B+	
Germany	A	E	D	B+	
Japan	B+	B+	C+	B	
Italy	C+	D	C	B	
Canada	C	C-	B+	B+	

In the first five G8 summits, nearly all the hosts were able to improve on their previous performance, thanks to the reforms to the summit process. The UK and Italy recorded their highest grades to date, Canada equalled its previous best and Germany had its best score since the 1970s. Though the last two summits, chaired by France and the US, only produced grades of C+, this was still the highest grade for the US for 20 years. The US has not scored highly in the past, while France's performance has been volatile, though sometimes extremely good. In both countries the presidential structure of government encourages independent initiatives, taking a risk that the rest of the G8 will buy into them. This has produced good results for France in the past, but less good for the US.[5] At Evian and Sea Island the individualistic instincts of Chirac and Bush - and the tension between them - had a negative effect.[6] Sea Island produced its best results, on the Middle East, when the US accepted modifications from its G8 partners.

It could be argued that the grading standards have become tougher over the years, just as new performance criteria have been added. The G8 now operates in a more complex environment and covers a wider range of issues than the G7 did when it was scoring A grades in the 1970s. On the basis of what they achieved, Cologne (for finance, debt and Kosovo) and Kananaskis (for Africa and a deal linking debt relief and action against WMD) should deserve A grades just as much as Rambouillet in 1975 or Bonn I in 1978. These arguments have some force. Even so, no A grades have yet been awarded to G8 summits because of their poor performance against the central summit aim of reconciling international and domestic pressures.[7] This point is developed further in the assessment of the G8's strengths and weaknesses in the chapter from now on.

Political Leadership

The most positive aspect of the G8 sequence has been the improvement in the summit's capacity for political leadership. This can be observed in the following ways:

- By greater innovation;
- By striking deals;
- By establishing linkage between issues.

Innovation

The overloading of the summits in the 1990s had not prevented the emergence of new ideas. The Halifax summit of 1995 launched reforms to the IMF, while Lyon in 1996 introduced the HIPC programme of debt relief. But the summits from Birmingham 1998 onwards show a stronger capacity to innovate, with new initiatives not only coming up through the preparations but also emerging at the summit itself.

In some areas the G8 heads were simply lending their authority to innovative ideas developed at lower levels, as noted in Chapter 13. For example, though the new international financial architecture was a major summit achievement, all the innovation emerged at the level of the G7 finance ministers, not the heads themselves. Likewise, the treatment of terrorism generated new approaches to penalising terrorist finance and improving transport security, but this did not really require the intervention of the heads.

The G8 heads made a far more important contribution when they were personally associated with innovative measures. There are examples of this from every summit in the sequence:

- Birmingham introduced new ideas on debt relief that were finally agreed as the Enhanced HIPC programme at Cologne in 1999. Although the main document was produced by the finance ministers, the heads added some new commitments of their own.
- Cologne also promoted new thinking on education, adopting a Charter for Lifelong Learning, and on conflict prevention.
- Okinawa launched the DOT-Force, to make IT more accessible to poor countries - a new and controversial idea. (A parallel task-force was set up to develop new ideas on renewable energy).
- Genoa built on the discussion of infectious diseases, which had begun at Okinawa. The main innovation was the launch of the Global Fund to fight AIDS, tuberculosis and malaria.
- Kananaskis agreed the Africa Action Plan, embodying a new set of measures for the benefit of African countries.
- Evian and Sea Island followed Kananaskis in promoting a sequence of innovative measures on non-proliferation of WMD, initiated by the US but backed and modified by the other G8 members.
- Sea Island launched the broader Middle East initiative, which developed a wholly new G8 approach to the region.

All these innovations came up to the summit through their preparatory work. In addition, the heads are now also innovating at the summit itself, although, as chapter 13 showed, this is more likely to be in procedure than in substance. While Kananaskis decided the content of the G8's policies towards Africa, the principle had been agreed at Genoa the year before. The G8 heads were deeply impressed by what they heard over their working dinner with African leaders. The following morning, without any advance preparation, they drew up and issued the 'Genoa Plan for Africa'. Though this was a procedural decision, which set an agenda rather than agreeing substantive measures, it was innovative in multiple ways that are explored later in this chapter. The G8 heads targeted Africa seriously for the first time; they established a new form of outreach; and they combined politics and economics in a way rarely done before.

Striking Deals

The G7 heads had become concerned that the bureaucratisation of the summit in the 1990s reduced their capacity to strike deals among themselves. Where agreements were reached at those summits, they emerged wholly from the preparatory work. The heads gave their authority to these deals, but added little of their own. As Chapter 13 noted, they sometimes showed their dissatisfaction with the summit process by procedural moves to speed it up. But they rarely achieved policy agreements that went beyond what had been agreed at lower levels.

The G8 summits showed that the heads were regaining their deal-making capacity. At Birmingham they were still finding their feet in the new format and the deal struck over Indian nuclear tests barely counts, as it was an agreement to differ. But thereafter deals were struck nearly every year. For example:

- At Cologne 1999 the agreements on Kosovo had been worked out at lower levels. But all depended on the assent of Yeltsin and that could only be obtained at the summit.
- At Genoa 2001, as described above, the innovative Genoa Plan for Africa emerged from what the heads did at the summit, without advance preparation.
- At Evian 2003 there was a tentative deal whereby Chirac and Blair undertook that the Europeans would match Bush's $1 billion pledge to the Global Fund. But this proved abortive, as it was based on a misunderstanding.
- At Sea Island 2004, the rest of the G8 would only agree to the American broader Middle East proposals if the peace process between Israel and the Palestinians could be restarted. This was agreed by the heads over their working dinner, following bilateral contacts between Blair and Bush.

The 2002 Kananaskis summit was particularly rich in deals struck among the heads. Three of the main agreements reached there were not available at lower levels and needed the intervention of the heads, while a fourth deal was concluded by the heads themselves without preparation. These agreements were:

- The G7 finance ministers had already discussed the replenishment of the World Bank's Trust Fund to finance the HIPC programme, but had failed to fix a figure. The summit agreed to a joint commitment of up to $1billion.
- The summit agreed the G8 Africa Action Plan to underpin NEPAD, largely as prepared in advance. But officials could not agree on the total aid funds that would support the Plan. That was only settled by the heads, after Bush was persuaded by the others to allocate to deserving African countries half of the extra aid funds pledged by the G8 members at Monterrey, producing a headline figure of $6 billion.
- The agreement to commit up to $20 billion over 10 years to cleaning up nuclear installations and chemical weapons in the former Soviet Union could only have been reached at the G8 summit. The Europeans, Canada and Japan were insisting on guarantees of support on the ground, which the Russians at

lower levels refused to give. It was only at the summit, when the other heads, especially Bush, leant on Putin, that the deal was struck.

- Without consulting their sherpas, the heads agreed that Russia could host the summit in 2006 and laid out the sequence of G8 Presidencies for the rest of the decade.[8]

The unusual number of deals struck at Kananaskis suggests that the practice of simpler, less cluttered summits was having a cumulative effect on decision-making. Evian and Sea Island were less productive, because the agenda had become overloaded again, but they still produced some results.

Linkage between Issues

G7 and G8 summits have the capacity to establish linkages between topics and to strike cross-issue deals, whereby a concession by one country in one topic is rewarded by a move by a different country in another. Cross-issue deals of this kind are regarded as the highest form of cooperation at the summit. The deal integrating macro-economic stimulus, energy policy and trade liberalisation agreed at the first Bonn summit of 1978 is the classic example.[9] But there were very few examples since then. Linkage was often used within a broad subject like trade or financial reform. But cross-issue linkage became almost unknown at the summit.

Two of the agreements from Kananaskis described above provide an excellent illustration of cross-issue linkage, though on a more modest scale than the 1978 case. The agreement on cleaning up nuclear material and chemical weapons in Russia was a very high priority for Bush. The US Congress had already earmarked funds up to $10 billion; Bush was looking for a matching commitment from the rest of the G7. On the other hand, the Americans were reluctant to set a figure for the replenishment of the HIPC programme and had prevented agreement on this among G7 finance ministers. They feared that this commitment would run into difficulties in Congress.

The Europeans and others strongly backed the HIPC replenishment, as essential to finance the programme. They were also convinced of the need to clean up installations in Russia and had already committed substantial sums for this purpose. Many of these funds remained unspent, however, because of Russian obstruction on the ground. This problem was removed by extracting firm guarantees from Putin, so that the rest of the G7 were ready for the sort of agreement the Americans wanted. They hesitated, however, to make a firm commitment of $10 billion. They were won over when Bush agreed to the $1 billion figure for the HIPC replenishment. He felt able to do this because he believed Congressional satisfaction at the $20 billion clean-up agreement would offset their reservations about the $1 billion for the HIPC. Such cross-issue deals are not likely to occur at every summit; there were none at Evian or Sea Island. But the record of Kananaskis shows that the G8, in its new format, is able to identify and strike them.

Collective Management

One original aim of the summit, right from 1975, was to bring about a transition from American hegemony to a regime of collective management of the international system, with responsibility shared between Europe, North America and Japan. But US hegemony cast a long shadow. For the first 15 years or so, the G7 process depended heavily on US initiative. If the Americans took the lead, with one or more G7 partners, there were good results. If the Americans tried to lead alone, the outcome was disappointing. If the Americans did not lead, nothing much happened.[10]

During the 1990s, however, as the summit revived after the end of the Cold War, this pattern changed and became much closer to real collective management. While the Americans usually led on monetary and financial issues, the Europeans began to take the lead in other areas, such as the environment and debt relief for poor countries. Genuine shared initiatives emerged, for example on drugs, crime and money-laundering.

The evolution of collective management in the first G8 sequence can be shown in two areas:

- The pattern of G8 initiative;
- The development of outreach.

Patterns of Initiative

Birmingham to Genoa The G8 summits of the sixth series showed a similar pattern to the mid-1990s. In some areas US initiative was still essential. In others the Europeans took the lead, sometimes with Canada, though the EU did not act collectively except in trade issues. Japan was especially active when it held the Presidency.[11] A breakdown of the main issues shows the following results:

- On *new financial architecture*, the Americans were the most active, creating the G22 and promoting the Contingent Credit Line. All other G7 members contributed ideas, though the EU participants did not act jointly, despite the creation of the Eurozone.
- On *debt relief*, the initiative came from the UK, France and Canada. The US was involved, but never in the lead. Germany and Japan had been sceptical, but moved to join the consensus at Cologne.
- On *trade*, the EU, exceptionally, took the initiative in the late 1990s, while the US dragged its feet. Divisions persisted until Genoa produced a joint EU/US approach.
- On *development*, the initiatives on IT and infectious diseases came from Japan in 2000, but both soon attracted collective support.
- On *Kosovo*, the Americans focused on security concerns, while the Europeans led on post-war Balkan reconstruction. Russian involvement was essential.

- *Crime*, which was a shared concern, got replaced by *conflict prevention*, which was driven by Germany and Italy because of fears aroused by Kosovo.
- On social issues, like *employment* and *education*, the impetus came from the UK and Germany.

In all these issues, financial architecture was the only one where American initiative was indispensable. The remaining items showed joint or collective initiative, or else other G8 countries were in the lead. When George W. Bush became US President in 2001, there were fears that he might draw back from the concept of collective management and insist that only US initiative counted. There were some backward moves before Genoa, notably the US withdrawal from the Kyoto Protocol on climate change. But in many G8 subjects the Americans were still ready to work for joint initiatives, as shown by the strong alliance on trade between Bob Zoellick and Pascal Lamy.

Kananaskis to Sea Island The summits of the seventh series, after the terrorist attacks of 11 September 2001, show a rather different pattern in the choice of subjects and the source of initiative. This breaks down as follows:

- *Africa* was the most important and original subject for this series. The initiative was shared between the UK, France and Canada. The Americans were active participants, but were not in the lead.
- The *terrorism* items - transport security, terrorist finance and capacity-building - were all promoted by the Americans.
- The cumulative approach to *non-proliferation* also derived from US initiative. But other G8 members - the Europeans, Japan and Russia - all had contributions to make.
- The broader *Middle East* initiative was launched by the Americans before Sea Island, but was extensively modified by the others, especially the Europeans.
- The *development* issues featured during the seventh series had various originators. France promoted clean water. The UK introduced ideas on transparency in governance. The US led on famine and was active on AIDS, though this was a shared concern for all the G8. Canada made a special contribution on the private sector and development.
- The *environment* yielded few results in either the sixth or seventh series. But the UK announced climate change as a major topic for Gleneagles 2005.

After the terrorist attacks of 11 September 2001, the Americans took a unilateralist line in their 'front-line' operations against terrorism. Afghanistan hardly came to the summit at all, while Iraq was first discussed seriously at Sea Island. But in wider counter-terrorist issues, especially non-proliferation, and in the broader Middle East initiative the United States sought the support of its G8 partners as the first step in winning wider international backing. The US was always the initiator, but actively worked to generate collective management involving the rest of the G8.

At first sight this looks like a throwback to the early G7 summits, when only US initiative counted. There is some truth in this, in that US hegemony has revived in military contexts. The early summits, after all, managed to produce some excellent results in those conditions. But the extent of American initiative today appears deceptively large because the US has just hosted a summit. Africa, which has become the single most important issue for the G8, is not based on US initiative, though the Americans are deeply involved and recognise the contribution that helping Africa makes to the fight against terrorism. In the growing development agenda there is a wide distribution of initiative, according to the subject, but all, including the Americans, see the value of collective management. For Gleneagles in 2005 Blair intends to keep the focus on Africa and related development topics, while seeking to revive G8 interest in the environment.

Even on Iraq, the Sea Island summit showed a welcome move away from unilateralism by the United States. The Americans realised that agreement on the broader Middle East depended on parallel progress on Iraq and Israel/Palestine. The emergence of the interim government in Iraq and the unanimous adoption of the UN Security Council resolution, just before the summit opened, created one essential foundation for agreement. On Israel/Palestine, the G8 summit essentially set the peace process back on track again, based on the Road Map and the Quartet of US, EU, Russia and the UN. Agreement on Iraq, Israel/Palestine and the broader Middle East became possible because the US showed greater readiness than before to accept collective, rather than sole, management in this area.

The Development of Outreach

G7 summits had been exclusive, so that no outsiders could take part in the proceedings, though international institutions were expected to follow up summit decisions. G8 summits realised that, in conditions of advancing globalisation, any attempts at collective management would be ineffective unless they engaged a wider range of participants from non-G8 countries as well as the private sector.

Non-G8 Countries The African initiative was the most advanced form of outreach to non-G8 governments. For the first time, the G8 heads entered into a structured relationship with a group of other leaders. This brought the Africans to meetings with the G8 heads at every summit from Genoa onwards, with a further meeting foreseen at Gleneagles in 2005. The G8 was deeply engaged in Africa, but took care to ensure that the Africans themselves retained ownership and responsibility for their own development programmes. This was one reason why joint G8/African machinery was slow to emerge, though the African Partners Group was formed in 2003.

In many of the other issues treated by the summits the G8 directly involved non-G8 countries, rather than simply relying on established institutions. For example:

- Countries that had renounced nuclear weapons were associated with the follow-up after Birmingham on Indian nuclear tests;

- Other EU and regional countries were involved in the Stability Plan for South-Eastern Europe, which formed part of the Kosovo settlement;
- The new financial architecture led to the creation of the FSF, where G7 finance ministers were joined by other monetary authorities, and the G20, where they sat down with their peers from 'systemically significant' countries;
- The task-forces on IT and renewable energy, as well as the Global Fund to fight AIDS, tuberculosis and malaria, had members from non-G8 countries and international institutions, as part of the 'multi-stakeholder' approach;
- Non-proliferation initiatives like the Global Partnership and the PSI associated other participating countries around a G8 core;
- The broader Middle East initiative was intended to engage as many countries as possible from Morocco to Afghanistan, in joint institutions and programmes.

In all these cases, non-G8 countries were involved because of their concern with the specific subject. In addition, the Evian summit associated the G8 with a group of major developing countries, including China, India, Brazil, Mexico and South Africa, in recognition that such countries would have a close interest in whatever was discussed at the summit. This meeting was not repeated at Sea Island, so that the shape of G8 links with this important group is not clear. As Chapter 13 noted, the G8 may not want to be committed to a wider meeting with a fixed participation. But there is little doubt that future summits, from Gleneagles onwards, will seek to build up such links.

The Private Sector The adaptation of collective management also involves greater outreach to the private sector, both business firms and civil society. This shows a similar dynamism and variety during the first G8 sequence:

- Birmingham and Cologne advocated the involvement of civil society in debt relief, which was picked up by the IMF and World Bank;
- The DOT-Force was instigated by private business, while the idea for the task-force on renewable energy originated from NGOs;
- Both firms and NGOs were well represented on the task-forces, following the 'multi-stakeholder' approach;
- The Global Fund had firms, foundations and both Western and local NGOs involved in its management;
- Private business and civil society were to be equal participants in the broader Middle East initiative, alongside government.

The active cooperation of firms and expert NGOs in the G8's work was in stark contrast with the opposition to the summit process shown by other civil society organisations.

Reconciling International and Domestic Pressures

So far the record of the summits since Birmingham 1998 shows an improvement in the G8's performance. But in reconciling international and domestic pressures the summits do not seem to be doing better; on balance, they are doing worse. The G8 heads have implicitly recognised this. They have shifted their discussions away from topics with major domestic impact towards ones where the decisions chiefly concern external policies. This judgement emerges from the following:

- The choice of agenda items;
- Implementation of commitments;
- Reactions to domestic pressures;
- Public presentation.

Choice of Agenda Items

The summits from Birmingham onwards were intended to respond to domestic worries about the advance of globalisation, as well as international ones. They were meant to address issues of concern to G8 members and their populations, like employment, crime, education, social protection and ageing, in addition to worldwide problems of financial disorder, crippling debt and persistent poverty.

In practice, the domestic issues went off the agenda very soon. From Okinawa onwards, almost all the items discussed were international, though of course with varying domestic repercussions. Crime, essentially a domestic anxiety, mutated into conflict prevention, where the concerns arose from foreign countries. Where the G8 heads still discussed domestic issues, as in their regular exchange on national economic policies, their exchanges had little practical impact.

Implementation of Commitments

One of the long-standing complaints against the G7 summits had been that they made commitments that they did not fulfil. The summit relied on others for follow-up, especially international institutions like the IMF or the WTO. But in the past G7 members had been guilty of preventing such institutions from carrying out promises that the heads had made at the summit. The most blatant example was when the heads, at their summits of 1990, 1991 and 1992, undertook to complete the Uruguay round of trade negotiations by the end of the year, only for this aim to be frustrated by their own disputes over agriculture. (A similar pledge made in 1993, however, was successfully honoured).

The new summit format could affect this problem in both positive and negative ways. Because the heads would be more personally involved in their decisions, this should improve the pattern of implementation. But because they were more detached from the G8 apparatus, that could make follow-up even more unreliable. The initial findings suggest that implementation has got worse, just as the capacity for innovation has expanded. The G8 produces more ideas, but does not always follow them through.

Right from the start, the summits often failed to resolve problems at a single meeting and had to return to the issue in later years to produce better results. This practice of iteration continued to be used successfully during the first G8 sequence. Financial architecture and debt relief required treatment at both Birmingham and Cologne. Action on IT and infectious diseases started at Okinawa but bore fruit at Genoa. Africa has received iterative treatment at five successive summits, from Genoa to Gleneagles. Non-proliferation and transport security provide further examples.

But alongside these successes, there are too many examples of the summit launching an initiative but then losing interest, as follows:

- Okinawa, as noted, launched an innovative task-force on renewable energy, which produced an agreed report for Genoa. But the United States and Canada refused to accept its findings and the report was shelved.[12]
- Genoa set up a task-force, of officials only, to recommend how to support primary education in developing countries. It worked closely with the World Bank, who identified a group of countries best able to absorb outside assistance. Kananaskis backed the recommendations on what poor countries should do to deserve assistance, but made only a weak commitment to provide such assistance, and did not endorse the World Bank's list of deserving countries. The World Bank programme was inadequately funded and later summits did not act to make up the shortfall.[13]
- Cologne produced a major achievement in debt relief - the Enhanced HIPC programme - that encouraged the Jubilee 2000 campaigners. But since then the terms of the programme have remained largely unchanged, though Kananaskis and Sea Island acted to ensure it could be financed. Development NGOs argue that the Enhanced HIPC programme is not working as generously as intended and the conditions facing poor debtor countries have got worse. But by October 2004 the G8 heads had not agreed on their response either to these arguments or to the new debt relief ideas in NEPAD.[14]
- Okinawa promised measures of capacity-building, to help poor countries benefit from the world trading system. Evian made comparable promises to build counter-terrorism capacity in poor countries. But the follow-up to both sets of promises has been disappointing.

These perceived failures to live up to G8 promises have damaged the summit's reputation. All these examples relate to development issues that are closely followed by civil society NGOs. These NGOs are discouraged by what they see as the summit's failure to live up to its pledges and have become increasingly critical of the G8, even though the violent riots have declined since 11 September 2001.[15]

Reacting to Domestic Pressures

The G8 heads of government have the ability to reconcile divergent domestic and international pressures on policy-making. The summits serve to remind the heads of their international responsibilities, so they do not become too inward-looking.

They also provide opportunities for the heads to mobilise international arguments to resolve domestic problems. This ability resides in the heads themselves, by virtue of their political authority and legitimacy, rather than in their bureaucracies or other ministers. Thus cutting the heads loose from their supporting apparatus should improve their ability to act in this way. But the record of the G8 summits shows no improvement here and too many cases of the heads allowing domestic pressures to frustrate agreement.

Environment The clearest example is in the global environment, where the G8 summits have a generally poor record, with few examples of productive decisions. This is because of conflicting domestic pressures on either side of the Atlantic. North American attitudes on energy issues, climate change, biodiversity and food safety are driven by producer interests. Thus the task-force on renewable energy created at Okinawa failed because of pressure from the energy industries in the US and Canada.

In Europe, on the other hand, as well as Japan, policy is shaped by pressure from consumers and environmental lobbies. So far the G8 governments have not been able to devise international agreements that reconcile these pressures. Evian did manage to agree documents on science for sustainable development and on the marine environment, while Sea Island endorsed a Japanese initiative against waste, but none of these were very substantial. Blair has taken a bold step in announcing climate change as a major item for Gleneagles.

International Trade The G8 summit record on trade policy also shows inadequate resistance to special domestic interests. At Birmingham and Cologne the heads failed to resolve their differences over the agenda for a new trade round. The Americans listened too much to lobbying from labour and environmental groups, the Europeans and Japanese to their farmers. The result was the fiasco at the Seattle WTO meeting.

Genoa produced a strong G8 consensus on international trade liberalisation, which facilitated the successful launch of the WTO's Doha Development Agenda two years after the failure of Seattle. But this was undermined by the later actions of G8 members. The US Administration secured negotiating authority from Congress, but only after imposing new tariffs on steel imports and enacting a Farm Bill that would greatly expand the subsidies paid to farmers. The European Union disagreed on the reform of its Common Agricultural Policy (CAP), holding up decisions in the WTO on how to negotiate on agriculture in the Doha Development Agenda. Though the G8 committed themselves at Evian to work for a successful WTO ministerial at Cancun, their attitude alienated the developing countries and contributed to the failure of the meeting. Sea Island similarly produced only a low-powered commitment to restarting the Doha negotiations.

Africa The G8's commitments to Africa are also weakest where they involve adjustments to domestic policy. At Kananaskis, the G8 leaders were unable to offer any improvement in access for agricultural imports, though that was what the Africans wanted most. They remained impervious to African pressure at Evian and Sea Island. The African request for improved terms of debt relief has also been resisted by the G8, because it involves financial decisions that could provoke resistance at home, especially in the US and Japan. While G8 countries have undertaken to increase their aid to Africa and are in fact doing so, they are more concerned to ensure that their aid programmes meet domestic standards than to respond to the African concept of 'enhanced partnerships'.

As a result, civil society's criticism of the summits extends to the G8's work on Africa. The NGO community was already sceptical, if not hostile, as regards NEPAD, which they saw as imposed from the top by African leaders without proper consultation.[16] NGOs criticised the G8's Africa Action Plan as being inadequate to the problems, short on precise commitments and unlikely to be implemented, on the G8's previous record.

Heads Intervene In these examples one would hope to find that the G8 heads were personally leading the search for ways round the domestic resistance. In fact they often turn out to be themselves the source of the obstacles. In the United States, Clinton contributed to the collapse of the Seattle meeting by incautious remarks to a journalist during his visit there.[17] Bush took the initiative to denounce the Kyoto Protocol, though others in the White House opposed this.[18] He backed the farm subsidies demanded by Congress, against the advice of his Secretary for Agriculture.[19]

In Europe, CAP reform was needed to enable the EU to negotiate constructively on agriculture in the WTO. But Chirac intervened to water down proposals on the table in 1999 before Seattle.[20] Later he struck a deal with Schroeder that constrained CAP reform after the EU's enlargement and forced this through at the European Council in October 2002, out-flanking Blair in the process. Though EU agriculture ministers, in late June 2003, finally reached an agreement on how to handle agriculture in the Doha negotiations, Chirac himself was holding this up until the last minute.[21] Despite the promise he gave at Sea Island, Chirac was again intervening to frustrate the talks in Geneva to revive the Doha Development Agenda, though fortunately he did not succeed.[22] G8 leaders show a disturbing readiness, on both sides of the Atlantic, to give in to special domestic interests instead of building coalitions to overcome them.

Public Presentation

Initially the summits were treated with respect by the media. But as their communiqués got longer and they became occasions for public display, the media became cynical. The G7 summits attracted journalists in huge numbers, especially from their national media. But the press showed little interest in the issues under discussion at the summit and was easily distracted. It was hoped that the reforms brought in at Birmingham, by making the summits more focused and less ceremonial, with shorter documents, would improve the G8 summits' public image. This has not happened; on the contrary, the media take the summits less seriously than before.[23]

Recent summits have not been successful in getting the media to focus on the issues. In 2000 the Japanese used the summit as the justification for massive public works in Western Japan and on Okinawa itself. The press portrayed this as huge sums being squandered on a summit intended to address the problems of poor countries. A year later the riots in the streets of Genoa monopolised media attention. The press largely ignored the content of the summit in their speculation about whether the summit could go on meeting in such conditions. In 2002 the Canadian hosts were obliged to take exceptional measures to protect the security of the G8 heads. While the heads themselves seemed pleased to have this greater privacy, the media were naturally unhappy at being stuck in Calgary 56 miles (90 km) away from the summit. At Evian the media were closer to the action, but they were much more interested in the personal chemistry between Bush and Chirac than in the content of the summit. At Sea Island the Americans alienated the press by charging for space in the media centre, so that only half the expected number of journalists turned up.

The underlying problem is that the G8 heads, in presenting their work to the public, pay more attention to the domestic rather than the international resonance of the summit. The G8 heads never conduct joint briefings - in contrast to the African presidents, who regularly appear together. Instead, they each give separate press conferences that are angled to their national press and play up their own achievements rather than common agreements. Journalists seeking an overall assessment turn to the NGOs present, who have often prepared briefing material that is more accessible than the summit documents. Since these NGOs are increasingly critical of the summits, this is reflected in the media treatment.

In short, by concentrating on their domestic image, the G8 heads have lost the opportunity to explain to their publics what they gain from international cooperation.[24] They have not used the summit as the place to develop a set of persuasive arguments that spell out the benefits of globalisation in the face of popular uncertainty and opposition.

Integrating International Economics and Politics

One of the advantages enjoyed by heads of government, as compared to their ministers, is the ability to integrate different aspects of policy. In the earliest days of the summit this capacity was limited to economic issues. But as soon as the summit developed its political agenda in the 1980s, the G7 had the potential to integrate issues from both economic and foreign policy domains. However, this potential was rarely used. In the early 1990s the economic assistance initiated by the G7 for Central and Eastern European countries, especially Russia, had a strong political motivation, to entrench democracy and prevent a revival of communism. But this was exceptional and usually the summit kept economics and politics apart.

During the G8 summit sequence, this position has been reversed. Perhaps to compensate for their poor performance in reconciling domestic and international pressures, the G8 heads seem to be deliberately looking for issues where politics and economics need to be combined or integrated. The first clear example was

Kosovo, where the G8 acted both to restore peace and security and to promote economic development. The focus on combined economic and political subjects has accelerated since Kananaskis.

Africa

Africa is the most obvious case of this new approach. In the G8's Africa programme politics and economics are closely enmeshed, as regards both aims and instruments. There were economic and ethical motives for helping Africa to overcome poverty and disease and enjoy some of the benefits of globalisation. But there was also a political motive, reinforced by the terrorist attacks of 11 September 2001. The misery and disorder prevailing in much of Africa, where there were many failed or failing states, was seen as fertile ground for terrorist movements.

The G8's Africa Plan, linked to the NEPAD, therefore aims to use economic revival to counter adverse political trends and mobilises a combination of economic and political measures for this purpose.[25] Alongside extensive provisions on economic development, the G8 Action Plan adopted at Kananaskis has one chapter dealing with conflict resolution in Africa, while a second aims to help the Africans meet their own objectives for improving their standards of government, democracy, legality and human rights. Evian and Sea Island kept up the momentum on all these fronts. In peace-keeping there was agreement on a joint G8/NEPAD Peace Support Plan, where African operations on the ground would be backed by substantial G8 help in training and logistics. In political governance a substantial nucleus of African countries undertook to submit themselves to the NEPAD peer review process. Economically, there were welcome increases in aid from all G8 members, though less progress on trade and debt relief.

Middle East

The principal topic chosen by the Americans for the 2004 summit - the broader Middle East initiative - also integrated politics and economics closely. The region it would cover, from Morocco to Afghanistan, is marked by both political unrest and economic sluggishness, with each feeding on the other. A programme of linked political and economic reform, to enhance democracy and stimulate market economies, was thus a very suitable subject for the G8 leaders. The American proposals were new, but they had the same objective as the 'Barcelona process' launched by the European Union in 1995 to enhance political and economic development round the Mediterranean. There was therefore the basis for a common G8 agreement, comparable with what had been done over Africa.

The great difference, however, was that in Africa the G8 were responding to an initiative that came from the African leaders themselves. The Africans had clear ownership of NEPAD and the G8 took care to preserve this. In the Middle East, however, as word of American intentions leaked out early in 2004, leading regional powers, like Egypt and Saudi Arabia, reacted strongly against the idea of reforms being imposed from outside. But thanks to intensive preparatory work, the programme agreed at the summit was re-designed to encourage indigenous movements towards political and economic reform in the Middle East.

The programme recognised that reform could not be imposed from outside and that each country was unique. Reform would be a long-term effort, supported by joint political, economic and social projects identified in the G8 documents and involving business and civil society as full partners. On that basis, the programme proved acceptable both to the regional powers that attended the summit and to the absentees, like Egypt and Saudi Arabia, who all expected to attend the first meeting of the 'Forum for the Future' later in 2004.

Terrorism

After the terrorist attacks of 11 September 2001, it was inevitable that political issues, like terrorism and non-proliferation, would move up the G8 agenda. Since the Kananaskis summit of 2002, political issues have had at least equal weight in the summit agenda with economic ones. Yet in much of the G8's terrorism agenda too, politics and economics are combined, though politics usually dominates.

The key outcome of Kananaskis was the programme to clean up nuclear material and chemical weapons in Russia and the rest of the former Soviet Union. This was clearly meant to reduce the security threat from these items falling into the wrong hands or leading to dangerous pollution. But the obstacles to be overcome were largely economic. The programmes required not only substantial financing, but also local measures of legal protection, insurance and other practical support, analogous to programmes of economic and technical assistance. The G8 summit was able to bring these two strands together. Other parts of the terrorism agenda also combined politics and economics, in that political objectives are sought through economic instruments. This applied to transport security, to penalising terrorist finance and to coordinating assistance to countries to build up their counter-terrorism capacity.

This analysis shows all the most innovative work of the G8 heads in the seventh summit series - on Africa, broader Middle East, terrorism and non-proliferation - exercised their new-found capacity to integrate politics and economics. This became a main focus of their activity, at the expense of reconciling domestic and international pressures.

Conclusions: Staying Together

The First G8 Sequence

This book has shown that the reform of the summit format begun at Birmingham in 1998 has had a lasting effect and continues to evolve. G8 performance has improved in many respects: the summits show greater innovative powers; they are reaching agreements not available at lower levels; non-G8 countries, private firms and NGOs are involved in the process; and the heads are using the summit's potential to integrate economics and politics. But other developments are less positive: the heads are less good at implementation than at innovation; they allow domestic obstacles to prevent or undermine agreement; the summit's public image has not improved. In short, these summits have largely reinforced the views of those who regard the G8 as useful, which include the heads themselves. But they have deepened the scepticism of the G8's critics, which include many NGOs and the media.

The G8's ability to meet its objectives therefore varies widely:

- The first objective, *political leadership*, had been losing ground to the bureaucratisation of the summit process. The Birmingham reforms have clearly sharpened the capacity of the G8 to exert leadership and have improved the G8's performance under this heading. The heads are now better at developing new ideas and launching innovative initiatives. They are also better at going beyond the preparatory work to strike agreements among themselves. They are reviving techniques, like cross-issue deals, where the summit's potential has not been used for many years.
- The second objective, *collective management*, showed variations through the sequence but has been preserved and adapted. The summits of the sixth series were not dependent on US initiative. The Europeans collectively were just as active, while Japan made good use of its time as host. After 11 September 2001, the United States took over the initiative in many of the areas treated by the seventh summit series, which inevitably focused on terrorism. But the Americans have favoured G8 collective management for issues like non-proliferation and the broader Middle East, while the most important issue, Africa, was a Euro-Canadian, not an US initiative. Meanwhile the G8 have begun involving outside forces, both state and non-state, in collective management, thus improving the quality and transparency of decision-making and responding to the new demands of globalisation.
- In the third objective of *reconciling domestic and international pressures* the performance has been much less satisfactory. The G8 heads are able to make progress with new issues, but their initial ideas are not always followed through. They have greater problems with mainstream economic issues like trade, agriculture and the environment, where they allow domestic pressures to frustrate agreement. Sometimes the heads themselves aggravate the problems. This trend greatly weakens the summit, as compared with its original aims. As globalisation advances, international pressures have increasingly moved 'within the border' and affect domestic decision-making far more than they did in 1975. But the summits' ability to deal with such issues is shrinking.
- The G8 summits have identified a fourth objective - *integrating international politics and economics*. This was not pursued by the G7 summits, which admitted politics only reluctantly and then kept economics and politics apart. But the integration of economics and politics fits well within the capacities of the G8 heads. It is very suitable for the fight against terrorism. This has to attack the roots as well as the symptoms of terrorism and therefore needs to

mobilise all available economic and political instruments. Both Africa and the broader Middle East are regions plagued by severe political and economic problems, which feed on one another and therefore require an integrated approach in their treatment.

Beginning the Second G8 Sequence

Pursuing the fourth objective, though valuable, does not compensate for the progressive loss of the G8's power to reconcile international and domestic pressures in mainstream economic issues. The G8 summit will not achieve its full potential (and hope to earn A grades) unless this capacity can be restored. It is clear that the United Kingdom has decided to use its summit Presidency in 2005 to revive the summit's capacity to pursue this objective and to confront the problem of conflicting domestic pressures between the G8 members. This can be seen in the agenda chosen and announced for the Gleneagles summit in 2005.

Environment One main item is climate change, where the conflict between domestic interests in North America and Europe (with Japan) has been sharpest and the G8 has never reached substantive agreements. Blair spelt out his strategy for Gleneagles in a speech on 14 September 2004.[26] He identified three aims: agreement on the science of climate change and the threat it poses; agreement on a process to speed up scientific, technological and other measures to meet the threat; and engaging with other non-G8 countries with growing energy needs, like China and India. He believed that agreement on that basis was achievable and the prospects have since been improved by Russia's long-delayed ratification of the Kyoto Protocol in October.[27] This means that the uncertainty about the Kyoto Protocol is over, because it will enter into force early in 2005. It now becomes possible to think about post-Kyoto strategies, in which the United States could become engaged once more.

Africa The second priority item is Africa. The advances made at Evian and Sea Island were more political, focused on peace-keeping capacity and peer review, than economic. The UK is bringing the attention back to economic aspects for Gleneagles, partly through the Commission for Africa, whose report is expected in March 2005. This economic focus will oblige the summit to address those issues that have hitherto been held back by domestic interests: better trade access, especially in agriculture and basic manufactures; improved conditions for debt relief; and official aid volume, where the UK will be pressing its ideas for an International Finance Facility.

After Gleneagles The Gleneagles summit will be shortly followed by a special UN General Assembly to review progress under the Millennium Development Goals and a WTO ministerial meeting hosted by Hong Kong (China). There will thus be strong external pressure on the G8 to make progress in these economic areas. If Gleneagles can show good results, it could provide the foundation for subsequent summits to continue the revival of the G8's ability to reconcile international and domestic pressures in mainstream economic issues.

The first summit hosted by Russia, in 2006, might focus on energy, where the Russians are major players. It could review progress with Middle East reform and perhaps extend this initiative to former Soviet Central Asia. The 2007 summit, with Germany in the chair, could concentrate on trade, either to complete the Doha Development Agenda or ensure its results are fully implemented.[28] It could return to African issues, as Schroeder promised to do at Evian. But as this would be the fifth summit after Kananaskis, it would almost certainly be time for the G8 to take a new direction and for a new summit series to begin.

Staying Together

The G8 summit still faces three distinct threats to its continued life. First, the summit has become much more costly and difficult to organise, because of the high level of security required since the riots in Genoa and the terrorist attacks of 11 September 2001. The media regularly suggest this as a reason for abandoning the summit. But in fact the media are the people who suffer most from the unreal seclusion forced upon the summit.[29] The heads themselves are most unlikely to abandon G8 summits for this reason. If they did so, they would hand a victory to the hostile demonstrators and the terrorists who want to stop them from meeting.

A second reason for abandoning the summit flows from the argument, advanced by many outside commentators, that the G8 is no longer a rational grouping, because no serious decisions can be taken without involving a wider circle of countries. There are now widespread calls for the G8 to be absorbed into a larger group including leading developing countries, on the grounds this would create a group that is much more representative of today's globalised world. The G8 heads understand perfectly well that their decisions only become effective if they are accepted by the international community at large. This will only happen if they devote time and effort to persuading other countries, starting with the major non-G8 powers. But the process of creating a larger representative group, whatever its merits, would destroy the present advantages of personal contact and informality, which enable the G8 to strike deals that are not attainable elsewhere. The G8 still value the summit as a vehicle for resolving disputes among themselves and for launching new collective ideas, without which no progress will be possible in a wider circle.

Thirdly, the summit could lapse because of a complete breakdown in cooperation among the participating heads. This is not inconceivable. In the spring of 2003 relations between Bush and Chirac were so bad that they were not speaking to each other. The Americans let it be known that while Bush would come to the Evian summit, he would prefer to stay in Geneva than be lodged on French soil. In the event, Bush came and stayed in Evian and the summit was the beginning of a slow reconciliation between Bush and the leading opponents of the invasion of Iraq. By Sea Island a year later, the rapprochement between Bush, Schroeder and Putin was essentially complete. Chirac, however, persisted in public criticism of Bush, in ways that ignored American moves back to better collective management. But even if leaders like Bush and Chirac clash on a personal level, that would be a bad reason for abandoning the summits. It is better for them to disagree openly and face-to-face than for real and imagined slights to fester at a distance.[30]

If the G8 disappeared or was absorbed into a G20, a valuable source of international initiative and conciliation would be lost. The value of the G8 summit lies in its personal quality. It brings together the leaders of eight of the world's most powerful nations and reminds them of their responsibility to cooperate internationally, rather than acting unilaterally or giving way to domestic pressures. The results are often oversold in advance and disappoint in practice. But without the discipline of this regular encounter, it would be very easy for tensions and disputes to spread and to poison the underlying relationships between the G8 members. A world which did not have the safety-valve of the G8 summit would be an increasingly fractious and dangerous place.[31] There is still great merit in the G8 staying together.

Notes

1 After Russia hosts the summit in 2006, a sequence will have eight summits.

2 This chapter draws on Bayne 2004a and Bayne 2005.

3 This table overlaps, as regards Birmingham and Cologne, with Bayne 2000, pp. 192-194 and Table 12.1.

4 I regard brevity in documentation as a merit in a summit. I differ here from Professor John Kirton (see Kirton 2005a), who regards extensive documentation as evidence of the G8's role as a centre of global governance.

5 One reason for this difference may be that French initiatives surface in good time, while internal turf battles delay American initiatives till the last moment.

6 For further evidence of individualistic approaches by Chirac and Bush, not shared by other leaders, see Chapter 13, p. 197 above and p. 227 below.

7 I have developed my view on grading since I moved from being a diplomat to an academic. I see a summit grade of A as a Distinction, B as a Merit, C as a Pass and D or E as a Fail. Several G8 summits score strong Merits, but none has reached Distinction level yet.

8 These were: France 2003, US 2004, UK 2005, Russia 2006, Germany 2007, Japan 2008, Italy 2009, Canada 2010. This made a complete sequence following Kananaskis.

9 For a full analysis, see Putnam and Henning 1989. This cross-issue deal is one main reason why Bonn I earns its A grade; the other is the strong interaction between domestic and international commitments.

10 See Putnam and Bayne 1987, pp. 272-273.

11 This passage should be compared with the analysis in Bayne 2000, pp. 194-198.

12 Agreement on a target for renewable energy also eluded the World Summit on Sustainable Development at Johannesburg in September 2002. The opposition was led by the US and the OPEC countries.

13 See above, Chapter 8 and Chapter 12, especially note 29.

14 However, the G7 finance ministers were charged by the Sea Island summit to resolve outstanding problems with the HIPC programme by the end of the year and they confirmed this remit when they met in October. See Chapter 12, note 31.

15 For a critical assessment of the Genoa summit on these lines, see Zupi 2001.

16 Hence NEPAD is seen as continuing 'neo-patrimonial' politics in Africa, as analysed by Chabal 2002.

17 Clinton spoke to the *Seattle Post-Intelligencer*. See Bayne 2000b, p.135 and note 6.

18 See N. Dunne, 'White House Split as Bush Rejects Kyoto', *Financial Times,* 30 March 2001.

19 See E. Alden and D. McGregor, 'A Cash Crop', *Financial Times,* 10 May 2002.

20 Chirac intervened at the Berlin European Council in March 1999. The consequence was that the EU could barely fulfil its obligations under the Uruguay round agreements and had nothing to offer for a new round. See M. Smith, 'Defeat for Champions of Liberalisation', *Financial Times,* 27 March 1999 and Bayne 2000b, p. 143.

21 On this, see T. Buck, 'EU Farm Deal Lifts Trade Deal Hopes', *Financial Times,* 27 June 2003, and 'France's Indefensible Support for the CAP', *The Economist,* 21 June 2003.

22 T. Buck and J. Johnson, 'Chirac Attacks Doha Framework Draft' and G. de Jonquieres, 'US Chides Chirac for Rekindling Doha Doubts', *Financial Times*, 22 July 2004.

23 The decline in media respect can be easily traced. See, for example, 'Genoa Must be the Last of These Overblown Summits', leader in *Independent on Sunday,* 22 July 2001; G. Baker, 'Scrap the G8 After a Pointless Summit', *Financial Times,* 5 June 2003; 'This Annual Gathering of the World's Richest Leaders Has Become Redundant', leader, *Independent,* 8 June 2004.

24 When the summits began, Kissinger considered this didactic role to be one of their greatest advantages. See Putnam and Bayne 1987, p. 35.

25 This justifies the comparison of the G8 Africa Plan and NEPAD with the Marshall Plan - see Bayne 2003.

26 See 'Hot Air and Blair', leader in *Financial Times,* 15 September 2004.

27 See F. Harvey and A. Ostrovsky, 'Russia's Kyoto Move Puts Spotlight on US', *Financial Times,* 1 October 2004.

28 Now that the Doha Development Agenda has missed its end-2004 deadline, its duration is hard to predict. US 'trade promotion authority' can be extended to 2007 - see F. Bergsten, 'A Competitive Approach to Free Trade', *Financial Times*, 5 December 2002.

29 See, for example, J. Chaffin, 'Trapped Inside the Summit's Trouble-Proof Bubble', *Financial Times,* 3 July 2004.

30 The personal antipathy between Schmidt and Carter did not prevent the sophisticated agreement between them at the first Bonn summit. See Putnam and Bayne 1987, pp. 68, 79-82 and 122.

31 German Chancellor Helmut Schmidt, joint founder of the original summit, commented: 'the economic summit conferences . . . did not bring about much, but what they avoided was of enormous importance.' *The Economist,* 29 September 1979, quoted in Putnam and Bayne 1987, pp. 33-34.

Bibliography

Note. All G7 and G8 documents, from the summits and supporting meetings, are accessible on the website of the University of Toronto G8 Research Group, www.g8.utoronto.ca. A full G8 bibliography is also to be found on the website, as well as in Hajnal, P. (1999), *The G7/G8 System*, for the period up to 1999.

Abbott, F. M. (2002), 'The Doha Declaration on the TRIPS Agreement and Public Health: Lighting a Dark Corner at the WTO', *Journal of International Economic Law*, vol. 3, no. 3, pp. 469-505.

Addison, T, Hansen, H. and Tarp, F. (eds.), (2004), *Debt Relief for Poor Countries*, United Nations University-Palgrave, Basingstoke.

Armijo, L. E. (ed.), (2002), *Debating the Global Financial Architecture*, State University of New York, Albany.

Attali, J. (1995), *Verbatim III*, Fayard, Paris.

Atwood, J. B., Browne, R. S. and Lyman, P. (2004), *Freedom, Prosperity and Security: The G8 Partnership with Africa - Sea Island 2004 and Beyond*, Council for Foreign Relations, New York.

Atwood, J. B. and Lyman, P. (2004), 'Relevant to All: G8 Partnership with Africa', *The World Today*, vol. 60, no. 6, pp. 26-27.

Bayne, N. (1998), 'Britain, the G8 and the Commonwealth: Lessons of the Birmingham Summit', *The Round Table*, no. 348, pp. 445-457.

Bayne, N. (2000), *Hanging In There: The G7 and G8 Summit in Maturity and Renewal*, Ashgate, Aldershot.

Bayne, N. (2000a), 'The G7 Summit's Contribution: Past, Present and Prospective', in K. Kaiser, J. J. Kirton and J. P. Daniels, (eds.), *Shaping a New International Financial System*, Ashgate, Aldershot, pp. 19-35.

Bayne, N. (2000b), 'Why Did Seattle Fail? Globalization and the Politics of Trade', *Government and Opposition*, vol. 35, no. 2, pp. 131–151.

Bayne, N. (2001), 'Managing Globalisation and the New Economy: The Contribution of the G8 Summit', in J. J. Kirton and G. M. von Furstenberg (eds.), *New Directions in Global Economic Governance*, Ashgate, Aldershot, pp. 23-38.

Bayne, N. (2001a), 'The G7 and Multilateral Trade Liberalisation: Past Performance, Future Challenges', in J. J. Kirton and G. M. von Furstenburg, (eds.), *New Directions in Global Economic Governance*, Ashgate, Aldershot, pp. 171-187.

Bayne, N. (2002), 'Reforming the International Financial Architecture: the G7 Summit's Successes and Shortcomings', in M. Fratianni, P. Savona and J. J. Kirton (eds.), *Governing Global Finance: New Challenges, G7 and IMF Contributions*, Ashgate, Aldershot, pp. 27-43.

Bayne, N. (2002a), 'The G8 and Global Governance: The Message of Okinawa', in J. J. Kirton and J. Takase (eds.), *New Directions in Global Political Governance*, Ashgate, Aldershot, pp. 21-34.

Bayne, N. (2002b), 'Impressions of the Genoa Summit', in M. Fratianni, P. Savona and J. J. Kirton (eds.), *Governing Global Finance: New Challenges, G7 and IMF Contributions*, Ashgate, Aldershot, pp. 199-210.

Bayne, N. (2003), 'The New Partnership for Africa's Development and the G8's Africa Action Plan: A Marshall Plan for Africa?', in M. Fratianni, P. Savona, and J. J. Kirton, (eds.), *Sustaining Global Growth and Development*, Ashgate, Aldershot, pp. 117-130.

Bayne, N. (2003a), 'Impressions of the Kananaskis Summit, 16-17 June 2002', in M. Fratianni, P. Savona, and J. J. Kirton, (eds.), *Sustaining Global Growth and Development*, Ashgate, Aldershot, pp. 229-240.

Bayne, N (2004), 'Concentrating the Mind: Decision-Making in the G7/G8 System', in J. J. Kirton and R. N. Stefanova, (eds.), *The G8, the United Nations and Conflict Prevention*, Ashgate, Aldershot, pp. 21-36.

Bayne, N. (2005 forthcoming), 'G7/G8 performance from Birmingham to Evian and Beyond', in M. Fratianni, P. Savona and J. J. Kirton, (eds.), *Governing Globalization: Corporate, Public and G8 Governance*, Ashgate, Aldershot.

Bayne, N. (2005a forthcoming), 'Impressions of the Evian Summit', in M. Fratianni, P. Savona and J. J. Kirton, (eds.), *Governing Globalization: Corporate, Public and G8 Governance*, Ashgate, Aldershot.

Bayne, N. (2005b forthcoming), 'Do We Need the G8 Summit? Lessons from the Past, Looking Forward to the Future', in M. Fratianni, P. Savona, A. Rugman and J. J. Kirton, (eds.), *New Perspectives on the G8*, Ashgate, Aldershot.

Bergsten, C. F. and Henning, C. R. (1996), *Global Economic Leadership and the Group of Seven*, Institute for International Economics, Washington.

Bhagwati, J. (2000), 'After Seattle: Free Trade and the WTO', *International Affairs*, vol. 77, no. 1, pp. 15-30.

Bhagwati, J. (2004), *In Defense of Globalization*, Oxford University Press, Oxford.

Bhagwati, J. (2004a), 'Don't Cry for Cancun', *Foreign Affairs*, vol. 83, no. 1, pp. 52-63.

Birdsall, N. and Williamson J. (2002), *Delivering on Debt Relief: From IMF Gold to New Aid Architecture*, Center for Global Development, Washington.

Bleiker, R. (2003), 'A Rogue is a Rogue is a Rogue: US Foreign Policy and the Korean Nuclear Crisis', *International Affairs*, vol. 79, no. 4, pp. 719-738.

Bowen, W. Q. and Kidd, J. (2004), 'The Iranian Nuclear Challenge', *International Affairs*, vol. 80, no. 2, pp. 257-276.

Bradford, C. and Linn, J. (2004), *Global Economic Governance at a Crossroads: Replacing the G7 with the G20*, Policy Brief 131, the Brookings Institution, Washington.

Budd, C. (2003), 'G8 Summits and Their Preparation' in Bayne, N. and Woolcock, S. *The New Economic Diplomacy: Decision-Making and Negotiation in International Economic Relations*, Ashgate, Aldershot, pp. 139-146.

Cable, V. (1999), *Globalisation and Global Governance*, Royal Institute for International Affairs, London.

Camdessus, M. and Wolfensohn, J. D. (1998), 'The Bretton Woods Institutions: Responding to the Asian Financial Crisis', in M. Fraser (ed.), *The G8 and the World Economy*, Strategems Publishing Ltd, London, pp. 6-8.

Centre for Economic Performance (CEP) (1998), *Employability and Exclusion: What Governments Can Do*, Papers from a Conference held on 6 May 1998 by the Centre for Economic Performance and the London School of Economics, London.

Chabal, P. (2002), 'The Quest for Good Government and Development in Africa: is NEPAD the Answer?' *International Affairs*, vol. 78, no. 3, pp. 447-462.

Cohn, T. H. (2002), *Governing Global Trade: International Institutions in Conflict and Convergence*, Ashgate, Aldershot.

Cooper, R. N. (1995), 'Reform of Multilateral Financial Institutions', in S. Ostry and C. R. Winham, (eds.), *The Halifax G7 Summit: Issues on the Table*, Centre for Policy Studies, Dalhousie University, Halifax, Nova Scotia, pp. 15-34.

Croome, J. (1995), *Reshaping the World Trading System: A History of the Uruguay Round*, World Trade Organization, Geneva.

Della Porta, D. and Reiter, H. (2002), '"You're the G8, We're Six Billion": The Genoa Demonstrations', in P. Bellucci and M. Bull (eds.), *Italian Politics 2000 (Volume 17): the Return of Berlusconi*, Berghahn Books, New York and Oxford, pp. 105-124.

De Menil, G. and Solomon, A. (1983), *Economic Summitry*, Council for Foreign Relations, New York.

Dent, M. and Peters, B. (1999), *The Crisis of Poverty and Debt in the Third World*, Ashgate, Aldershot.

De Waal, A. (2002), 'What's New in the "New Partnership for Africa's Development"?', *International Affairs*, vol. 78, no. 3, pp. 463-476.

DFID (2000), *Eliminating World Poverty: Making Globalisation Work for the Poor,* White Paper on International Development, The Stationery Office, London.

Dobson, W. (1991), *'Economic Policy Coordination: Requiem or Prologue?'*, Institute for International Economics, Washington.

DOT-Force (2001), *Digital Opportunities for All: Meeting the Challenge*, Report of the Digital Opportunity Task-Force (DOT-Force) including a proposal for a Genoa Plan of Action, May 2001, accessible on www.dotforce.org.

DOT-Force (2002), *Report Card: Digital Opportunities for All*, June 2002, accessible on www.dotforce.org.

DTI (2004), *Making Globalisation a Force for Good,* Trade and Investment White Paper, The Stationery Office, London.

Eichengreen, B. (1999), *Towards a New International Financial Architecture: A Practical Post-Asia Agenda*, Institute for International Economics, Washington.

English, J., Thakur, R. and Cooper, A. F. (eds.), (2005 forthcoming), *A Leaders G20 Summit: Why, How, Who and When?'*, Centre for International Governance Innovation, Waterloo, Ontario.

Evans, H. (1999), 'Debt Relief for the Poorest Countries: Why Did It Take So Long?', *Development Policy Review*, vol. 17, no.3, pp. 267-279.

Evans, H. (2000), *Plumbers and Architects*, FSA Occasional Papers, Financial Services Authority, London.

Evans, P. B., Jacobson, H. K. and Putnam, R. D. (1993), *Double-Edged Diplomacy: International Bargaining and Domestic Politics,* University of California Press, Berkeley.

Everts, S. (2004), 'The Ultimate Test Case: Can Europe and America Forge a Joint Strategy for the Wider Middle East?', *International Affairs,* vol. 80, no. 4, pp. 665-686.

Feldstein, M. (1998), 'Refocusing the IMF', *Foreign Affairs*, vol. 77, no. 2, pp. 20-33.

Fischer, S. (1998), 'In Defence of the IMF', *Foreign Affairs*, vol. 77, no. 4, pp. 103-106.

Fowler, R. (2004), 'The Intricacies of Summit Preparation and Consensus Building', in Kirton, J. J. and Stefanova, R. N. (eds.), *The G8, the United Nations and Conflict Prevention,* Ashgate, Aldershot, pp. 39-42.

Funabashi, Y. (1988), *Managing the Dollar: From the Plaza to the Louvre*, Institute for International Economics, Washington.

Gresser, E. (2002), 'Toughest on the Poor: America's Flawed Tariff System', *Foreign Affairs*, vol. 81, no. 6, pp. 9-14.

Haggard, S. (2000), *The Political Economy of the Asian Financial Crisis*, Institute for International Economics, Washington.

Hajnal, P. (1999), *The G7/G8 System: Evolution, Role and Documentation*, Ashgate, Aldershot.

Hajnal, P. (2002), 'Civil Society Encounters the G7/G8' in Hajnal, P. (ed.), *Civil Society in the Information Age*, Ashgate, Aldershot.

Hamill, J. (2002), 'Despots or Aid?', *The World Today*, vol. 58, no. 6, pp. 17-18.

Hart, J. A. (2005 forthcoming), 'The G8 and the Governance of Cyberspace', in M. Fratianni, P. Savona, A. Rugman and J. J. Kirton, (eds.), *New Perspectives on the G8*, Ashgate, Aldershot.

Hoekman, B. and Kostecki, M. (2001), *The Political Economy of the World Trading System*, second edition, Oxford University Press, Oxford.

Hollis, R. 'The Israeli-Palestinian Road Block: Can Europeans Make a Difference', *International Affairs*, vol. 80, no. 2, pp. 191-201.

Jackson, J. H. (1998), *The World Trade Organization: Constitution and Jurisprudence*, Royal Institute of International Affairs, London.

Julius, D. (1998), 'Trade and Investment in the Light of the Asian Crisis', *Bank of England Quarterly Bulletin*, vol. 38, no. 3, pp. 280-282.

Kenen, P. B. (ed.) (1994), *Managing the World Economy: Fifty Years After Bretton Woods*, Institute for International Economics, Washington.

Kenen, P. B. (ed.) (1996), *From Halifax to Lyons: What Has Been Done About Crisis Management?* Essays in International Finance no. 200, Princeton University, Princeton.

Kenen, P. B. (2001), *The International Financial Architecture: What's New? What's Missing?*, Institute for International Economics, Washington.

Kenen, P. B. and Swoboda, A. K., (eds.), (2000), *Reforming the International and Financial System*, International Monetary Fund, MF, Washington.

Kenen, P. B., Shafer, J. R., Wicks, N. L. and Wyplosz, C. (2004), *International Economic and Financial Cooperation: New Issues, New Actors, New Responses,* Centre for Economic Policy Research, London.

Kirton, J. J. (2001), 'The G20: Representativeness, Effectiveness and Leadership in Global Governance', in J. J. Kirton, J. P. Daniels and A Freytag, (eds.), *Guiding Global Order: G8 Governance in the Twenty-first Century*, Ashgate, Aldershot, pp. 143-171.

Kirton, J. J. (2001a), 'The G7/8 and China: Toward a Closer Association', in J. J. Kirton, J. P. Daniels and A. Freytag (eds.), *Guiding Global Order: G8 Governance in the Twenty-first Century*, Ashgate, Aldershot, pp. 189-222.

Kirton, J. J. (2004), 'Getting the L20 Going: Reaching Out from the G8', paper accessible on www.g8.utoronto.ca.

Kirton, J. J. (2005, forthcoming), 'Towards Multilateral Reform: The G20's Contribution', in J. English, R. Thakur and A. F. Cooper (eds.), *A Leaders G20 Summit: Why, How, Who and When?'*, Centre for International Governance Innovation, Waterloo, Ontario.

Kirton, J. J. (2005a forthcoming), 'America at the G8: From Vulnerability to Victory at the Sea Island Summit', in M. Fratianni, P. Savona, A. Rugman and J. J. Kirton, (eds.), *New Perspectives on the G8*, Ashgate, Aldershot.

Kokotsis, E. (1999), *Keeping International Commitments: Compliance, Credibility and the G7, 1988-1995*, Garland Publishing, Levittown.

Kurosawa, M. (2002), 'Curbing Nuclear Proliferation: Japanese, G8 and Global Approaches', in J. J. Kirton and J. Takase, (eds.), *New Directions in Global Political Governance*, Ashgate, Aldershot, pp. 117-140.

Laird, S. (2002), 'A Round by Any Other Name', *Development Policy Review*, vol. 20, no. 1, pp. 41-62.

Lockwood, M., Donlan, E., Joyner K. and Simms, A. (1998), *Forever in Your Debt? Eight Poor Nations and the G8*, Christian Aid, London.

Maxwell, S. and Christiansen, K. (2002), 'Negotiation as Simultaneous Equation': Building a New Partnership with Africa,' *International Affairs*, vol. 78, no. 3, pp. 477-492.

Mbirimi, I., Chilala, B. and Grynberg, R. (2003). *From Doha to Cancun: Delivering a Development Round*, Commonwealth Secretariat, London.

Meltzer, A. (Chairman) (2000), *Report of the International Financial Institutions Advisory Commission*, United States Congress, Washington.

The Monitor (2004), 'The Proliferation Security Initiative: Promise and Performance', vol. 10, no. 1, Center for International Trade and Security, University of Georgia, Athens, Georgia.

OECD (2004), *African Economic Outlook* 2003-2004, Organisation for Economic Cooperation and Development, Paris.

O'Neill, J. and Hormats, R. (2004), *The G8: Time for A Change,* Global Economics Paper 112, Goldman Sachs, accessible on www.gs.com.

Preeg, E. (1995), *Traders in a Brave New World*, University of Chicago Press, Chicago.

Putnam, R. D. and Bayne, N. (1984), *Hanging Together: the Seven-Power Summits*, Heinemann for Royal Institute for International Affairs, London.

Putnam, R. D. and Bayne, N. (1987), *Hanging Together: Cooperation and Conflict in the Seven-Power Summits*, SAGE, London.

Putnam, R. D. (1988), 'Diplomacy and Domestic Politics: the Logic of Two-Level Games', *International Organization*, vol. 42, no. 3, pp. 427-460.

Putnam, R. D. and Henning, C. R. (1989), 'The Bonn Summit of 1978: A Case Study in Coordination', in R. N. Cooper and others (eds.), *Can Nations Agree? Issues in International Economic Cooperation*, the Brookings Institution, Washington, pp. 12-140.

Reinalda, B. and Verbeek, B. (eds.) (2004), *Decision Making Within International Organizations*, Routledge, London.

Rogoff, K. (2004), 'The Sisters at 60: the IMF and World Bank', *The Economist*, 24 July 2004.

Sachs, J. (1999), 'Helping the World's Poorest', *The Economist*, 14 August 1999.

Sachs, J. (2000), 'Globalisation - A New Map of the World', *The Economist*, 24 June 2000.

Sachs, J. (2004), 'Doing the Sums on Africa', *The Economist*, 22 May 2004.

Schott, J. J. (1994), *The Uruguay Round: An Assessment*, Institute for International Affairs, Washington.

Sherifis, R. F. and Astraldi, V. (2001), *The G7/G8 from Rambouillet to Genoa*, FrancoAngeli, Milan.

Stiglitz, J. (2002), *Globalization and its Discontents*, Allen Lane, London.

Teunissen, J. J. and Akkerman, A. (eds.) (2003), *The Crisis That Was Not Prevented: Lessons for Argentina, the IMF and Globalisation,* Forum on Debt and Development, The Hague.

Van der Westhuizen, J. (2003), 'How (Not) to Sell Big Ideas: Argument, Identity and NEPAD', *International Journal*, vol. LVIII, no. 3, pp. 369-394.

Vines, D. and Gilbert, C. L. (eds.), (2004), *The IMF and its Critics: Reform of Global Financial Architecture,* Cambridge University Press, Cambridge.

Von Furstenberg, G. M. and Daniels, J. P. (1992), *Economic Summit Declarations, 1975-1989: Examining the Written Record of International Cooperation*, Princeton University, Princeton, NJ.

Wechsler, W. (2001), 'Follow the Money', *Foreign Affairs*, vol. 80, no. 4, pp. 40-57.

Wolf, M. (2004), *Why Globalisation Works*, Yale University Press, New Haven and London.

Wolfe, R. (1998), *Farm Wars: The Political Economy of Agriculture and the International Trade Regime*, Macmillan, Basingstoke.

Zupi, M. (2001), 'The Genoa G-8 Summit: Great Expectations, Disappointing Results', *International Spectator*, vol. XXXVI, no. 3, pp. 57-68.

Index

Entries shown in **bold** indicate the principal treatment of a subject.